SECOND EDITION

face2face

Elementary Student's Book

Chris Redston & Gillie Cunningham

Contents

Lesson			Vocabulary	Grammar	Real World
	Welcome!	p6	numbers 0–20; the alphabet; things in the classroom; days of the week		introducing yourself; classroom instructions; names; saying goodbye
1A	How are you?	p8	countries and nationalities	*be* (1): positive and *Wh-* questions; subject pronouns and possessive adjectives	introducing people
1B	Coffee break	p10	jobs; *a* and *an*	*be* (2): negative, *yes/no* questions and short answers	
1C	Personal details	p12	numbers 20–100		asking for personal details; asking people to repeat things
1D	Lost property	p14	personal possessions; plurals; *this, that, these, those*		
Extra Practice 1 and Progress Portfolio 1		**p115**			
2A	What's important?	p16	adjectives (1); adjective word order and *very*	*have got*: positive and negative, questions and short answers	
2B	The Browns	p18	family	possessive *'s*	
2C	Time and money	p20	time words		telling the time; talking about the time; saying prices; buying tickets at the cinema
2D	Where's the baby?	p22	things in a house; prepositions of place		
Extra Practice 2 and Progress Portfolio 2		**p116**			
3A	My day	p24	daily routines	Present Simple (1): positive and *Wh-* questions (*I/you/we/they*)	
3B	Free time	p26	free time activities (1); time phrases with *on, in, at, every*	Present Simple (2): negative and *yes/no* questions (*I/you/we/they*)	
3C	Special days	p28	months; dates		phrases for special days; talking about days and dates; suggestions
3D	Early bird?	p30	frequency adverbs	subject and object pronouns	
Extra Practice 3 and Progress Portfolio 3		**p117**			
4A	Away from home	p32	free time activities (2)	Present Simple (3): positive and negative (*he/she/it*)	
4B	First Date!	p34	things you like and don't like; verb+*ing*	Present Simple (4): questions and short answers (*he/she/it*)	
4C	Eating out	p36	food and drink (1)		requests and offers
4D	Breakfast time	p38	food and drink (2); countable and uncountable nouns		
Extra Practice 4 and Progress Portfolio 4		**p118**			
5A	Three generations	p40	adjectives (2); years	Past Simple (1): *be* (positive and negative, questions and short answers)	
5B	Famous films	p42	life events	Past Simple (2): regular and irregular verbs (positive and *Wh-* questions)	
5C	Four weekends	p44	weekend activities		showing interest; asking follow-up questions
5D	Competitions	p46	adjectives (3); adjectives with *very, really, quite, too*		
Extra Practice 5 and Progress Portfolio 5		**p119**			
6A	Google it!	p48	the internet	Past Simple (3): negative, *yes/no* questions and short answers	
6B	Changing technology	p50	mobile phones and TVs; past time phrases	*can/can't; could/couldn't*	
6C	The news	p52	verbs from news stories		talking about the news
6D	Mario Man	p54	articles; *a, an* and *the*		
Extra Practice 6 and Progress Portfolio 6		**p120**			

VIDEO See Teacher's DVD

Speaking	Listening and Video	Reading	Writing
Introducing yourself What's your first name? Saying goodbye	Conversations in a classroom First names and surnames		
Names and countries	At the conference	At the conference	
Phone numbers and jobs The conference list	Phone numbers What do you do?	Three conversations	Sentences about you
Numbers Hiring a car	**Help with Listening** Sentence stress (1) **VIDEO** Hiring a car	Personal information	Filling in a form
Things in the classroom			
HELP WITH PRONUNCIATION Word stress and syllables p15		**Reading and Writing Portfolio 1** At the hotel Workbook p64	
Personal possessions	What's important to me? A survey in a shop	What's important to me?	My friend's possessions
My family	Family photos **Help with Listening** Sentence stress (2)	The Brown family	Questions with How many ... ?
Buying tickets	What time is it? Times and prices **VIDEO** At the cinema	Adverts for an exhibition and for a cinema	
Whose mobile phone is this? Where's Robbie's bag?	Where's the baby?		Sentences with prepositions
HELP WITH PRONUNCIATION The schwa /ə/ in words p23		**Reading and Writing Portfolio 2** My favourite thing Workbook p66	
Daily routines		Behind the camera	My daily routine Questions about routines
Free time activities Find two people	The office party **Help with Listening** Weak forms (1): do you ... ?		Questions with Do you ... ?
My important dates What shall we get her?	What's the date today? **VIDEO** A birthday present		Dates A conversation
My habits	Early bird or night owl?	Early bird or night owl?	
HELP WITH PRONUNCIATION How we say th p31		**Reading and Writing Portfolio 3** All about me Workbook p68	
My free time activities My partner's free time	Life at the observatory **Help with Listening** Linking (1)		Questions with Do you ... ?
Things I like and don't like I've got a friend for you!	First Date!	First Date! Mark's first date	Questions with Does he/she ... ?
My favourite café Ordering food and drink	**Help with Listening** Would you like ... ? **VIDEO** At the Sun Café	A café menu Conversations in a café	A conversation in a café
Breakfasts around the world My perfect breakfast	What's for breakfast?		
HELP WITH PRONUNCIATION /ʃ/, /tʃ/ and /dʒ/ p39		**Reading and Writing Portfolio 4** Going out Workbook p70	
When was he born? When I was thirteen	Albert's thirteenth birthday **Help with Listening** Weak forms (2): was and were	My birthday party	Questions with was and were
Questions about the past My timeline	**Help with Listening** Present Simple or Past Simple	Cameron's world	
What I did last weekend Asking follow-up questions	**VIDEO** How was your weekend?	Four weekends	Writing notes about the past
Too expensive or quite cheap?		Winners and losers	
HELP WITH PRONUNCIATION The letter o p47		**Reading and Writing Portfolio 5** A night to remember Workbook p72	
My internet Find someone who ...	Planet Google	The Google guys	Negative Past Simple sentences Past Simple yes/no questions
My mobile, computer and TV	**Help with Listening** can and can't	Our first colour TV The first mobile phones	My first mobile
Telling news stories	Here is the news **VIDEO** Talking about the news **Help with Listening** Sentence stress (3)	Two news reports	
Video games	The father of video games	Shigeru Miyamoto fact file	
HELP WITH PRONUNCIATION Past Simple of regular verbs p55		**Reading and Writing Portfolio 6** Text me! Workbook p74	

Lesson			Vocabulary	Grammar	Real World
7A	Where I live	p56	places in a town	there is/there are	
7B	A new home	p58	rooms and things in a house	How much …? and How many …?; some, any, a	
7C	At the shops	p60	shops; things to buy		what sales assistants say; what customers say
7D	What to wear	p62	clothes; colours; plural nouns		
Extra Practice 7 and Progress Portfolio 7 p121					
8A	The meeting	p64	work	Present Continuous: positive and negative, questions and short answers	
8B	It's snowing!	p66	types of transport; travelling verbs and phrases	Present Simple or Present Continuous	
8C	On the phone	p68			talking on the phone
8D	Life outdoors	p70	indoor and outdoor activities; adjectives and adverbs		
Extra Practice 8 and Progress Portfolio 8 p122					
9A	Holiday South Africa	p72	holiday activities	infinitive of purpose	
9B	A trip to Egypt	p74	natural places	comparatives	
9C	A day out	p76	animals		deciding what to do
9D	Time for a change	p78	verb patterns (like doing, would like to do, etc.)		
Extra Practice 9 and Progress Portfolio 9 p123					
10A	Stay fit and healthy	p80	verb phrases; frequency expressions	imperatives; should/shouldn't	
10B	What's she like?	p82	appearance; character	questions with like	
10C	I feel ill	p84	health problems; treatment		talking about health
10D	Winter blues	p86	seasons; weather; word building		
Extra Practice 10 and Progress Portfolio 10 p124					
11A	Happy New Year!	p88	New Year's resolutions	be going to (1): positive, negative and Wh- questions	
11B	No more exams!	p90	studying	be going to or might; be going to (2): yes/no questions and short answers	
11C	Directions	p92			directions; asking for and giving directions
11D	An invitation	p94	collocations		
Extra Practice 11 and Progress Portfolio 11 p125					
12A	It's a world record	p96	big and small numbers	superlatives	
12B	Have you ever … ?	p98	past participles	Present Perfect: positive and negative; Have you ever … ? questions and short answers	
12C	See you soon!	p100	things and places at an airport		at the airport; saying goodbye
End of Course Review		p103			
Extra Practice 12 and Progress Portfolio 12 p126					

Pair and Group Work p104   **LANGUAGE Summaries** p127   **Audio and Video Scripts** p155

Speaking	Listening and Video (VIDEO See Teacher's DVD)	Reading	Writing
Places near my home My favourite place	Three places **Help with Listening** Weak forms (3): prepositions		
Spot the difference My shopping habits	Renting a flat At the supermarket	An advert for a flat	Questions with *Is there ... ?/Are there ... ?*
Buying things in a department store	VIDEO Can I help you?	A conversation in a department store	A conversation in a department store
What I wear		Me and my clothes	
HELP WITH PRONUNCIATION /ɔː/ and /ɜː/ p63		**Reading and Writing Portfolio 7** Renting a flat Workbook p76	
Spot the difference	The contract	Conversations in the office and at home	
My travel habits Usually and today	Snow day A day at home **Help with Listening** Linking (2)	A day at home	Questions in the Present Simple or Present Continuous
A phone conversation	**Help with Listening** Phone messages Emily's phone calls VIDEO Can I call you back?	A list, a business card and an advert Conversations on the phone	A phone conversation
What can you do?		A reference letter	Sentences with adjectives and adverbs
HELP WITH PRONUNCIATION /ɪ/ and /iː/ p71		**Reading and Writing Portfolio 8** Finding a job Workbook p78	
My last holiday Four places	A holiday in Cape Town **Help with Listening** Weak forms: review		Sentences with the infinitive of purpose
Natural places Two people I know	Choosing a holiday Back from holiday	Two holiday places	Sentences with comparatives
What would you like to do? Planning a day out Deciding what to do	VIDEO Planning a day out	Places to go for a day out	
Questions with *like* and *would like*		The grass is always greener	Questions with *like* and *would like*
HELP WITH PRONUNCIATION Silent letters p79		**Reading and Writing Portfolio 9** Places to go Workbook p80	
People I know What should I do?	At the doctor's	Get fit for free	Tips on how to stay fit and healthy
Describing people in my family Three friends	The *Break* advert Leo's new girlfriend **Help with Listening** Sentence stress (3)		A description of a person
I'm not very well	VIDEO Get well soon **Help with Listening** Being sympathetic		
What's the weather like?		If you're SAD, see the light!	
HELP WITH PRONUNCIATION The letter *a* p87		**Reading and Writing Portfolio 10** The advice page Workbook p82	
Plans for the future	New Year's resolutions		
Next weekend Find one person who ...	The final exam Future plans **Help with Listening** *going to*		My plans for next month *Yes/No* questions with *be going to*
Asking for and giving directions	Which holiday home? VIDEO Giving directions	Two holiday homes An email giving directions	
My last wedding or party	Going to the wedding **Help with Listening** Linking: review	An email about a wedding	An email to my friends
HELP WITH PRONUNCIATION /ʊ/ and /uː/ p95		**Reading and Writing Portfolio 11** A town by the sea Workbook p84	
My superlatives	The World Quiz **Help with Listening** Sentence stress: review	Record breakers The World Quiz	
My life experiences	Being self-employed Holiday experiences	Being self-employed	My life experiences *Have you ever ... ?* questions
My travel experiences Saying goodbye	VIDEO At the airport VIDEO Saying goodbye		A conversation saying goodbye
HELP WITH PRONUNCIATION Vowel sounds: review p102		**Reading and Writing Portfolio 12** At the airport Workbook p86	

Phonemic Symbols p167   **Irregular Verb List p167**

Welcome!

Vocabulary numbers 0–20; the alphabet; things in the classroom; days of the week
Real World introducing yourself; classroom instructions; names; saying goodbye

Hello!

1 a CD1 ▶1 Look at conversation 1 and listen.

b Practise conversation 1 with your teacher. Use your name.

2 a CD1 ▶2 Look at conversation 2 and listen.

b Practise conversation 2 with four students. Use your name.

Numbers 0–20

3 a Work in pairs. How do we say these numbers?

0 1 2 3 4 5
6 7 8 9 10
11 12 13 14 15
16 17 18 19 20

b CD1 ▶3 PRONUNCIATION Listen and check. Listen again and practise.

c Work in the same pairs. Say five numbers. Write your partner's numbers. Are they correct?

Classroom instructions

4 a Work in new pairs. Which of these instructions do you understand? Check in Language Summary Welcome REAL WORLD 0.2 ▶ p127.

Open your book.
Look at the photo on page 11.
Do exercise 6 on your own.
Look at the board.
Work in pairs.
Work in groups.
Fill in the gaps.
Compare answers.
Listen and check.
Listen and practise.
Match the words to the pictures.
Ask and answer the questions.

b CD1 ▶4 Listen and tick (✓) the instructions when you hear them.

1
TEACHER Hello. What's your name, please?
DENIZ My name's Deniz Aslan.
TEACHER I'm Peter Adams. Welcome to the class.
DENIZ Thank you.

2
HASSAN Hello, my name's Hassan.
OLGA Hi, I'm Olga.
HASSAN Nice to meet you.
OLGA You too.

The alphabet

5 a CD1 ▶5 PRONUNCIATION Listen and practise the alphabet.

Aa Bb Cc Dd Ee Ff Gg Hh Ii
Jj Kk Ll Mm Nn Oo Pp Qq Rr
Ss Tt Uu Vv Ww Xx Yy Zz

b CD1 ▶6 Listen and write the words.

TIP • ss = *double s*

3 MARCOS Hello. Sorry I'm late.
   TEACHER No problem.

First names and surnames

6 a Look at conversation 3. Then match the teacher's questions 1–3 to Marcos's answers a–c.

1 What's your first name?   a F–U–E–N–T–E–S.
2 What's your surname?   b Fuentes.
3 How do you spell that?   c It's Marcos.

b CD1 ▶ 7 Listen and check.

c CD1 ▶ 8 Listen to two conversations, A and B. Write the names.

7 a CD1 ▶ 9 PRONUNCIATION Listen and practise the questions in **6a**.

b Ask four students these questions and write the names.

Things in the classroom

8 a Match these words to pictures a–j.

a table *b*   a chair   a book   a pencil
a pen   a dictionary   a CD player
a TV   a DVD player   a computer

b Work in pairs. Test your partner.

What's picture e?   It's a chair.

Goodbye!

9 a Put the days of the week in order.

Friday   Tuesday   Thursday   Monday *1*
Wednesday   Saturday   Sunday

b CD1 ▶ 10 PRONUNCIATION Listen and check. Listen again and practise. What day is it today? What day is it tomorrow?

10 CD1 ▶ 11 Listen and write the day. Then practise with other students.

MARCOS Bye, Olga.
OLGA   Goodbye. See you on _____ .
MARCOS Yes, see you.

Progress Portfolio Welcome!

Tick (✓) the things you can do in English.

☐ I can say hello, introduce myself and say goodbye.
☐ I can say numbers 0–20.
☐ I can understand classroom instructions.
☐ I can say the alphabet.
☐ I can spell my name.
☐ I can say the days of the week.

1A How are you?

Vocabulary countries and nationalities
Grammar be (1): positive and Wh- questions; subject pronouns and possessive adjectives
Real World introducing people

QUICK REVIEW **The alphabet** Write five words in English. Work in pairs. Spell the words to your partner. He/She writes them down. Are they correct?

Listening and Speaking

1 a CD1 12 PRONUNCIATION Read and listen to conversation 1. Listen again and practise.

b Practise conversation 1 with four students. Use your name.

2 a CD1 13 PRONUNCIATION Read and listen to conversation 2. Listen again and practise.

b Work in groups. Take turns to introduce students to each other.

Vocabulary and Speaking
Countries and nationalities

3 a Tick (✓) the countries you know.

countries I'm from …	nationalities I'm …
Brazil	Brazili **a n**
Australia	Australi __ __
Argentina	Argentini __ __
the USA	Americ __ __
Germany	Germ __ __
Italy	Itali __ __
Mexico	Mexic __ __
Russia	Russi __ __
Egypt	Egypti __ __
the UK	Brit **i s h**
Spain	Span __ __
Poland	Pol __ __
Turkey	Turk __ __
China	Chin **e s e**
Japan	Japan __
France	French

b Write the missing letters in the nationalities. Check in Language Summary 1 **VOCABULARY 1.1** p128.

c Where are you from? What's your nationality?

> I'm from Colombia.   I'm Korean.

4 a CD1 14 Listen and notice the word stress (•) in the countries and nationalities in **3a**.

Brazil   Brazilian

b PRONUNCIATION Listen again and practise. Copy the word stress.

Reading and Listening

5 a CD1 15 Read and listen to conversations 3, 4 and 5. Write the countries.

b Work in pairs. Compare answers.

1
LISA Hello, Tom.
TOM Hi, Lisa. How are you?
LISA I'm fine, thanks. And you?
TOM I'm OK, thanks.

2
PAOLO Bianca, this is Toshi.
BIANCA Hello, Toshi. Nice to meet you.
TOSHI You too.

3
RECEPTIONIST Good morning. What's your name, please?
CARLOS It's Carlos Moreno.
RECEPTIONIST And where are you from?
CARLOS I'm from _____.

HELP WITH GRAMMAR
be (1): positive and Wh- questions

6 a Fill in the gaps with 'm, 're or 's.

POSITIVE (+)

1 I _'m_ from Spain. (= I am)
2 You____ in room 6. (= you are)
3 He____ from Italy. (= he is)
4 She____ from Brazil. (= she is)
5 It____ Carlos Moreno. (= it is)
6 We____ from Australia. (= we are)
7 They____ from the UK. (= they are)

b Fill in the gaps with are or 's.

WH- QUESTIONS (?)

1 Where _are_ you from?   4 What____ your name?
2 Where____ he from?   5 What____ your names?
3 Where____ she from?   6 Where____ they from?

c Check in GRAMMAR 1.1 ▶ p129.

4
RECEPTIONIST What are your names, please?
DANIEL My name's Daniel Ross and this is Kelly Easton.
RECEPTIONIST Where are you from?
DANIEL We're from _____ .
RECEPTIONIST Welcome to the conference. You're in room 6.

5
EMMA Where's he from?
DAVE He's from _____ .
EMMA OK. And where's she from?
DAVE She's from _____ .
EMMA Right. And where are they from?
DAVE They're from _____ , I think.

---

7 a CD1 ▶16 PRONUNCIATION Listen and practise the sentences in **6a** and the questions in **6b**. Copy the contractions (I'm, you're, What's, etc.).

I'm from Spain.

b Work in pairs. Practise conversations 3, 4 and 5.

8 Fill in the gaps with 'm, 're, are or 's.

EMMA Where ¹ _are_ they from?
DAVE They ²____ from Egypt.
EMMA What ³____ **their** names?
DAVE **His** name ⁴____ Hanif and **her** name ⁵____ Fatima.

RECEPTIONIST What ⁶____ **your** names, please?
DIETER **Our** names ⁷____ Dieter Koller and Mehmet Kaya.
RECEPTIONIST Where ⁸____ you from?
DIETER I⁹____ from Germany and he¹⁰____ from Turkey.

HELP WITH GRAMMAR
Subject pronouns and possessive adjectives

9 Fill in the table with the words in **bold** in **8**.

subject pronouns	I	you	he	she	it	we	they
possessive adjectives	my				its		

GRAMMAR 1.2 ▶ p129

10 a Choose the correct words.

RECEPTIONIST What are ¹you/your names, please?
MARTIN ²We/Our names are Martin and Julia Green.
RECEPTIONIST Where are ³you/your from?
MARTIN ⁴We/Our 're from the USA.

LISA Where are ⁵they/their from?
TOM ⁶He/His 's from France and ⁷she/her 's from Japan.
LISA What are ⁸they/their names?
TOM ⁹He/His name's Louis and ¹⁰she/her name's Hiroko.

b Work in pairs. Compare answers.

Get ready … Get it right!

11 Work in pairs. Student A p104. Student B p109.

1B Coffee break

Vocabulary jobs; *a* and *an*
Grammar *be* (2): negative, *yes/no* questions and short answers

QUICK REVIEW Numbers 0–20
Work in pairs. Count from 0 to 20:
A *Zero*. **B** *One*. **A** *Two*. **B** *Three*.
Then count backwards from 20 to 0:
A *Twenty*. **B** *Nineteen*. **A** *Eighteen*.

Listening and Speaking

1 a Work in pairs. Look at A–D. How do we say the phone numbers?

TIP • In phone numbers 0 = *oh* or *zero* and 11 = *double one*.

b CD1 ▶ 17 PRONUNCIATION Listen and check. Listen again and practise.

2 a CD1 ▶ 18 Listen to four conversations. Write the phone numbers.

b Ask three students their phone numbers. You can invent numbers if you like!

What's your mobile number? It's …

What's your home number? It's …

Vocabulary and Speaking
Jobs

3 a Work in pairs. Which of these jobs do you know? Then do the exercise in VOCABULARY 1.2 ▶ p128.

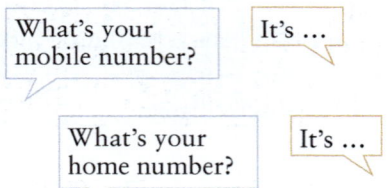

a manager   a doctor   an engineer
a sales assistant   a waiter/a waitress
a cleaner   a police officer
an actor/an actress   a musician
a teacher   a student   a housewife
an accountant   a lawyer
a builder   a mechanic

TIPS • In these vocabulary boxes we only show the main stress.
• We can also say *I'm unemployed.* not *I'm an unemployed.* and *I'm retired.* not *I'm a retired.*

b CD1 ▶ 19 PRONUNCIATION Listen and practise. Copy the word stress.

HELP WITH VOCABULARY *a* and *an*

4 Look at the jobs in **3a**. Then complete the rules with *a* or *an*.

• We use _____ with nouns that begin with a **consonant** sound. (The consonants are *b, c, d, f,* etc.)
• We use _____ with nouns that begin with a **vowel** sound. (The vowels are *a, e, i, o, u.*)

VOCABULARY 1.3 ▶ p128

5 Fill in the gaps with *a* or *an*.

1 ____ job   4 ____ book
2 ____ student   5 ____ English book
3 ____ answer   6 ____ room

6 a Look again at the pictures in VOCABULARY 1.2 ▶ p128. Take turns to cover the words and test your partner.

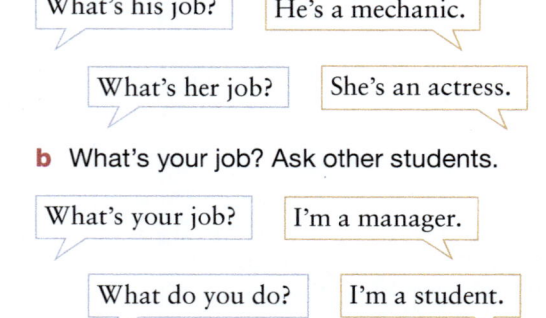

What's his job?   He's a mechanic.
What's her job?   She's an actress.

b What's your job? Ask other students.

What's your job?   I'm a manager.
What do you do?   I'm a student.

Listening and Speaking

7 a CD1 20 Read and listen to these conversations. Fill in the gaps with the correct jobs.

1. A Are you from New York?
   B No, we aren't from the USA. We're from Canada.
   A Oh, really? What do you do?
   B I'm an ¹_____ and Jane's a ²_____ .

2. A Who's she?
   B Her name's Sally Andrews.
   A Is she a ³_____ ?
   B Yes, she is. But she isn't famous.

3. A What do you do?
   B I'm a ⁴_____ . And you?
   A I'm an ⁵_____ .
   B Are you from Mexico?
   A No, I'm not. I'm from Colombia.

b Look at the photo. Match conversations 1–3 to the groups of people A–C.

HELP WITH GRAMMAR
be (2): negative, *yes/no* questions and short answers

8 a Look again at **7a**. Underline all the parts of *be* in the conversations.

b Fill in the gaps in these negative sentences with *'m, aren't* and *isn't*.

1. I_____ not a teacher.
2. You/We/They _____ from the USA. (= are not)
3. He/She/It _____ famous. (= is not)

c Fill in the gaps in these questions and answers with *'m, Is, Are, isn't* or *aren't*.

1. _Are_ you from Spain?
   Yes, I am./No, I _____ not.
2. _____ she a musician?
   Yes, she is./No, she _____ .
3. _____ you from New York?
   Yes, we are./No, we _____ .

d Check in GRAMMAR 1.3 p129.

9 CD1 21 PRONUNCIATION Listen and practise. Copy the contractions (*I'm, aren't*, etc.).

I'm not a teacher.
We aren't from the USA.

10 Work in pairs. Ask and answer questions about the people in the photo.

| Is he a doctor? | No, he isn't. He's an engineer. |

11 a Tick (✓) the sentences that are true for you. Make the other sentences negative. Write the correct sentences.

1. I'm an English student. ✓
2. I'm from the UK.
   I'm not from the UK. I'm from Poland.
3. My English class is in room 12.
4. I'm an accountant.
5. My teacher's from Australia.
6. My language school is in London.
7. My English lessons are on Tuesdays and Thursdays.
8. The students in my class are all from my country.

b Work in groups. Compare sentences.

Get ready ... Get it right!

12 Work in pairs. Student A p104. Student B p109.

REAL WORLD
1C Personal details

Real World asking for personal details; asking people to repeat things
Vocabulary numbers 20–100

QUICK REVIEW Jobs Work in pairs. Write all the jobs you know. Which pair in the class has the most words?

What number is it?

1 a Work in pairs. How do we say these numbers? Check in **VOCABULARY 1.4** ▶ p128.

> 20   30   40   50   60   70   80   90   100

b Work in the same pairs. Say these numbers.

> 28   34   47   51   63   75   86   92

2 a CD1 ▶22 Listen to these numbers. Notice the stress.

> thirteen   thirty   fifteen   fifty   nineteen   ninety

b CD1 ▶23 Listen and write the numbers.

c CD1 ▶24 **PRONUNCIATION** Listen and practise the numbers in **2a** and **2b**.

3 Work in pairs. Say a number between 1 and 100. Your partner says the next three numbers.

> fifty-eight   fifty-nine, sixty, sixty-one

What's her address?

4 a Look at the photo of Emma. Then match these words to Emma's things 1–3.

> a credit card   a business card   a mobile phone

b Match these words/phrases to the letters a–j in the pictures.

1 first name *b*
2 surname
3 home number
4 work number
5 mobile number
6 home address
7 email address
8 postcode at work
9 credit card number
10 job

c Work in pairs. Ask questions about 1–10 in **4b**.

> What's her first name?   Emma.

1 Webber & Webber Ltd
89 Villiers Street
Liverpool
a L14 6Y2

b Emma Mitchell
c Sales Manager

d Tel 0151 496 0814
e Mobile 07974 610771
f email emma.mitchell@wwl.co.uk

2 HOME BANK CREDIT
g 4589 2300 6754 7961
4550
VALID FROM 02/12   EXPIRES END 01/20
MRS EMMA R MITCHELL **h**

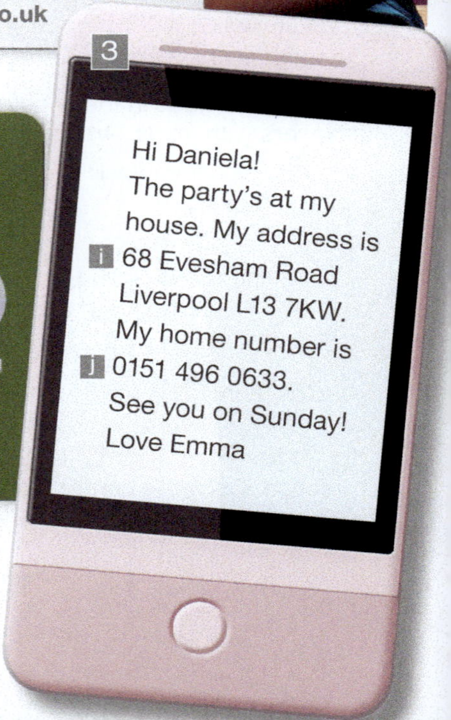

3 Hi Daniela!
The party's at my house. My address is **i** 68 Evesham Road Liverpool L13 7KW. My home number is **j** 0151 496 0633. See you on Sunday! Love Emma

Hiring a car

HELP WITH LISTENING Sentence stress (1)

5 CD1 ▶25 Look at the photo of Paul. Then listen to the woman's questions. Notice the sentence stress. We stress the important words.

1 What's your surname, please?
2 What's your first name?
3 And what's your nationality?
4 What's your address?
5 And what's your postcode?
6 What's your mobile number?
7 And what's your home number?
8 What's your email address?

6 a VIDEO ▶1 CD1 ▶26 Watch or listen to Paul's conversation. Tick (✓) the sentences in **5** when you hear them.

b Watch or listen again. Complete the form.

Car Hire Form
Customer ref: 00349

surname
first name — Paul
nationality
address — _____ Road
           Bristol
mobile number — 07969
home number
email address — paul99@webmail.com

REAL WORLD Asking people to repeat things

7 a CD1 ▶27 Listen to these sentences from the conversation in the car hire office. Fill in the gaps with these words.

| repeat | again | please | Could | sorry |

1 I'm _____ ?
2 _____ you say that _____ , please?
3 Could you _____ that, _____ ?

b PRONUNCIATION Listen again and practise.

REAL WORLD 1.3 ▶ p129

8 CD1 ▶28 PRONUNCIATION Listen and practise the questions in **5**. Copy the sentence stress.

9 Work in pairs. Interview your partner and fill in the form. Use the questions in **5**.

Car Hire Form
Customer ref: 00350

surname
first name
nationality
address
mobile number
home number
email address

VOCABULARY AND SKILLS 1D
Lost property

Vocabulary personal possessions; plurals; *this, that, these, those*

QUICK REVIEW Numbers 0–100
Work in pairs. Count from 0 to 51 in threes: A *Zero*. B *Three*. A *Six*. Then count from 0 to 98 in sevens: B *Zero*. A *Seven*. B *Fourteen*.

1 Look at the picture of the lost property room in the conference hotel. Match these words to 1–17.

> diaries 12   wallets
> an MP3 player   a mobile
> watches   an umbrella   bags
> shoes   a camera   coats
> a bike/bicycle   a radio
> suitcases   a laptop
> dresses   ID cards   false teeth

HELP WITH VOCABULARY
Plurals

2 a Write the missing letters. When do we add -s, -es and -ies? Which plurals are irregular?

singular	plural
a bag	bag _
a wallet	wallet _
a suitcase	suitcase _
a watch	watch _ _
a dress	dress _ _
a diary	diar _ _ _
a man	m _ n
a woman	wom _ n
a child	childr _ n
a person	p _ _ ple
a tooth	t _ _ th

b Check in VOCABULARY 1.6 p128.

3 CD1 29 PRONUNCIATION Listen and practise the singular and plural words in **2a**.

4 Write the plurals.
a a bike *bikes*
b a credit card
c a nationality
d a waitress
e a person
f a camera
g an address
h a man
i a country
j a woman

5 Work in pairs. Take turns to test each other on 1–17.

Number 12.   They're diaries.

Number 17.   It's an MP3 player.

6 Eva's got a job at the hotel. Look at the pictures and fill in the gaps with words from **1**.

A What's this in English?
It's an _____.

B What's that in English?
It's a _____.

C What are these in English?
They're _____.

D What are those?!
They're _____!

HELP WITH VOCABULARY
this, *that*, *these*, *those*

7 Fill in the table with *this*, *that*, *these* and *those*.

	here ↓	there ↗
singular		
plural		

8 a CD1 ▶ 30 **PRONUNCIATION** Listen and practise. Copy the stress.

this → *What's this?* → *What's this in English?*

b Choose three things in the classroom or from your bag. Ask your teacher what they are in English.

What's that in English?   It's a poster.

What are these in English?   They're keys.

HELP WITH PRONUNCIATION
Word stress and syllables

1 CD1 ▶ 31 Listen to these words. Notice the stress and number of syllables. Listen again and practise.

Brit-ish   Ja-pan
bi-cy-cle   com-pu-ter   sev-en-teen

2 a Work in pairs. Write the words in the table.

~~teacher~~	musician	address	thirty
thirteen	umbrella	engineer	manager
Brazil	Germany	Japanese	mobile
Mexican	mechanic	unemployed	

Brit-ish	*teacher*
Ja-pan	
bi-cy-cle	
com-pu-ter	
sev-en-teen	

b CD1 ▶ 32 Listen and check. Listen again and practise.

3 a Write five words. Mark the stress on each word.

b Work in pairs. Compare words. Is the stress on your partner's words correct?

continue2learn

■ Vocabulary, Grammar and Real World
- **Extra Practice 1 and Progress Portfolio 1** p115
- **Language Summary 1** p128
- **1A–D** Workbook p5

■ Reading and Writing
- **Portfolio 1** At the hotel Workbook p64
  Reading addresses; hotel registration forms
  Writing capital letters (1); addresses; filling in a hotel registration form

2A What's important?

Vocabulary adjectives (1); adjective word order and *very*
Grammar *have got*: positive and negative, questions and short answers

QUICK REVIEW Personal possessions
What's in the lost property room at the conference hotel? Write all the things you can remember. Work in pairs. Compare lists. Then check on p14.

Vocabulary Adjectives (1)

1 a Tick the adjectives you know. Then do the exercise in VOCABULARY 2.1 p130.

new	old	big	small
good	bad	early	late
cheap	expensive	fast	slow
beautiful	ugly	young	old
easy	difficult	right	wrong
nice	great	important	favourite

b Work in pairs. Take turns to test your partner on the opposites.

old → new

HELP WITH VOCABULARY
Adjective word order and *very*

2 Look at these sentences. Then choose the correct words in the rules.

She's late.
It's a small bag.
It's a very difficult question.
Those are my new shoes.

- We put adjectives *before/after* the verb *be*.
- We put adjectives *before/after* a noun.
- We put *very before/after* adjectives.
- Adjectives *are/aren't* plural with plural nouns.

VOCABULARY 2.2 p130

3 a Make sentences with these words.
1 very / 's / It / early .
   It's very early.
2 answer / right / That / 's / the .
3 very / are / Those / dresses / expensive .
4 cheap / a / It / watch / 's .
5 very / They / good / 're / cameras .
6 question / very / a / difficult / 's / That .

b Work in pairs. Compare sentences.

ALAN What things are important in my life? Well, I've got <u>an old car</u>. It isn't very fast, but I love it. What else? Well, my mobile's very important to me. It's got all my friends' phone numbers on it, my photos, music, everything! I haven't got a laptop, but I've got an old computer. That's important to me for school. And I've got a big TV in my room. That's very important because I love football!

Reading and Listening

4 a CD1 ▶33 Read and listen to Alan and his grandmother, Mary. <u>Underline</u> the things that are important to each person.

b Read the texts again. Find all the adjectives.

c Work in pairs. Compare answers.

HELP WITH GRAMMAR *have got*: positive and negative

5 a Look again at the texts about Alan and Mary. Find all the examples of *'ve got* (= *have got*), *'s got* (= *has got*), *haven't got* and *hasn't got*.

b Fill in the gaps with *'ve, 's, haven't* and *hasn't*.

POSITIVE (+)
I/you/we/they _____ got (= have got)
he/she/it _____ got (= has got)

NEGATIVE (−)
I/you/we/they _____ got (= have not got)
he/she/it _____ got (= has not got)

GRAMMAR 2.1 p131

MARY What's important to me? I've got this very expensive watch. It's from Ben, my husband, and I love it. And my diary – that's important to me too. Ben hasn't got a diary, he's got everything on his mobile these days. And my new bicycle is important to me because we haven't got a car. What else? Well, we've got a beautiful cat, Lily. She's very important!

Listening and Speaking

9 **a** Work in pairs. Look at the table and guess which things Alan and Mary have got. Put a tick (✓) or a cross (✗) in the *guess* columns.

product	Alan guess	Alan answer	Mary guess	Mary answer
laptop	✗	✗		
camera				
MP3 player				
radio				
DVD player				

b CD1 ▶35 Listen to Alan and Mary answer questions for a survey. Complete the *answer* columns. Are your guesses correct?

HELP WITH GRAMMAR
have got: questions and short answers

10 **a** Fill in the gaps with *have, has, haven't* or *hasn't*.

QUESTIONS
Have you got a camera?
_____ he/she got a DVD player?
_____ they got any cheap TVs?
What _____ you got in your bag?

SHORT ANSWERS
Yes, I _____ .
No, I _____ .
Yes, he/she _____ .
No, he/she _____ .
Yes, they _____ .
No, they _____ .

TIP • We use *any* with plural nouns in *yes/no* questions.

b Check in GRAMMAR 2.2 ▶ p131.

6 CD1 ▶34 PRONUNCIATION Listen and practise. Copy the stress and contractions (*I've, he's,* etc.).
I've got an old car.

7 Fill in the gaps with the correct form of *have got*.
1 I *'ve got* (+) a new camera.
2 She _____ (–) a very big house.
3 You _____ (+) a nice car.
4 We _____ (–) a computer.
5 I _____ (–) your mobile number.
6 He _____ (+) a very good TV, but he _____ (–) a DVD player.
7 Mary and Ben _____ (+) a beautiful cat called Lily.
8 They _____ (–) a dog.

8 **a** Think of a friend and write five things he/she has got or hasn't got.

b Work in pairs. Compare lists. Are any of the things the same?

11 CD1 ▶36 PRONUNCIATION Listen and practise the questions and short answers in **10a**.

12 Work in pairs. Ask questions about Alan and Mary.

Has Alan got a new car?   No, he hasn't.

Get ready ... Get it right!

13 Work in pairs. Student A p104. Student B p109.

2B The Browns

Vocabulary family
Grammar possessive 's

QUICK REVIEW *have got* Work in pairs. Ask questions with *have got*. Find five things you've got but your partner hasn't got.

Ben   Mary

~~husband~~   ~~son~~   daughter   father
mother   brother   children

PAM We're a typical British family, I think. My ¹ *husband* 's name is Nick and we've got two ² _____ , a boy and a girl. Our ³ *son* 's name is Robbie and Florence is our ⁴ _____ – she's just a baby. And my parents? Well, Ben is my ⁵ _____ and Mary is my ⁶ _____ . I've got one ⁷ _____ , his name's Greg, and one sister, Jill.

~~wife~~   ~~parents~~   sisters   granddaughter
grandsons   grandchildren

GREG My ⁸ *wife* 's name is Martina and we've got one son, Alan. He's nineteen years old now. I've got two ⁹ _____ , Pam and Jill. Pam's married with two kids and Jill's divorced. My ¹⁰ *parents* ' names are Ben and Mary. They've got three children and three ¹¹ _____ , two ¹² _____ , Alan and Robbie, and a ¹³ _____ , Florence.

Nick   Pam

Jill

Greg   Martina

Robbie   Florence

~~aunts~~   ~~grandparents~~   cousins
grandmother   grandfather   uncle

ALAN My mum and dad's names are Greg and Martina. I've got two ¹⁴ *aunts* , Pam and Jill, and one ¹⁵ _____ . His name's Nick and he's a doctor. I've also got two ¹⁶ _____ , Robbie and Florence. My ¹⁷ *grandparents* ' names are Ben – he's my ¹⁸ _____ – and Mary, my ¹⁹ _____ .

Alan

Vocabulary, Reading and Listening
Family

1 a Look at the family tree. Then read about the family. Fill in the gaps with the words in the boxes.

b CD1▶37 Listen and check your answers.

2 Look again at the family tree. Put the words in the boxes in three groups. Then check in VOCABULARY 2.3 ▶ p130.

1 ♂ male *father/dad*
2 ♀ female *mother/mum*
3 ⚥ male and female *parents*

3 a Write four questions with *How many … ?* about the people in the family tree.

How many brothers and sisters has Pam got?
How many children have Mary and Ben got?

b Work in pairs. Ask and answer your questions.

4 Tick the correct sentences. Change the words in bold in the incorrect sentences.

1 Jill is Pam's ~~cousin~~. *sister*
2 Ben is Mary's **husband**.
3 Jill is Alan's **cousin**.
4 Alan is Martina's **son**.
5 Nick and Pam are Robbie's **grandparents**.
6 Mary is Robbie and Florence's **grandmother**.

HELP WITH GRAMMAR Possessive 's

5 a Look at these sentences. Then read the rule.

Jill is Pam's sister.   My husband's name is Nick.

- We use a name + **'s** (*Pam's*, etc.) or a noun + **'s** (*husband's*, etc.) for the possessive.

b *'s* can mean *is*, *has* or the possessive. Match 1–3 to a–c.

1 Ben is Pam**'s** father.   a *'s = is*
2 Jill**'s** her sister.   b *'s = has*
3 She**'s** got one brother.   c *'s = possessive*

GRAMMAR 2.3 ▶ p131

6 Make sentences about these people.

1 Pam / Alan   3 Robbie / Florence
  Pam is Alan's aunt. 4 Mary / Ben
2 Greg / Martina   5 Florence / Ben and Mary

7 CD1 ▶ 38 **PRONUNCIATION** Listen and practise. Copy the stress.

Ălan's → Păm is Ălan's aunt.

Listening and Speaking

8 Jill wants to show her new boyfriend, Luke, some photos. Look at photos A–D. Who are the people?

A

B

C

D

9 a CD1 ▶ 39 Listen to Jill and Luke's conversation. Put photos A–D in order.

b Listen again and choose the correct words.

1 Jill's sister Pam is an *English/French* teacher.
2 Pam's husband Nick is a *lawyer/doctor*.
3 Their son Robbie is *six/seven*.
4 Jill's brother Greg is an *engineer/accountant*.
5 His wife Martina is *Spanish/Italian*.
6 Jill's mother is *retired/a sales assistant*.
7 Jill's father is *seventy/seventy-three*.

HELP WITH LISTENING
Sentence stress (2)

10 a CD1 ▶ 39 Listen to the first sentence of the conversation again. Notice the sentence stress. We stress the important words.

Lŭke, cŏme and lŏok at thĕse phŏtos of my fămily.

b Look at Audio Script CD1 ▶ 39 p156. Listen to the whole conversation and follow the stressed words.

Get ready ... Get it right!

11 a Write your name and the names of five people in your family on a piece of paper. Think what you can say about these people (age, job, married, etc.). Don't write this information.

b Choose a partner, but don't talk to him/her. Swap papers. Make questions to ask about your partner's family.

Who's (Claudia)?

Is she married?

Has she got any children?

12 a Work with your partner. Take turns to ask questions about his/her family. Make notes on your partner's answers.

b Tell another student about your partner's family.

REAL WORLD 2C — Time and money

Real World telling the time; talking about the time; saying prices; buying tickets at the cinema
Vocabulary time words

QUICK REVIEW Family words Work in pairs. Write all the family words you know. Which words are for men/boys, women/girls, or both?

What's the time?

1 a Put these time words in order.

| a minute | a year | a day | a week |
| an hour | a second | 1 | a month |

b Work in pairs. Ask and answer these questions.
1 How many minutes are in an hour?
2 How many hours are in a day?
3 How many months are in a year?
4 How many weeks are in a year?
5 How many hours are in a week?
6 How many days are in a year?

2 a Match the times to pictures A–F.

one o'clock A   quarter to ten   twenty past five
half past seven   quarter past four   twenty to nine

b We can say times in a different way. Match these times to pictures A–F.

four fifteen   five twenty   seven thirty
eight forty   nine forty-five   one

3 a Complete the times.

1 five past _____   2 twenty-five to _____   3 ten _____

4 _____ eleven   5 _____ -five   6 _____ _____

b Check in REAL WORLD 2.1 ▶ p131.

4 CD1 ▶ 40 Listen and match conversations 1–3 to three of the pictures A–F in **2a**.

REAL WORLD Talking about the time

5 a Fill in the gaps in the questions and answers.

What time ¹_____ it?   It's ²_____ o'clock.

What's the ³_____, please?   It's about half ⁴_____ seven.

Excuse me. Have you ⁵_____ the time, please?   Yes, it's four fifteen.

b Fill in the gaps with *to*, *from* or *at*.
1 My English class is _____ ten.
2 My son's class is _____ seven _____ nine thirty.

REAL WORLD 2.2 ▶ p132

6 a CD1 ▶ 41 **PRONUNCIATION** Listen and practise the questions and answers in **5a**. Copy the polite intonation in the questions.

b Write six times. Work in pairs. Ask and answer the questions in **5a**. Write your partner's times. Are they correct?

BRENT GALLERY
Mexican Art
July 20th–September 3rd

Opening times
10.00–1_____ Mon–Fri
10.00–2_____ Sat & Sun
Adults a £9.50 / £10.50
Children b £5.60 / £6.50
Ticket office: 08081 570570
Book online: www.brentgallery.org.uk   A

FilmWorld
Acton Lane, London W3 5HU

Now showing
A New Day (12)
3_____, 7.00, 9.20
The Brothers (15)
5.00, 4_____, 9.30

Tickets: Adults c £10.50 / £11.50
Children d £7.25 / £8.25

For more information phone
08081 570203
www.filmworld.co.uk   B

An evening out

7 a Look at adverts A and B. Which is for a cinema and which is for an exhibition?

b CD1 42 Listen and write the missing times 1–4 on the adverts.

8 a Work in pairs. How do we say these prices?

£20	£7.50	40p	£29.99
€9	€6.50	$35	50c

b CD1 43 **PRONUNCIATION** Listen and check. Listen again and practise.

c CD1 44 Listen and choose the correct ticket prices a–d on adverts A and B.

9 a Before you watch or listen, check these words with your teacher.

buy   popcorn   a screen   start

b VIDEO 2 CD1 45 Look at the photo in a cinema. Watch or listen to the people's conversations with the ticket seller. Which film do Chris and Louise want to see? Which film do Alison and Josh want to see?

10 VIDEO 2 CD1 45 Watch or listen again. Complete the table.

	price of tickets	time film starts	screen number
Chris and Louise			
Alison and Josh			

REAL WORLD Buying tickets at the cinema

11 a Read the sentences. Fill in the gaps with these words.

~~Can~~   adults   time   are
Thanks   please   is   welcome

CUSTOMER

1 _Can_ I have (two) tickets for (*The Brothers*), please?

(Two) tickets for (*A New Day*), 2_____. One adult and one child.

How much 3_____ that?
How much 4_____ the tickets?

Here you are. What 6_____ is the film?

Right. 7_____ a lot. Thank you very much.

TICKET SELLER

Yes, of course.

That's (£23), please.
(£11.50) for 5_____ and (£8.45) for children. So that's (£19.95), please.

It starts at (seven fifteen).
It starts in (two minutes).

You're 8_____. Enjoy the film.

b Check in **REAL WORLD 2.4** p132.

12 CD1 46 Listen and practise the customer's sentences in **11a**.

13 Work in pairs. Student A p105. Student B p110.

REAL WORLD

VOCABULARY 2D AND SKILLS > Where's the baby?

Vocabulary things in a house; prepositions of place
Skills listening: a conversation

QUICK REVIEW Times and prices Write four times and four prices. Work in pairs. Say them to your partner. He/She writes them down. Are they correct?

1 Work in pairs. Which of these words do you know? Then do the exercise in VOCABULARY 2.5 > p130.

> a mirror   a desk   a sofa   a carpet   a door   a bookcase
> a window   the floor   a plant   a coffee table   a lamp   curtains

HELP WITH VOCABULARY Prepositions of place

2 Where's the cat? Match the prepositions to pictures 1–6. Then check in VOCABULARY 2.6 > p131.

> in   on   by   under   behind   in front of

1  2  3

4    5    6

3 a Look at the picture. Choose six of these things. Write sentences to say where they are.

Nick's suitcase is behind the sofa.

> Nick's suitcase
> Nick's keys
> Nick's mobile phone
> Pam's coat
> Robbie's new shoes
> the cat
> Robbie's bag
> Robbie's books
> Nick's passport
> Robbie's MP3 player
> the lamp
> the DVDs

b Work in pairs. Compare sentences. Are your partner's sentences correct?

4 Work in pairs. Cover the box in **3a**. Point at things in the picture and ask questions with *Whose …?*

- Whose mobile phone is this?
- It's Nick's.
- Whose shoes are these?
- They're Robbie's.

5 a CD1 ▶47 Listen and tick the things in the box in **3a** that the family talk about.

b Listen again. Three things are in the wrong place in the picture. What are they?

c Where's the baby?!

6 Look at Audio Script CD1 ▶47 p156. Listen again and underline all the prepositions of place.

7 Look at the picture for one minute. Then cover the picture. Work in pairs. Take turns to ask where things are in the living room.

- Where's Robbie's bag?
- It's by the door.

HELP WITH PRONUNCIATION
The schwa /ə/ in words

1 a CD1 ▶48 The schwa /ə/ is very common in English. Listen to these words. Notice the schwas. Is the schwa stressed?

address   mechanic   Poland   teacher
/ə/   /ə/   /ə/   /ə/

doctor   number   manager   accountant
/ə/   /ə/   /ə//ə/   /ə/

b Listen again and practise.

2 a Work in pairs. Underline the schwa in each word.

China   seven   actor   important   second
daughter   parents   Japan   police   sofa

b CD1 ▶49 Listen and check. Listen again and practise.

3 a Look at these words. (Circle) the word with a schwa.

1 email / (letter)   5 laptop / computer
2 dentist / cleaner   6 Italy / Egypt
3 seventy / ninety   7 window / mirror
4 Spanish / German   8 Saturday / Tuesday

b Work in pairs. Compare answers.

c CD1 ▶50 Listen and check. Listen again and practise.

continue2learn

■ **Vocabulary, Grammar and Real World**
- **Extra Practice 2 and Progress Portfolio 2** p116
- **Language Summary 2** p130
- **2A–D** Workbook 2 p10

■ **Reading and Writing**
- **Portfolio 2** My favourite thing Workbook p66
  Reading people's favourite things
  Writing capital letters (2); punctuation; a description of your favourite thing

3A My day

Vocabulary daily routines
Grammar Present Simple (1): positive and Wh- questions (I/you/we/they)

QUICK REVIEW Prepositions of place
Work in pairs. Say where something is in the classroom: A *It's on the floor behind the teacher's desk.* Your partner guesses what it is: B *Is it a bag?* A *Yes, it is./No, it isn't.*

Vocabulary Daily routines

1 a Tick the words/phrases you know. Then do the exercise in VOCABULARY 3.1 ▶ p132.

> get up   go to bed   leave home   get home
> have breakfast   have lunch   have dinner
> start work/classes   finish work/classes
> work   study   sleep   live

TIP • In these vocabulary boxes we only show the main stress in phrases.

b Match two of the words/phrases from **1a** to these times of day.

1 in the morning *get up*   3 in the evening
2 in the afternoon   4 at night

c Work in pairs. Compare answers. Are they the same?

Reading and Speaking

2 a Look at the photos of Kari Matchett. What's her job?

b Before you read, check these words/phrases with your teacher.

> glamorous   a TV show   a studio
> hair   make-up   learn your lines

c Work in pairs. Guess the times that TV actors do these things.

1 get up   3 start work
2 have breakfast   4 have lunch

d Read the article and check your answers.

3 Read the article again. Are these sentences true (T) or false (F)? Correct the false sentences.

                Canada
1 Kari Matchett is from ~~Los Angeles~~.   *F*
2 TV actors get up very late.
3 They have breakfast at the studio.
4 They work for six hours before lunch.
5 They have half an hour for lunch.

Behind the Camera
by David Ross

This week I talk to Kari Matchett, star of the TV shows *24* and *ER*, about a typical day at the studio and her glamorous life as an actress.

DAVID Where are you from, Kari?
KARI I'm from Canada, but I live and work in Los Angeles.
D Can you tell us about your day-to-day life?
K Well, TV actors work very long days and we start work very early.
D What time do you get up?
K I get up at 4.30 in the morning.
D Wow! You get up very early.

HELP WITH GRAMMAR
Present Simple (1): positive (I/you/we/they)

• We use the Present Simple to talk about daily routines.

4 a Find the verbs in these sentences. They are in the Present Simple.

1 I (get up) at 4.30 in the morning.
2 You get up very early.
3 We start work at about 7.00.
4 They have an hour for lunch.

b Is the Present Simple the same or different after *I*, *you*, *we* and *they*?

GRAMMAR 3.1 ▶ p134

5 CD1 ▶51 **PRONUNCIATION** Listen and practise the sentences in **4a**. Copy the stress.

I get up at four thirty in the morning.

6 a Look at Kari's answers in the article again. Underline all the verbs in the Present Simple.

b Work in pairs. Compare answers.

HELP WITH GRAMMAR Present Simple (1): Wh- questions (I/you/we/they)

9 **a** Look at the table. Notice the word order in questions.

question word	auxiliary	subject	infinitive	
What time	do	you	get up?	
When	do	you	have	lunch?

TIP • Present Simple questions are the same for I, you, we and they.

b Write questions 1–3 in the table.
1 When do you finish work?
2 What time do you get home?
3 Where do you have dinner?

c Check in GRAMMAR 3.2 ▶ p134.

10 **a** Make questions with these words.
1 Where / live / you / do ? *Where do you live?*
2 you / do / Where / work ?
3 What time / get up / you / do ?
4 start / When / do / you / work or classes ?
5 do / What time / get / you / home ?
6 dinner / do / When / you / have ?

b CD1 ▶ 52 **PRONUNCIATION** Listen and check. Notice how we say *do you* /djə/. Then listen again and practise.

Where do you /djə/ live?

c Work in pairs. Ask and answer the questions in **10a**.

K Yes, and I'm not very good in the morning, so it's always difficult! I leave home at 5.30 and I get to the studio at about 6.00. That's when people do my hair and make-up.
D What about breakfast?
K I have breakfast at about 6.15 in the make-up room. Then we start work at about 7.00.
D When do you have lunch?
K We have lunch at 1.00 and we start work again at 2.00.

7 Read about Kari's afternoon and evening routine. Fill in the gaps with these verbs.

| ~~finish~~ | get | go | start | finish | sleep |

D When do you finish work?
K Most days we ¹ *finish* at about 9.00.
D You ² _____ work at 7.00 and you ³ _____ work at 9.00!
K Yes, it's a very long day, but sometimes I ⁴ _____ for an hour in the afternoon.
D What time do you get home?
K I ⁵ _____ home at about 9.30.
D Where do you have dinner?
K Usually at home while I learn my lines for the next day. Then I ⁶ _____ to bed at 11.00.
D So do you have a glamorous life?
K Not when I'm at work, no – definitely not!

8 **a** Write six sentences about your daily routine. Use words/phrases from **1a**.

I start work at half past eight.

b Work in pairs. Compare sentences.

Get ready … Get it right!

11 Write eight questions about people's routines in the week or at the weekend. Use words/phrases from **1a**.

What time do you go to bed in the week?
When do you get up at the weekend?

12 **a** Ask other students your questions. For each question, find one student who does this at the same time as you.

b Tell the class two things that you and other students do at the same time.

25

3B Free time

Vocabulary free time activities (1); time phrases with *on*, *in*, *at*, *every*
Grammar Present Simple (2): negative and *yes/no* questions (*I/you/we/they*)

QUICK REVIEW Daily routines Work in pairs. Ask and answer questions about your Sunday routines: **A** *What time do you get up on Sundays?* **B** *At about eleven. And you?* Are the times the same or different?

Vocabulary Free time activities (1)

1 a Work in pairs. Which of these phrases do you know? Then do the exercise in VOCABULARY 3.2 > p133.

> stay in   go out (a lot)   eat out
> go for a drink   go to the cinema
> go to concerts   go shopping
> phone friends/my family
> visit friends/my family
> have coffee with friends
> do (a lot of) sport
> watch (a lot of) TV/DVDs

b Work in new pairs. What are your five favourite things to do on Saturdays?

Listening

2 Look at the photo of Freddie and Jeanette. Where are they? Are they good friends, do you think?

3 a CD1 ▶ 53 Listen to Freddie and Jeanette's conversation. Are these sentences true (T) or false (F)?
1 Freddie and Jeanette are good friends. *F*
2 They work in the same office.
3 They watch a lot of DVDs.
4 Freddie's got tickets for a concert on Saturday.
5 Freddie and Jeanette are single.

b Listen again. Tick the things in **1a** that Jeanette does in her free time.
1 go out after work
2 watch TV in the evenings
3 go to the cinema
4 watch a lot of DVDs ✓
5 go shopping on Saturday morning
6 go out on Saturday evening
7 visit her parents on Sunday afternoon
8 go to concerts

HELP WITH GRAMMAR
Present Simple (2): negative (*I/you/we/they*)

4 a Look at the table. Notice the word order.

subject	auxiliary	infinitive	
I	don't (= do not)	go out	on Saturday evening.
You	don't	work	in this office.

b Write sentences 1 and 2 in the table.
1 We don't stay in at the weekend.
2 They don't watch TV in the day.

c Check in GRAMMAR 3.3 > p134.

5 a Tick the sentences that are true for you. Make the other sentences negative.
1 I study English. ✓
2 I phone my family every day
   I don't phone my family every day.
3 I go shopping on Saturdays.
4 I watch TV every evening.
5 I eat out with my friends a lot.
6 I live near this school.
7 I have lunch at 12.00 every day.
8 I work at the weekends.

b Work in pairs. Compare sentences.

HELP WITH GRAMMAR Present Simple (2): yes/no questions and short answers (I/you/we/they)

6 a Look at the table. Notice the word order in the questions.

YES/NO QUESTIONS (?)				SHORT ANSWERS
auxiliary	subject	infinitive		
Do	you	eat out	a lot?	Yes, I do. No, I don't.
				Yes, we _____. No, we _____.
				Yes, they _____. No, they _____.

b Write questions 1 and 2 in the table.
1 Do you go to concerts?   2 Do they watch TV a lot?

c Fill in the gaps in the *short answers* column with *do* or *don't*.

d Check in GRAMMAR 3.4 p134.

HELP WITH LISTENING
Weak forms (1): *do you ... ?*

7 a CD1 54 Listen to how we usually say *do you*.

YOU EXPECT TO HEAR	YOU USUALLY HEAR
Do you /duː juː/	Do you /djə/
Do you /duː juː/ go out after work?	Do you /djə/ go out after work?

b CD1 55 Listen to these questions. Fill in the gaps. You will hear each sentence twice.
1 What _____ _____ _____ in the evenings?
2 _____ _____ _____ to the cinema?
3 What _____ _____ _____ at the weekends?
4 _____ _____ _____ to concerts?

8 a Fill in the gaps with *do*, *don't* or a verb from the box.

~~go out~~   visit   go out   watch   go (x2)

1 A *Do* you *go out* a lot in the week?
   B Yes, we _____ .
2 A _____ you _____ your parents at the weekend?
   B Yes, I _____ .
3 A _____ you _____ to concerts at the weekend?
   B No, we _____ .
4 A _____ you _____ shopping on Saturdays?
   B Yes, I _____ .
5 A _____ your parents _____ on Saturday evenings?
   B No, they _____ . They stay in and _____ TV.

b CD1 56 PRONUNCIATION Listen and check. Listen again and practise. Copy the stress and weak forms.

Do you /djə/ gò out a lòt in the wèek?

c Work in pairs. Take turns to ask the questions in **8a**. Answer for you.

Vocabulary and Speaking
Time phrases with *on, in, at, every*

9 a Write these words and phrases in the correct place. Some words and phrases can go in more than one place. Then check in VOCABULARY 3.3 p133.

~~Saturday~~   ~~the morning~~   ~~nine o'clock~~
~~week~~   the afternoon   day
the evening   month   half past three
night   the week   Mondays
Monday mornings   the weekend
morning   Sunday afternoon

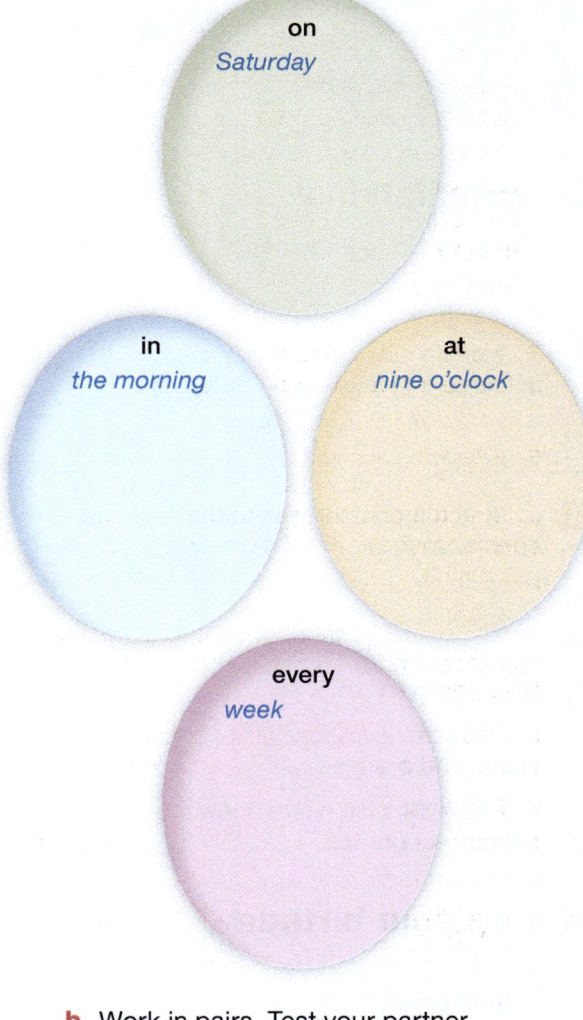

b Work in pairs. Test your partner.

the weekend   at the weekend

Get ready ... Get it right!

10 Work in two groups. Group A p105. Group B p110.

3C REAL WORLD — Special days

Real World phrases for special days; talking about days and dates; suggestions
Vocabulary months; dates

QUICK REVIEW Free time activities Write four ways to end this sentence: *On a perfect day I … .* Work in pairs. Compare your days.

Congratulations!

1 Match cards A–E to special days 1–5.
1 a birthday
2 a wedding
3 the birth of a new baby
4 a New Year's Eve party
5 a wedding anniversary

2 a Match these phrases to the special days in **1**.
Happy birthday!
Happy New Year!
Congratulations!
Happy anniversary!

b CD1 ▶ 57 PRONUNCIATION
Listen and practise.

c CD1 ▶ 58 Listen and answer with the correct phrase.

When's your birthday?

3 a Put the months in the correct order.

July   March   December
January 1 April   October
August   June   February
November   May   September

b CD1 ▶ 59 PRONUNCIATION
Listen and check. Listen again and practise.

4 a Match the dates with the words. Then check in VOCABULARY 3.5 ▶ p133.

1st	second	13th	twentieth
2nd	twelfth	20th	thirty-first
3rd	fourth	21st	thirtieth
4th	fifth	22nd	twenty-second
5th	first	30th	twenty-first
12th	third	31st	thirteenth

b CD1 ▶ 60 PRONUNCIATION Listen and practise the dates in **4a**.

REAL WORLD Talking about days and dates

5 a Match questions 1–4 to answers a–d. Notice the words in bold.
1 What day is it today?
2 What's the date today?
3 What's the date tomorrow?
4 When's your birthday?

a (It's) **the** fifth **of** March.
b (It's) March **the** sixth.
c (It's **on**) June the third.
d It's Wednesday.

b CD1 ▶ 61 PRONUNCIATION Listen and check. Listen again and practise.

REAL WORLD 3.2 ▶ p134

6 CD1 ▶ 62 Listen to six conversations. Which dates do you hear?
1 September 5th / 15th
2 December 13th / 30th
3 March 4th / 14th
4 July 2nd / 22nd
5 October 13th / 30th
6 February 1st / 5th

7 a Write four dates that are important to you every year.

b Work in pairs. Say your dates to your partner. Write your partner's dates. Then ask why they are important.

Why is May 6th important to you?

Because it's my wedding anniversary.

Chris | Louise

What shall we get her?

8 a VIDEO 3 CD1 63 Watch or listen to Louise and her husband, Chris. What do they decide to buy their friend Sophie for her birthday?

b Watch or listen again and choose the correct answer.
1 The date today is the *19th/29th*.
2 It's Sophie's birthday on *Tuesday/Thursday*.
3 Louise *has got/hasn't got* Sophie a birthday card.
4 Sophie *has got/hasn't got* an MP3 player.
5 Sophie *has got/hasn't got* lots of books.
6 Sophie and Marcus *watch/don't watch* a lot of DVDs.

REAL WORLD Suggestions

9 Read these sentences. Fill in the gaps with these words.

| ~~get~~ | good | What | Why | think | her |

What shall we ¹ *get* her?
² _____ about (an MP3 player)?
✗ No, I don't ³ _____ so.
⁴ _____ don't we get her (a book)?
✓✗ Maybe.
Let's get ⁵ _____ (a DVD).
✓ Yes, that's a ⁶ _____ idea.

TIP • We can say *get* or *buy*: *What shall we get/buy her?*

REAL WORLD 3.3 ▶ p134

10 CD1 64 PRONUNCIATION Listen and practise the sentences in **9**.

What shall we get her?

11 Sophie and Marcus want to buy their son Liam a birthday present. Fill in the gaps with the correct words.

SOPHIE It's Liam's ¹ *birthday* next week. What ² _____ we get him?
MARCUS ³ _____ don't ⁴ _____ get him a laptop?
S No, I ⁵ _____ think ⁶ _____ . Let's ⁷ _____ him a new mobile.
M Maybe. But his mobile's only a year old.
S I know! What ⁸ _____ a new bike?
M Yes, ⁹ _____ a good ¹⁰ _____ .

12 a Work in pairs. It's Louise's birthday next week. Sophie and Marcus want to buy her a present. Write their conversation. Use language from **9**.

b Practise the conversation until you remember it.

c Work in groups of four. Role-play your conversations for the other pair. What present do the other pair choose?

VOCABULARY 3D AND SKILLS > Early bird?

Vocabulary frequency adverbs
Grammar subject and object pronouns
Skills reading: a questionnaire; listening: a conversation

QUICK REVIEW Dates Work in pairs. Take turns to say the dates 1st–31st: A *First*. B *Second*. A *Third* … . Then say them backwards! A *Thirty-first*. B *Thirtieth*. A *Twenty-ninth* … .

1 Put these frequency adverbs on the line. Then check in VOCABULARY 3.6 > p133.

~~hardly ever~~   never   always   sometimes   often   usually

hardly ever 
100% ——————————————————— 0%

2 a Read the questionnaire. Tick your answers.

b Look at p114. What's your score? Are you an early bird or a night owl?

c Work in groups. Compare scores. How many of your answers are the same?

3 a CD1 > 65 Listen to Jeanette and her husband, Dominic. Write *J* by Jeanette's answers to the questionnaire.

b Work in pairs. Compare answers. What's Jeanette's score? What kind of person is she?

HELP WITH VOCABULARY
Word order of frequency adverbs

4 a Underline the frequency adverbs (*often*, etc.) in the questionnaire.

b Choose the correct words in the rules.
- Frequency adverbs go *before/after* the verb *be*.
- Frequency adverbs go *before/after* other verbs.

VOCABULARY 3.7 > p133.

5 a Put a frequency adverb in these sentences and make them true for you.
1 I get up at eight in the morning.
   I never get up at eight in the morning.
2 I have breakfast before 9 a.m.
3 I'm tired on Friday evenings.
4 I study English in the evening.
5 I'm happy on Monday mornings.
6 I go to the cinema at the weekend.
7 I'm late for my English class.
8 I watch TV on Sunday afternoons.

b Work in pairs. Compare sentences. How many are the same?

Are you an early bird or a night owl?
Do the questionnaire to find out!

1 When I get up in the morning …
a I'm always happy and I have a lot of energy.
b I'm sometimes happy, but I don't have a lot of energy.
c I'm not very happy and I never have a lot of energy.

2 At the weekend …
a I sometimes get up before 9 a.m.
b I always get up before 9 a.m.
c I hardly ever get up before 9 a.m.

3 When I go to a party …
a I always stay to the end.
b I sometimes stay to the end.
c I never stay to the end.

4 When there's a good film on TV late at night …
a I always watch **it** to the end.
b I usually record **it** and go to bed.
c I often watch the beginning but I never see the end.

5 When I see friends at the weekend …
a I usually see **them** in the afternoon.
b I sometimes have coffee with **them** in the morning.
c I hardly ever see **them** before 9 p.m.

6 When a friend phones me before 8 a.m. …
a I'm always happy to talk to **him**/**her**.
b I'm sometimes happy to talk to **him**/**her**.
c I never answer the phone.

30

HELP WITH GRAMMAR
Subject and object pronouns

6 **a** Look at the words in pink and blue in these sentences. Which are subject pronouns? Which are object pronouns?

I usually see them in the afternoon.
We hardly ever see him in the week.

b Look at questions 4–6 in the questionnaire. Fill in the table with the object pronouns in blue.

subject pronouns	object pronouns
I	me
you	you
he	
she	
it	
we	us
they	

c Check in **GRAMMAR 3.5** p134.

7 **a** Choose the correct words.
1 Lauren's my sister and (I)/me see she/her every Sunday.
2 Ian and I phone Eve a lot, but she/her never phones we/us.
3 My name's Zachariah, but my friends always call I/me Zak.
4 Alexander's our son and we/us see he/him every weekend.
5 Rob and Andy are my cousins, but I/me hardly ever talk to they/them.

b Work in pairs. Compare answers. Underline the object pronouns. Who do they refer to?

1 her → Lauren

8 **a** Write two things you: always, usually, sometimes, hardly ever do in the morning.

always – get up early, have coffee

b Work in new pairs. Compare answers. Are any the same?

I always get up early in the morning.

Me too.

HELP WITH PRONUNCIATION
How we say *th*

1 **a** **CD1 ▶ 66** Listen to these sounds and words. Notice the two ways we say *th*.

/θ/	/ð/
fourth thirteenth	the this that
month birthday	these those
think thing	they their
Thursday teeth	with mother
	father brother

b Listen again and practise.

2 **a** **CD1 ▶ 67** Listen to these sentences. Listen again and practise.
1 Who's that over there with Matthew's father?
2 It's Kathy's thirty-third birthday this Thursday.
3 I think Beth's three brothers are with their mother.
4 That's the sixth or seventh time this month.
5 Thanks for taking those things to Theo's brother.
6 I think those are their father's things.

b Work in pairs. Take turns to say the sentences. Is your partner's pronunciation correct?

c Say one of the sentences for the class.

continue2learn

■ **Vocabulary, Grammar and Real World**
- **Extra Practice 3 and Progress Portfolio 3** p117
- **Language Summary 3** p132
- **3A–D** Workbook p15

■ **Reading and Writing**
- **Portfolio 3** All about me Workbook p68
  Reading learner profiles
  Writing connecting words (1): *and*, *but*, *because*; a learner profile

4A Away from home

Vocabulary free time activities (2)
Grammar Present Simple (3): positive and negative (*he/she/it*)

QUICK REVIEW **Frequency adverbs** Write sentences about things you: never, sometimes, always, often do on Saturdays. Work in pairs. Take turns to say your sentences. Are any the same?

Vocabulary and Speaking
Free time activities (2)

1 a Tick the phrases you know. Then do the exercise in VOCABULARY 4.1 p135.

> take photos   go to the gym
> watch sport on TV   play video games
> play tennis   read books or magazines
> go cycling   go swimming   go running
> go clubbing   listen to music
> listen to the radio

TIP • We can say *play video games* or *play computer games*.

b Work in pairs. Ask and answer questions about the free time activities in **1a**.

> Do you watch sport on TV?
> No, never.
> Yes, every weekend.

Listening and Speaking

2 a Before you read and listen, check these words with your teacher.

> an observatory   stars   the weather
> a holiday   hot   rain

b Read the email and look at the photo. Where is Trevor? Who is Polly, do you think?

c CD1 ▶68 Listen to Polly and her friend, Lorna. Choose the correct answers.
1 Trevor is in *Argentina/Chile*.
2 Trevor and Polly *are/aren't* married.
3 Trevor's got *three/four* weeks' holiday.
4 The hotel *is/isn't* very good.

3 a Work in pairs. What does Trevor do in his free time, do you think? Choose six activities from **1a**.

b CD1 ▶69 Listen to the rest of Polly and Lorna's conversation. Are your guesses correct?

HELP WITH LISTENING Linking (1)
• We usually link consonant (*b, c, d, f,* etc.) sounds at the end of a word with vowel (*a, e, i, o, u*) sounds at the beginning of the next word.

4 a CD1 ▶70 Listen and notice the linking.

YOU EXPECT TO HEAR	YOU USUALLY HEAR
And all of	And‿all‿of
the people are nice	the people‿are nice
And all of the people are nice.	And‿all‿of the people‿are nice.

b Look at Audio Script CD1 ▶69 p157. Listen again and notice the linking in Polly's part of the conversation.

HELP WITH GRAMMAR
Present Simple (3): positive and negative (*he/she/it*)

5 a Look at these sentences. Then complete the rules.
*He **plays** video games.*
*He **doesn't like** the weather.*
*He **watches** lots of DVDs.*
*She **doesn't talk** to him very often.*

• In positive sentences with *he*, *she* and *it* we add _____ or _____ to the infinitive.
• In negative sentences with *he*, *she* and *it* we use _____ + infinitive.

TIP • *have* is irregular: *he/she/it **has** …* : *He **has** tennis lessons every week.*

b Check in GRAMMAR 4.1 p137.

To: polly.carr@gomail.co.uk

Hi Polly

Here's a photo of Cerro Paranal observatory this evening. Isn't it beautiful? What a great place to work. The only problem is – you're not here!

Lots of love
Trevor

6 **a** Check the spelling rules in GRAMMAR 4.2 p137. Then write the *he/she/it* forms of these verbs.

| watch | play | go | write | phone | get |
| finish | have | study | start | do | live |

b CD1 71 PRONUNCIATION Listen and practise the infinitives and the *he/she/it* forms of the verbs in **6a**. Which have the sound /ɪz/ at the end?
*watch, watch**es** /ɪz/*

7 Fill in the gaps with the correct form of the verbs in brackets.

Lorna and Polly are both sales assistants in London, but they ¹ *don't work* (not work) in the same shop. Polly ² _____ (work) in a shoe shop and Lorna ³ _____ (work) in a bookshop. In their free time they ⁴ _____ (read) a lot. Lorna ⁵ _____ (not like) sport, but Polly ⁶ _____ (play) tennis a lot and she ⁷ _____ (watch) sport on TV. At the weekend Lorna ⁸ _____ (not stay) in London. She ⁹ _____ (go) to see her parents in Bath. Polly ¹⁰ _____ (not visit) her parents very often because they ¹¹ _____ (not live) in England.

Get ready ... Get it right!

8 **a** Choose a partner, but don't talk to him/her. Look at the words/phrases in the box. Guess what your partner does or doesn't do in his/her free time. Complete the sentences with the positive or negative form of the verbs in brackets.

My partner's name _____

He/She _____ swimming. (go)
He/She _____ tennis. (play)
He/She _____ sport on TV. (watch)
He/She _____ to the gym. (go)
He/She _____ books/magazines. (read)
He/She _____ video games. (play)
He/She _____ cycling. (go)
He/She _____ a lot of DVDs. (watch)
He/She _____ clubbing. (go)

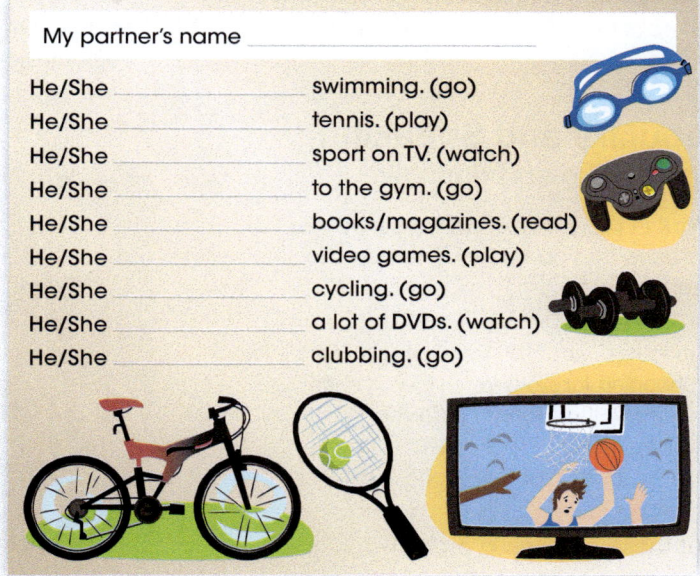

b Make questions with *you* for each sentence in the box.
Do you go swimming?

9 **a** Work with your partner. Take turns to ask your questions. How many of your guesses are correct?

Do you go swimming?   Yes, I do.   No, I don't.

Yes, sometimes.

b Tell another student about your partner.

Alex doesn't go swimming, but she plays tennis a lot.

4B First Date!

Vocabulary things you like and don't like; verb+*ing*
Grammar Present Simple (4): questions and short answers (*he/she/it*)

QUICK REVIEW Free time activities
Write eight free time activities. Work in pairs. Tell your partner when you do the things on your list: *I play tennis on Fridays. I watch sport on TV at the weekend.*

Vocabulary and Speaking
Things you like and don't like

1 Work in pairs. Which of these words/phrases do you know? Then do the exercise in VOCABULARY 4.2 ▶ p135.

> reading   football   travelling   cats
> shopping for clothes   video games
> animals   dancing   cooking
> dance music   rock music   jazz
> Italian food   Chinese food   fast food

2 Put these phrases in order 1–7.

> I love … 1   I hate … 7   I like …
> … is/are OK.   I don't like …
> I really like …   I quite like …

HELP WITH VOCABULARY
Verb+*ing*

3 a With the phrases in 2 we can use verb+*ing* or a noun. Look at these sentences.
*I love **reading**.* (verb+*ing*)
*I like **books**.* (noun)

b Find all the verb+*ing* words in 1.

TIP • We use *enjoy* + verb+*ing* to say we like doing something: *I enjoy travelling.*

VOCABULARY 4.4 ▶ p135

4 Work in pairs. Talk about the things in 1 and your own ideas. Do you like the same things?

> I really like video games.
> Me too./I don't. I hate them.
> Do you like dance music?
> Yes, I love it./It's OK./No, not really.

PRESENTER Hello and welcome to *First Date!*. Tonight you choose a date for Mark Skipper. Mark is 28 years old and he's a teacher. In his free time he watches TV and plays video games. He also goes to the cinema a lot and he plays football and tennis every weekend. He loves rock music and Chinese food, but he hates shopping for clothes! He also likes animals – he's got a dog and three cats. So, Mark – who do you want to ask about first?

MARK Er, Kim, please.

PRESENTER OK. Remember, you can only ask six questions.

Reading, Listening and Speaking

5 CD1 ▶ 72 Read and listen to the TV game show, *First Date!*. Find four things Mark likes and one thing he doesn't like.

6 a Match Mark's questions about Kim to the presenter's answers.

1 What does she do in her free time?
2 Does she watch TV a lot?
3 Does she like films?
4 What music does she like?
5 Does she like animals?
6 And what does she do?

a Yes, she does. She's got two dogs.
b Yes, she goes to the cinema every Saturday evening.
c She loves dance music, but she doesn't like rock music.
d She plays tennis and she eats out a lot. She loves Italian food.
e No, she doesn't. She hates watching TV!
f She's a vet.

b CD1 ▶ 73 Listen and check.

HELP WITH GRAMMAR Present Simple (4): questions and short answers (*he/she/it*)

7 **a** Look at **6a**. Then fill in the gaps with *does* or *doesn't*.

QUESTIONS | SHORT ANSWERS
1 _____ she **like** animals? | Yes, she _____ .
2 _____ she **watch** TV a lot? | No, she _____ .
3 What _____ she **do** in her free time?

b Look at the table. Notice the word order in questions. Then write questions 3 and 4 from **6a** in the table.

question word	auxiliary	subject	infinitive	
What	does	she	do	in her free time?
	Does	she	watch	TV a lot?

c Check in GRAMMAR 4.3 p137. Then read GRAMMAR 4.4 p137.

8 **a** Write questions with *she*.
1 What / do? *What does she do?*
2 / like rock music?
3 What food / like?
4 / like sport?
5 / have any animals?
6 What / do on Saturday evenings?

b CD1 74 PRONUNCIATION Listen and check. Listen again and practise. Copy the stress.

What does she do?

c Work in pairs. Ask and answer the questions in **8a** about Kim. Find her answers in **6a**.

9 **a** Work in pairs. Student A, read about Jo on p105. Student B, read about Susie on p110. Find the answers to the questions in **8a**.

b Work with your partner. Ask and answer the questions in **8a** about Jo or Susie.

c Tell your partner three more things about Jo or Susie.

10 **a** Work in groups. Which woman do you want to choose for Mark's first date – Kim, Jo or Susie? Why?

b Tell the class which woman your group wants for Mark's first date and why. The class must agree on one person!

c Read about Mark's date with the woman the class chose. (Kim p106, Jo p111, Susie p114). Answer these questions.
1 Does Mark like her? Why? / Why not?
2 Does she like Mark? Why? / Why not?
3 Do they want to see each other again?

Get ready … Get it right!

11 **a** Work in pairs, but don't talk to your partner. Choose a friend to introduce to your partner. Tick the things in the box that your friend does or likes.

I've got a friend for you!

My friend's name: _____
- [ ] watches TV a lot
- [ ] likes travelling/cooking/clubbing
- [ ] plays tennis/football
- [ ] likes shopping for clothes
- [ ] goes to the cinema a lot
- [ ] likes cats/dogs/animals
- [ ] reads a lot of books
- [ ] likes rock music/dance music/jazz
- [ ] eats out a lot
- [ ] likes Chinese/Italian/fast food

b Choose eight things you do or like from the box. Make questions with *he* or *she*.

Does he/she watch TV a lot?

Does he/she like Italian food?

12 **a** Work with your partner. Ask and answer questions about your friends. First, ask about the friend's name, age, job and where he or she lives. Then ask your questions from **11b**.

b Do you and your partner's friend do or like the same things? Tell another student.

We both eat out a lot.

He likes rock music, but I don't.

4C ▶ REAL WORLD — Eating out

Real World requests and offers
Vocabulary food and drink (1)

QUICK REVIEW Present Simple questions with *he/she* Write the names of three people in your family. Work in pairs. Ask questions about the people on your partner's list: *What does Marcia do in her free time?*

The Sun Café

Pizzas	Margherita	£8.50
	Neapolitan	£9.25
Burgers	Burger and chips	£8.75
	Cheeseburger and chips	£9.50
Salads	Tuna	£9.50
	Chicken	£10.25
	Mixed	£4.50
Sandwiches	Egg mayonnaise	£5.75
	Cheese and tomato	£6.25
Desserts	Apple pie with cream	£5.25
	Fruit salad	£4.75
	Vanilla, chocolate or strawberry ice cream	£3.25
Drinks	Red/White wine (Glass)	£4.75
	(Bottle)	£14.50
	Bottle of beer	£3.75
	Bottle of mineral water (still or sparkling)	£2.75
	Tea or coffee	£2.50

See you at the Sun Café!

1 Work in groups. Discuss these questions.
 1 When do you usually eat out?
 2 What's your favourite café or restaurant?
 3 Is it cheap or expensive?
 4 What do you usually eat there?

2 a Work in pairs. Match photos 1–13 to food and drink on the menu. Check in **VOCABULARY 4.5** p136.

b Work in pairs. Take turns to point to photos 1–13 and test your partner.

> What's number 1?

> A cheese and tomato sandwich.

3 Work in pairs. Take turns to choose something to eat and drink from the menu. Ask your partner questions with *How much …?*

> How much is a tuna salad and a bottle of mineral water?

> Twelve pounds twenty-five.

HELP WITH LISTENING Would you like … ?

4 a CD1 ▶75 We use *Would you like … ?* for offers. Listen and notice how we say *would you* in questions.

YOU EXPECT TO HEAR	YOU USUALLY HEAR
would you /wʊd juː/	would you /wʊdʒə/
Would you /wʊd juː/ like to order now?	Would you /wʊdʒə/ like to order now?

b CD1 ▶76 Listen and put these questions in the order you hear them.
 a Would you like tea or coffee?
 b Would you like anything else?
 c Would you like a dessert?
 d What would you like to drink?

5 a VIDEO ▶4 CD1 ▶77 Close your books. Watch or listen to Paul and Clare at the Sun Café. What do they order?

b Work in pairs. Compare answers.

REAL WORLD
Requests and offers

7 a Look at sentences 1–3. Which sentences are requests (we want something)? Which sentence is an offer (we want to give something or help someone)?

1 **Would you like** to order now?
2 **I'd / We'd like** a bottle of mineral water, please.
3 **Can I / we have** the bill, please?

b Complete the rules with the phrases in bold in **7a**.

- We use _____ and _____ for requests.
- We use _____ for offers.

c Look at the conversation in **6a** again. Find four more requests.

REAL WORLD 4.1 ▶ p137

8 a CD1 ▶ 78 Listen to the sentences in **7a**. Notice the stress and polite intonation.

Would you like to order now?

b CD1 ▶ 79 **PRONUNCIATION** Listen and practise the offers and requests in the conversation in **6a**. Copy the stress and polite intonation.

9 a Work in groups of three. Decide who is the waiter/waitress and who are the customers. Practise the conversation in **6a** until you remember it.

b Close your book. Practise the conversation again.

10 a Work in the same groups. Look at the menu. Write a new conversation between a waiter/waitress and two customers.

b Swap conversations with another group. Correct any mistakes.

c Practise the new conversation with your partner. Then role-play it for the other group.

---

6 a Read Paul and Clare's conversations with the waitress. Fill in the gaps with the questions from **4b**.

WAITRESS Would you like to order now?
CLARE Yes, I'd like the chicken salad, please.
PAUL Can I have the cheeseburger and chips, please?
WAITRESS ¹_____?
CLARE We'd like a bottle of mineral water, please.
WAITRESS Still or sparkling?
CLARE Sparkling, please.
WAITRESS ²_____?
PAUL No, that's all, thanks.

WAITRESS ³_____?
CLARE Yes, I'd like the fruit salad, please.
PAUL And can I have the apple pie with cream?
WAITRESS Certainly.

WAITRESS ⁴_____?
CLARE Not for me, thank you.
PAUL No, thank you. Can we have the bill, please?
WAITRESS Yes, of course.

b VIDEO ▶ 4 CD1 ▶ 77 Watch or listen again. Check your answers.

VOCABULARY 4D AND SKILLS > Breakfast time

Vocabulary food and drink (2); countable and uncountable nouns
Skills listening: a conversation

QUICK REVIEW Food and drink Work in pairs. What's on the Sun Café menu? Work with another pair. Which pair has the most things? Check the menu on p36.

1 Tick the food and drink you know. Then do the exercise in VOCABULARY 4.6 > p136.

> biscuits   milk   an apple   rice   yogurt
> sugar   toast   bread   fish   eggs   coffee
> sausages   soup   cheese   a banana
> orange juice   a croissant   tea   jam   meat
> fruit   cereal   olives   tomatoes   vegetables

2 Which of the things in **1** do you usually have for breakfast? Is this typical for your country? Compare answers in groups.

3 a What do you think people in Japan, France and Turkey have for breakfast? Work in pairs and make three lists. Use words from **1**.

b CD1 > 80 Listen to a chef and his assistant, Dylan, at a language school in the UK. Tick the food and drink on your lists that they talk about.

c Listen again. Complete your lists of the three breakfast menus.

4 a Look at the pictures in the table. Then choose the correct words.

1 We *can/can't* count biscuits and apples.
2 We *can/can't* count milk and rice.

COUNTABLE NOUNS		UNCOUNTABLE NOUNS	
singular	plural		
a biscuit	*biscuits*	*milk*	*rice*
an apple	*apples*		

b Write the words from **1** in the table. Write the singular and plural if possible.

HELP WITH VOCABULARY
Countable and uncountable nouns

5 a Look at the table in **4a**. Choose the correct words in these rules.

COUNTABLE NOUNS

- Countable nouns *have/don't have* a plural form.
- We *use/don't use* **a** or **an** with singular countable nouns.
- We *use/don't use* **a** or **an** with plural countable nouns.

UNCOUNTABLE NOUNS

- Uncountable nouns *are/aren't* usually plural.
- We *use/don't use* **a** or **an** with uncountable nouns.

b Check in VOCABULARY 4.7 > p136.

6 Choose the correct answer: *a*, *an* or – (no article).
1 Sue never has *a* / – milk in her tea.
2 I have *an* / – egg for breakfast every day.
3 Do you want *a* / – biscuit?
4 I love *a* / – cheese sandwiches.
5 Ted usually has *a* / – soup for lunch.
6 Would you like *a* / – banana?
7 Do you eat *a* / – fruit?

7 a Fill in the gaps with *a*, *an* or – .
1 I often have _____ rice with my main meal.
2 My friends and I sometimes go out for _____ burger.
3 I always have _____ toast and jam for breakfast.
4 I never have _____ sugar in coffee.
5 I like _____ olives in my salad.
6 I have _____ apple every day.
7 I often have _____ sandwich for lunch.
8 I never eat _____ meat.

b Make the sentences in **7a** true for you. Change the underlined words if necessary.

I often have chips with my main meal.

c Work in pairs. Compare sentences. Are any the same?

8 Work in groups. Tell the other students which food and drink you like/don't like.

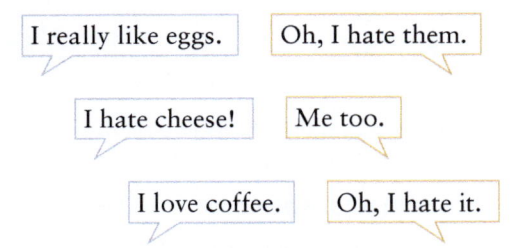

I really like eggs.
Oh, I hate them.
I hate cheese!
Me too.
I love coffee.
Oh, I hate it.

9 a Imagine your perfect breakfast. Answer these questions.
1 Where are you?
2 What time is it?
3 Who are you with?
4 What do you have for breakfast?
5 What do you do after breakfast?

b Work in groups. Tell the other students about your perfect breakfast.

HELP WITH PRONUNCIATION
/ʃ/, /tʃ/ and /dʒ/

1 CD1 81 Listen to the sounds and words. Listen again and practise.
1 /ʃ/ **sh**opping fini**sh** Turki**sh**
2 /tʃ/ **ch**eap wat**ch** **ch**ildren
3 /dʒ/ **G**ermany **J**apan sausa**g**es

2 a Work in pairs. Match the letters in bold in these words to sounds 1–3 in **1**.

English 1   **ch**eese   **j**am   **ch**icken
ve**g**etables   sandwi**ch**   musi**c**ian   en**g**ineer
tea**ch**er   Ru**ss**ia   **j**azz   na**t**ionality

b CD1 82 Listen and check. Listen again and practise.

3 a CD1 83 Listen to these sentences. Listen again and practise.
1 My Russian teacher loves jazz.
2 George eats a lot of jam sandwiches.
3 Jane loves chocolate and Turkish coffee.
4 Janet's got a cheap Japanese watch.
5 Joe often has chicken and vegetables.
6 Roger likes Spanish sausages, French cheese and German beer.

b Work in pairs. Take turns to say the sentences. Is your partner's pronunciation correct?

continue2learn

■ **Vocabulary, Grammar and Real World**
- **Extra Practice 4 and Progress Portfolio 4** p118
- **Language Summary 4** p135
- **4A–D** Workbook p20

■ **Reading and Writing**
- **Portfolio 4** Going out Workbook p70
  Reading restaurant adverts
  Writing messages (1): an email

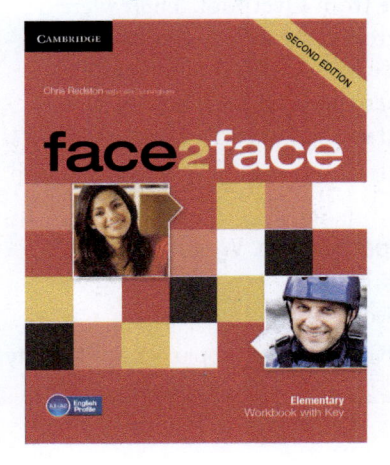

5A Three generations

Vocabulary adjectives (2); years
Grammar Past Simple (1): *be* (positive and negative, questions and short answers)

QUICK REVIEW Food and drink Work in pairs. Write all the words for food and drink you know. Compare answers with another pair. Which pair has more words? Which words are countable/uncountable?

Vocabulary Adjectives (2)

1 a Work in pairs. Which of these adjectives do you know? Then do the exercise in VOCABULARY 5.1 ▶ p138.

hot	cold
noisy	quiet
well	ill
short	tall
lucky	unlucky
different	the same
happy	unhappy
boring	interesting
friendly	unfriendly
terrible/awful	fantastic/amazing/wonderful

b Work in pairs. Test your partner on the opposites.

happy — unhappy

Listening and Reading

2 a Look at photo A. Where are the people? What's their relationship, do you think?

b CD2 ▶ 1 Listen and read. Who is talking? How old is he?

> I live in Bristol with my parents and my sister. It was my thirteenth birthday yesterday and there was a big party at our house. About thirty people were here, and we were lucky because it was a very hot day. I was happy because my granddad was here from Liverpool. There were only two things wrong. My best friend Robert wasn't here because he was ill. And my two brothers weren't here because they're in the USA. But it was a fantastic party!

c Read about the party again. Which of these things are <u>not</u> in the text?

- where the family lives
- the weather
- people at the party
- people not at the party
- food and drink
- birthday presents

Photo A: Albert, Matt, Jason

HELP WITH GRAMMAR
Past Simple (1): *be* (positive and negative)

3 a Look at the text in **2b** again. Underline all the examples of *was*, *wasn't*, *were* and *weren't*.

b Fill in the gaps with *was*, *wasn't*, *were* and *weren't*.

POSITIVE (+)	NEGATIVE (–)
I was	I _____ (= was not)
you/we/they _____	you/we/they _____ (= were not)
he/she/it _____	he/she/it _____

c Check in GRAMMAR 5.1 ▶ p139.

4 Read about Matt's thirteenth birthday party. Choose the correct words.

> I ¹(*was*)/*were* born in Liverpool in 1974 and I ²*was*/*were* thirteen in 1987. Our house ³*wasn't*/*weren't* very big, so my party ⁴*was*/*were* at my grandparents' house. The house ⁵*was*/*were* cold and the food ⁶*wasn't*/*weren't* very nice. Only about twelve people ⁷*was*/*were* at the party and there ⁸*wasn't*/*weren't* any girls my age. So the party ⁹*was*/*were* a bit boring.

Listening and Speaking

5 **a** CD2 2 Look at photo B. Listen to Jason ask his grandfather, Albert, about his thirteenth birthday party. Where was he? Why was his birthday a special day?

b Listen again and answer the questions.
1 When was Albert's 13th birthday?
2 Where was the party?
3 Were his friends there?
4 Was the food good?
5 Where were his grandparents?

HELP WITH LISTENING
Weak forms (2): *was* and *were*

6 **a** CD2 3 Listen and notice the weak forms of *was* and *were*.
I was /wəz/ in Liverpool with my parents.
All my friends were /wə/ there.
Was /wəz/ the food good?
Were /wə/ your grandparents there?

b Look at Audio Script CD2 2 p158. Listen again and notice the weak forms of *was* and *were* in pink.

HELP WITH GRAMMAR Past Simple (1): *be* (questions and short answers)

7 **a** Look at the table. Notice the word order. Then write questions 2, 4 and 5 from **5b** in the table.

question word	was/were	subject	
When	was	Albert's	13th birthday?
	Were	his friends	there?

b Fill in the gaps in these short answers with *was*, *were*, *wasn't* or *weren't*.

Yes, I/he/she/it _____ .   No, I/he/she/it _____ .
Yes, you/we/they _____ .   No, you/we/they _____ .

c Fill in the gaps with *was* or *were*.
1 A When _____ you born?
  B I _____ born in 1940.
2 A Where _____ Matt born?
  B He _____ born in Liverpool.

d Check in GRAMMAR 5.2 p139.

8 CD2 4 PRONUNCIATION Listen and practise. Copy the stress and weak forms.
I was /wəz/ in Liverpool with my parents.

9 **a** Work in pairs. How do we say these years?

| 1835 | 1900 | 1990 | 2000 | 2005 | 2018 |

b CD2 5 PRONUNCIATION Listen and check. Listen again and practise.

c Write the names of five people in your family. Then work in pairs. Swap papers. Ask your partner when and where the people were born.

When was Miguel born?   In 1986.

10 **a** Make questions with *you*.
1 / at work yesterday? *Were you at work yesterday?*
2 Where / last night?
3 / at home yesterday afternoon?
4 Where / on your last birthday?
5 Where / last New Year's Eve?

b Work in new pairs. Ask and answer the questions. Give more information if possible.

Get ready … Get it right!

11 Work in pairs. Student A p105. Student B p110.

5B Famous films

Vocabulary life events
Grammar Past Simple (2): regular and irregular verbs (positive and Wh- questions)

QUICK REVIEW Past Simple (1): *be* Write six times of the day. Work in pairs. Ask your partner where he/she was at these times yesterday: *Where were you at six in the evening?*

Vocabulary
Life events

1 a Work in pairs. Fill in the gaps in the phrases with these verbs. Check in VOCABULARY 5.3 p138.

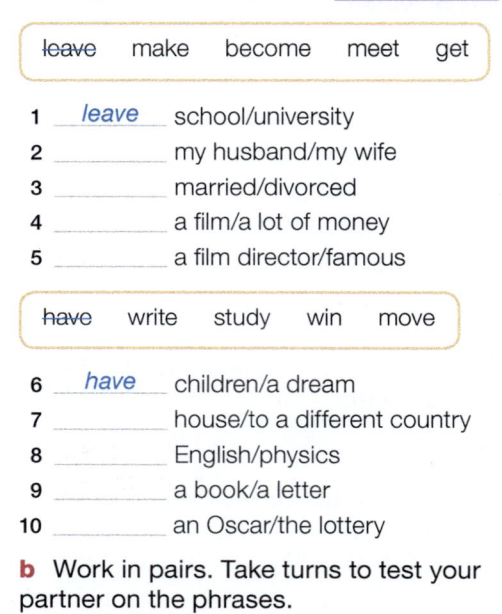

| leave | make | become | meet | get |

1. _leave_ school/university
2. _____ my husband/my wife
3. _____ married/divorced
4. _____ a film/a lot of money
5. _____ a film director/famous

| have | write | study | win | move |

6. _have_ children/a dream
7. _____ house/to a different country
8. _____ English/physics
9. _____ a book/a letter
10. _____ an Oscar/the lottery

b Work in pairs. Take turns to test your partner on the phrases.

married | get married

Speaking, Reading and Listening

2 Work in groups. Look at posters A–D. What do you know about these films? What do you know about the director James Cameron?

3 a Check these words with your teacher.

a script | a robot | successful
diving | 3D | a billion

b Read the article about James Cameron's life. Fill in the gaps with these dates and numbers.

1971 | twelve | 1999 | two
August 16th | 1986 | $2 billion

c Work in pairs. Compare answers.

d CD2 ▶ 6 Listen and check your answers.

CAMERON'S WORLD

James Cameron was born in Ontario, Canada, on ᵃ_____ 1954. His family moved to the USA in ᵇ_____. James went to California State University and studied physics and English. He left university after only ᶜ_____ years because he wanted to become a film director. He worked as a bus driver in the day and wrote film scripts at night. James's first job as a director was on a film called *Piranha 2*. One night after filming he had a bad dream about a robot from the future. The next day James started writing the script of *The Terminator*. The film was very successful and Cameron became famous all around the world.

He then made *Aliens* in ᵈ_____, *Terminator 2* in 1991 and *Titanic* in 1997. At that time James loved diving, and he visited the Titanic ᵉ_____ times before he started making the film. *Titanic* made ᶠ_____ and won eleven Oscars. His next film was the first *Avatar* movie in 2009, which he made in 3D.

James met Linda Hamilton – Sarah Connor in the *Terminator* films – in 1984 and she became his fourth wife in 1997. They had one daughter, but they got divorced in ᵍ_____. A year later he married actress Suzy Amis, who was in *Titanic*. They have two daughters and a son.

HELP WITH GRAMMAR
Past Simple (2): regular and irregular verbs (positive)

4 a Look at the regular Past Simple forms in blue in the article. Then answer these questions.
1. How do we make the Past Simple of regular verbs?
2. What do we do when the verb ends in -e (*move*, *love*, etc.)?
3. What do we do when the verb ends in -y (*study*, *marry*, etc.)?

b Look at the irregular Past Simple forms in pink in the article. Match them to verbs 1–9.

1. become _____
2. get _____
3. go _____
4. have _____
5. leave _____
6. make _____
7. meet _____
8. win _____
9. write _____

TIP • The Past Simple is the same for all subjects (*I, you, he, she, it, we, they*).

c Check in GRAMMAR 5.3 ▶ p139 and in the Irregular Verb List, p167.

7 Fill in the gaps with the Past Simple of these verbs.

| ~~love~~ | marry | write | win | be | get | start | make |

1 James Cameron _loved_ films when he _____ a child.
2 He _____ the film director Kathryn Bigelow in 1989, but they _____ divorced in 1991.
3 He _____ the script for the second *Rambo* film.
4 He _____ a film called *True Lies* in 1994.
5 His film *Aliens* _____ two Oscars.
6 He _____ writing the script for *Avatar* in 1995.

8 a Cover the article. Choose the correct answers.
1 What did James study at university?
   a Physics.   b English.   c Physics and English.
2 When did he make *Terminator 2*?
   a In 1986.   b In 1991.   c In 1999.
3 Which film did he make in 3D in 2009?
   a *Aliens*   b *Titanic*   c *Avatar*
4 Who did he marry in 1997?
   a Sarah Connor.   b Suzy Amis.   c Linda Hamilton.

b Look at the article. Check your answers.

HELP WITH GRAMMAR
Past Simple (2): *Wh-* questions

9 a Look at the table. Notice the word order in questions. Then write questions 3 and 4 from **8a** in the table.

question word	auxiliary	subject	infinitive	
What	did	James	study	at university?
When	did	he	make	*Terminator 2*?

b Check in GRAMMAR 5.4 p139.

10 a Make questions with these words.
1 yesterday / did / you / What / do ?
2 go on holiday / you / did / last year / Where ?
3 What / you / last weekend / do / did ?
4 see / last month / How many films / you / did ?
5 meet / you / your best friend / did / Where ?

b CD2 11 PRONUNCIATION Listen and check. Notice how we say *did you* /dɪdʒə/. Listen again and practise.
What did you /dɪdʒə/ do yesterday?

c Work in pairs. Ask and answer the questions in **10a**.

Get ready ... Get it right!

11 Work in pairs. Look at p114.

5 a CD2 7 PRONUNCIATION Listen and practise the regular verbs in the article and their Past Simple forms. Which end with the sound /ɪd/?

b CD2 8 PRONUNCIATION Listen and practise the irregular verbs in **4b** and their Past Simple forms.

HELP WITH LISTENING
Present Simple or Past Simple

6 a CD2 9 Listen to these sentences. Notice the difference between the Present Simple and the Past Simple.
1 I **love** all his films. I **loved** all his films.
2 They **live** in L.A. They **lived** in L.A.

b CD2 10 Listen to six pairs of sentences. Which do you hear <u>first</u>, the Present Simple or the Past Simple?
1 Present Simple

5C REAL WORLD — Four weekends

Real World showing interest; asking follow-up questions
Vocabulary weekend activities

QUICK REVIEW Past Simple Write six verbs you know. Work in pairs. Say the verb to your partner. He/She says a sentence with the Past Simple form: **A** go **B** I went to England last year.

Weekend activities

1 a Work in pairs. Look at phrases 1–8. Then fill in the gaps with these words/phrases. Check in **VOCABULARY 5.4** p138.

> a run   for a couple of days
> the house   a bad cold   a report
> at home all weekend   your homework
> your parents' house for lunch

1 go for — a walk / *a run*
2 clean — the car
3 do — the washing
4 write — an email
5 go away — for the weekend
6 have — a great time
7 go to — a party
8 stay — with friends

b What are the Past Simple forms of the verbs in **1a**?

2 a Think of five things you did last weekend. Use phrases from **1a** or your own ideas.

b Work in pairs. Ask your partner what he or she did last weekend. Find three things you both did.

> What did you do last weekend?
> I went for a walk on Sunday.
> Me too.

A
To: Clive Roberts
Hi Clive
Just a note to say I'm sorry I wasn't at the party. I was ill all weekend. I think it was because I worked every evening last week!

B goldfish
Had a quiet weekend. Stayed in and watched TV on Saturday. Last night I went to the cinema to see *A Day in the Life*.
10th June at 07.46   Like Comment Share

Emily   *Tim*

How was your weekend?

3 a VIDEO 5 CD2 12 Look at the photos and read A–D. Then watch or listen to two conversations and match the people to A–D.

b Watch or listen again. Are these sentences true (T) or false (F)?

CONVERSATION 1
1 Tim had a terrible weekend. *T*
2 Emily did the washing on Saturday.
3 She went to the theatre.
4 She didn't like the film.

CONVERSATION 2
5 Rachel went to Madrid with a friend.
6 She stayed in a hotel.
7 Simon had an interesting weekend.
8 He finished the report on Sunday evening.

5 CD2 ▶14 **PRONUNCIATION** Listen and practise the responses in **4b**. Copy the intonation.

REAL WORLD
Asking follow-up questions

6 a Look at these follow-up questions from the conversations in **3b**. Fill in the gaps with *did*, *was* or *are*.

1 What _____ wrong?
2 _____ you OK now?
3 What _____ you do?
4 What _____ you see?
5 What *was* it like?
6 Where _____ you go?
7 Who _____ you go with?
8 Where _____ you stay?

b Which of the questions in **6a** can you ask someone who:

a was ill at the weekend?
b stayed at home?
c went to the cinema?
d went away for the weekend?

c Check in REAL WORLD 5.2 ▶ p139.

7 a Work in pairs. Look at VIDEO ▶5 CD2 ▶12 p158. Choose one of the conversations. Underline all the responses from **4a** and follow-up questions from **6a**.

b Practise the conversation with your partner.

8 a Make notes on what you did at these times.

- last weekend
- last week
- yesterday
- before you came to this lesson
- on Friday evening

b Work in new pairs. Ask and answer questions about the times in **8a**. Use the follow-up questions from **6a**. How long can you continue each conversation?

> What did you do last weekend?

> Well, I went to a party on Saturday.

> Oh, nice. What was it like?

> It was great!

c Tell the class three things about your partner.

C **Things to do**
- go shopping ✓
- clean the car ✓
- check emails ✓
- go to gym ✓
- write report ✓

D 9.17am All Contacts Edit

Hi Pablo and Marta! It was great to go away for the weekend. We had a wonderful time with you in Madrid. Thanks again!

REAL WORLD Showing interest

4 a CD2 ▶13 Listen to parts of the conversations in **3b** again. Match sentences 1–8 to responses a–h.

1 I was ill all weekend.
2 I had a really bad cold.
3 I stayed at home on Saturday.
4 I went to the cinema.
5 I went away for the weekend – to Spain!
6 We went to Madrid. It was wonderful!
7 I worked all Sunday.
8 It took me ten hours.

a Oh, right.
b Wow!
c Oh, dear.
d What a shame.
e Really?
f You're joking!
g Oh, nice.
h Oh, great!

b Fill in the table with responses a–h.

I'm happy for you.	I'm sorry for you.	I'm surprised.	I'm not surprised.
			Oh, right.

c Check in REAL WORLD 5.1 ▶ p139.

VOCABULARY 5D AND SKILLS > Competitions

Vocabulary adjectives (3); adjectives with *very, really, quite, too*
Skills reading: a magazine article

QUICK REVIEW Past Simple Work in pairs. Take turns to tell your partner five things you did last week: **A** *I went to a concert on Saturday.* Ask follow-up questions to get more information: **B** *What was it like?*

1 a Work in pairs. Which of these adjectives do you know? Then do the exercise in **VOCABULARY 5.5 ▶ p138**.

bored   crowded   busy   comfortable
dirty   rich   dangerous   clean
poor   excited   safe   empty

b Put the words in **1a** into groups a–c:
a adjectives for people   *bored*
b adjectives for places   *crowded*
c adjectives for places and people   *busy*

c Work in pairs. Compare answers. Which words in **1a** are opposites?

2 a Before you read, check these words/phrases with your teacher.

enter a competition   win a prize
a castle   a queue   a receptionist

b Work in pairs. Discuss these questions.
1 Do you think you're a lucky person? Why?/Why not?
2 Do you (or people you know) enter competitions in magazines or on the internet?
3 What prizes do people win in competitions?
4 What prize would you like to win?

c Look at the magazine article. Read the first paragraph only. What is the article about?

3 a Work in pairs. Student A, read about Bruce. Student B, read about Sally. Answer these questions.
1 What did he/she win?
2 Who did he/she go with?
3 Did he/she like the hotel?
4 What did they do on Saturday?
5 Where did they have dinner?
6 Was the food good?
7 What did Bruce/Craig do on Sunday?

b Work with your partner and ask the questions. Student A, ask about Sally. Student B, ask about Bruce. Give more information if possible.

c Read your partner's text. Check his/her answers.

Winners and Losers

A lot of people enter competitions every year and 99% of them never win anything. But what about the winners? Do they always enjoy their prizes? We talked to two people with very different experiences.

BRUCE I won a weekend for two in Kraków, in Poland. I went with my girlfriend, Olivia, and we stayed in a very nice hotel by the river. The rooms were really comfortable and the people were very friendly. On Saturday we went for a walk in the Old Town. It was quite crowded, but all the shops and buildings were really interesting. We wanted to visit Wawel Castle, but the queues were quite long, so we had lunch instead. In the evening we went back to the hotel and had dinner in the restaurant. It was very busy, but the food was fantastic! Then on Sunday I asked Olivia to marry me – and she said yes! We were very happy when we got home. It was a wonderful weekend in a beautiful city!

SALLY I'm not usually very lucky, but last year I won a weekend for two in Cardiff. I went with my boyfriend, Craig. I was really excited because I love Wales, but the hotel was really awful. It was in a poor part of town and the rooms were very small and quite noisy. On Saturday we didn't leave the hotel because it was too cold. Craig watched sport on TV all day and I was really bored! We had dinner in the hotel, but the restaurant was quite dirty and the food was awful. I went to bed early, but Craig stayed up and talked to the receptionist for hours. She was very young and friendly – too friendly! On Sunday Craig left me and went away with her. It was a terrible weekend!

HELP WITH VOCABULARY
Adjectives with *very*, *really*, *quite*, *too*

4 a Look at pictures 1–3 and read the sentences. Which word in bold means 'more than you want'?

1 It's **quite** big.   2 It's **very/really** big.   3 It's **too** big.

b Complete the rule with *before* and *after*.
- *Very*, *really*, *quite* and *too* come _____ the verb *be* and _____ adjectives.

VOCABULARY 5.6 ▶ p138

5 a Read the article again and underline all the examples of *very*, *really*, *quite*, *too* + adjective.

b Work in pairs. Compare answers.

6 Choose the correct words.
1 Don't go out on your own at night. It's *quite*/*too* dangerous.
2 He's a famous musician and he's *too/very* rich.
3 Let's go to that new café. It's *really/too* nice.
4 Sorry, sir, you're *quite/too* late. The restaurant is closed.
5 This sofa's *very/too* comfortable.
6 Jill's got a new job and she's *really/too* happy.
7 It's a nice town and the people are *very/too* friendly.
8 You're only 15. You're *quite/too* young to drive.

7 a Write the name of a place in the town or city where you are now that is:
1 too expensive or quite cheap
2 really beautiful or really ugly
3 too crowded or quite empty
4 really boring or really interesting
5 too noisy or very quiet
6 very safe or quite dangerous

b Work in groups and compare places. Do you know any of the places the other students talk about? If so, do you agree?

> I think the new coffee shop is very cheap.

> Me too.

> Really? I think it's quite expensive!

HELP WITH PRONUNCIATION
The letter *o*

1 CD2 ▶ 15 Listen and notice four ways we say the letter *o*. Listen again and practise.

/ɒ/ h**o**t l**o**ng **o**ften   /ʌ/ s**o**n m**o**nth m**o**ther
/əʊ/ **o**ld h**o**me ph**o**ne   /ə/ act**o**r p**o**lice sec**o**nd

2 a Work in pairs. Write the words in the table.

~~coffee~~ sofa tomato wonderful
shopping sometimes mobile computer
open director bottle comfortable

/ɒ/	h**o**t	*coffee*
/əʊ/	**o**ld	
/ʌ/	s**o**n	
/ə/	act**o**r	

b CD2 ▶ 16 Listen and check. Listen again and practise.

3 Work in pairs. Cover **1** and **2a**. Say these words. Which letter *o* sound is different?
1 tomato actor (sometimes) director
2 phone wonderful mobile old
3 son month bottle comfortable
4 mother often hot shopping
5 police second computer long
6 open home sofa coffee

continue2learn

■ **Vocabulary, Grammar and Real World**
   ■ **Extra Practice 5 and Progress Portfolio 5** p119
   ■ **Language Summary 5** p138
   ■ **5A–D** Workbook p25

■ **Reading and Writing**
   ■ **Portfolio 5** A night to remember Workbook p72
   Reading a student's composition
   Writing paragraphs (1); connecting words (2): *after*, *when* and *then*; a composition

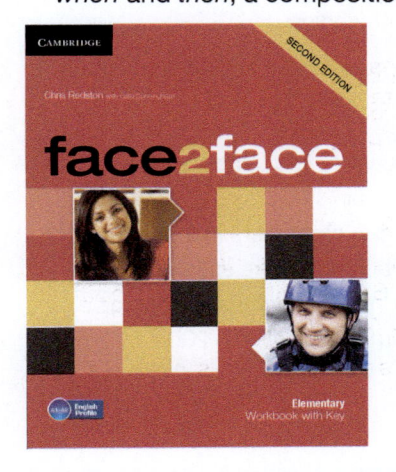

6A Google it!

Vocabulary the internet
Grammar Past Simple (3): negative, yes/no questions and short answers

> **QUICK REVIEW** Adjectives with *very, really, quite, too*
> Think of three places you went to last year. Work in pairs. Tell your partner about the places. Use adjectives with *very, really, quite* and *too*: *I went to Istanbul last year. It was really beautiful.*

Vocabulary and Speaking
The internet

1 a Choose the correct verbs in these sentences about the internet. Then check in **VOCABULARY 6.1** p140.

1. Do you *use*/*send* the internet every day?
2. How many emails do you *go*/*send* every day?
3. How many emails do you *get*/*chat* every day?
4. When did you last *chat*/*read* a blog?
5. Do you *download*/*go* videos or music onto your computer?
6. When did you last *go*/*send* online?
7. Do you *get*/*have* a favourite website?
8. Do you *send*/*chat* to your friends online?
9. Which places in your town or city *have*/*download* WiFi?
10. Which search engine do you usually *write*/*use*?

b Work in pairs. Ask and answer the questions. Ask follow-up questions if possible.

Reading and Speaking

2 a Before you read, check these words/phrases with your teacher.

| launch | computer science | build (past: built) |
| a cheque | a bank account | a billionaire |

b Read the article about the Google Guys. Match headings a–d to paragraphs 1–4.

a. Starting the business
b. How Page and Brin met
c. The internet before 1998
d. Building a new search engine

c Read the article again. Tick the true sentences. Correct the false sentences.

1. Before 1998 it was ~~easy~~ *difficult* to find things on the internet. *F*
2. Page and Brin first met in 1997.
3. They had a lot of cheap computers in their room.
4. They built Google when they were students.
5. Google was the first name for their search engine.
6. Page and Brin became billionaires in 2004.

THE Google GUYS

1 What did we do before Google? In the early days of the internet, search engines weren't very good and it wasn't easy for people to find the information they wanted. Then in 1998, Larry Page and Sergey Brin launched the Google search engine. Suddenly it was easy to find the right website in seconds.

Larry Page — *Sergey Brin*

HELP WITH GRAMMAR
Past Simple (3): negative

3 Complete the rules with words from these sentences.

Search engines weren't very good.
They didn't like each other at first.

- To make the Past Simple negative of the verb *be*, we use *wasn't* or _____ .
- To make the Past Simple negative of all other verbs, we use _____ + infinitive.

GRAMMAR 6.1 p141

4 a Find six more Past Simple negatives in the article.

b Work in pairs. Compare answers.

5 **CD2 17 PRONUNCIATION** Listen and practise.

They didn't like each other at first.

2 So how did it all begin? Page and Brin met in 1995 when they started studying computer science at Stanford University in California. They didn't like each other at first, but they became friends when they shared a room together at university.

3 While Page and Brin were at Stanford, they got a lot of cheap computers and started to build a new search engine in their room. At first they called it BackRub, but they weren't happy with the name so they changed it to Google. They didn't finish their course and left Stanford in 1997.

4 Page and Brin wanted to start a business together, but they didn't have any money. At first their families and friends helped them. Then in August 1998 a businessman wrote a cheque to Google Inc for $100,000. But Page and Brin didn't get the money for a month because they didn't have a bank account. Six years later they were billionaires!

6 a Tick the sentences that are true for you. Make the other sentences negative.

1 I got lots of emails yesterday.
I didn't get lots of emails yesterday.
2 I watched a DVD on my computer last Saturday.
3 I used the internet every day last week.
4 I downloaded a lot of music last weekend.
5 I got a new laptop last year.
6 I chatted online with a friend last night.

b Work in pairs. Compare sentences. How many are the same?

Listening and Speaking

7 a CD2 18 Listen to a radio interview with the writer, Wes Clark. Put these people, places and things in the order you hear them.

Michigan State University	Wes Clark's new book 1
Russia	Sergey's mother	Maryland University
Larry's parents	Sergey's father	

b Listen again. Answer the questions.
1 Did Sergey leave Russia in 1978?
2 Did his father teach mathematics?
3 Were Sergey and his father at the same university?
4 Did Larry go to Maryland University?
5 Did his parents teach computer science?
6 Was Larry at the same university as his parents?

HELP WITH GRAMMAR Past Simple (3): yes/no questions and short answers

8 Fill in the gaps in these yes/no questions and short answers with *did* or *didn't*.

1 A _Did_ Sergey leave Russia in 1978?
  B Yes, he _____./No, he _____.
2 A _____ his parents teach computer science?
  B Yes, they _____./No, they _____.

GRAMMAR 6.2 p141

9 a Make yes/no questions with these words.
1 in 1994 / Sergey and Larry / meet / Did ?
Did Sergey and Larry meet in 1994?
2 they / at first / each other / Did / like ?
3 Sergey / Did / Maryland University / go to ?
4 Larry's parents / teach / mathematics / Did ?
5 study / Sergey / Did / computer science ?
6 launch / Google / in 1999 / Sergey and Larry / Did ?

b CD2 19 PRONUNCIATION Listen and practise the questions in **9a** and the short answers. Copy the stress.
Did Sérgey and Lárry méet in 1994?

c Work in pairs. Ask and answer the questions in **9a**.

Get ready ... Get it right!

10 Write yes/no questions with *you* and these ideas. Use these verbs.

| ~~go~~ | play | have | read |
| watch (x2) | go to (x2) | | |

1 shopping last weekend?
Did you go shopping last weekend?
2 a good book last month?
3 sport on TV last weekend?
4 a concert last month?
5 tennis or football last week?
6 a DVD last weekend?
7 the cinema last week?
8 dinner at home last night?

11 a Ask other students your questions. Find one person who did each thing. Ask follow-up questions.

b Tell the class two things about the people you talked to.

Beata went shopping last weekend. She bought a new laptop.

6B Changing technology

Vocabulary mobile phones and TVs; past time phrases
Grammar can/can't; could/couldn't

QUICK REVIEW Past Simple yes/no questions
Write five questions with *Did you … ?* about yesterday. Choose a partner and guess his/her answers. Then work with your partner and ask the questions. How many guesses were correct?

Vocabulary and Speaking
Mobile phones and TVs

1 a Work in pairs. Which of these words/phrases do you know? Check in **VOCABULARY 6.2** p140.

> send/get a text   charge your phone   GPS
> a channel   a TV programme   a battery
> an app   turn on   turn off   record

b Work on your own. Put the words/phrases into three groups: TVs, mobile phones, TVs and mobile phones.

c Work in pairs. Compare answers. Did you put the words/phrases in the same groups?

2 a Put these past time phrases in order.

> twenty minutes ago 1   in 1986
> two years ago   last year
> in May 2002   last Monday
> in the eighteenth century   yesterday
> the day before yesterday   in the nineties

b Fill in the gaps with *ago*, *last* or *in*.
1 I left school four years *ago* .
2 I went to bed quite late _____ Saturday.
3 My parents were born _____ the sixties.
4 My parents got married _____ 1985.
5 I didn't have a holiday _____ year.
6 I started learning English six years _____ .
7 I got my mobile _____ March.
8 I bought my computer two years _____ .

c Tick the sentences in **2b** that are true for you. Change the time phrases in the other sentences to make them true for you.

I left school ten years ago.

d Work in pairs. Compare sentences. Are any the same?

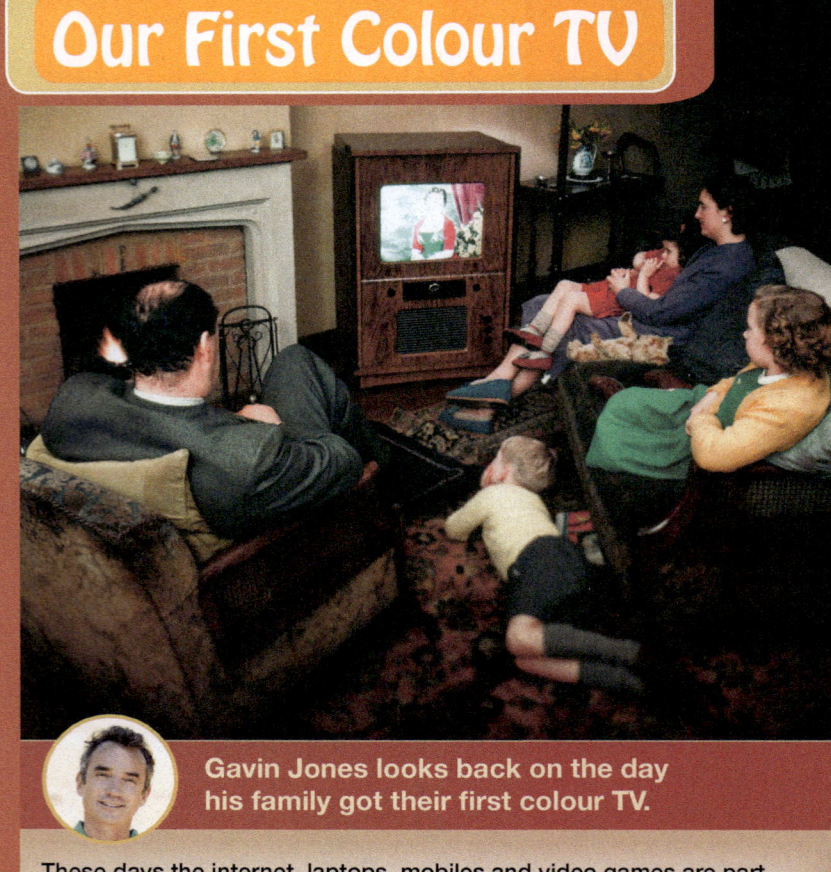

Our First Colour TV

Gavin Jones looks back on the day his family got their first colour TV.

These days the internet, laptops, mobiles and video games are part of normal life. My son and daughter can't understand how people lived without them. But life wasn't always like this. I was a child in the seventies, when things were very different.

I remember my family's first TV very well. In the seventies you could only get three channels – and they were in black and white. Everybody watched live TV all the time because you couldn't record TV programmes. And you couldn't watch TV all night because there weren't any programmes after midnight!

Reading and Speaking

3 a Before you read, check these words/phrases with your teacher.

> without   colour   black and white   live TV   explain

b Read the article. How was TV different in the seventies?

c Read the article again. Answer these questions.
1 How many children has Gavin got?
2 When was Gavin a child?
3 When did his family get their first colour TV?
4 What did his family do that evening?
5 What type of TV has Gavin got now?

Then, in June 1974, my life changed for ever. I came home from school and there it was – our family's first colour TV. I was really excited because I could watch all my favourite programmes in colour! After dinner my father turned on the TV for the first time and my grandfather took a photo. Then the whole family watched TV together until midnight with biscuits and cups of hot chocolate. It was one of the best evenings of my life – and I've still got the photo!

Of course, now you can choose from hundreds of TV channels and watch anything you want at any time of day. You can watch TV programmes online and download them onto your mobile. So I think children today are very lucky – but I can't explain this to my kids because they're too busy watching football on our 3D TV!

HELP WITH GRAMMAR
can/can't; could/couldn't

4 a Look at the phrases in blue in the article. Complete the rules with *can* and *could*.

- We use _____ + infinitive to say that something is possible in the present.
- We use _____ + infinitive to say that something was possible in the past.

b Look at the phrases in pink in the article. What is the negative of *can*? What is the negative of *could*?

c Fill in the gaps in these questions and short answers with *can*, *can't*, *could* or *couldn't*.

1 A _Can_ you watch TV online?
   B Yes, you _____./No, you _____.
2 A _____ you record programmes in 1974?
   B Yes, you _____./No, you _____.

TIP • *Can/can't* and *could/couldn't* are the same for all subjects (*I, you, he, she, it, we, they*).

d Check in **GRAMMAR 6.3** p141.

HELP WITH LISTENING *can* and *can't*

5 a CD2 ▶20 Listen to these sentences. Notice how we say *can* and *can't*. When is *can* stressed?

You can /kən/ watch TV programmes online.
I can't /kɑːnt/ explain how lucky they are.
Can /kən/ you watch TV online?
Yes, you can /kæn/. No, you can't /kɑːnt/.

b CD2 ▶21 Listen to these sentences. Do you hear *can* or *can't*?

1 can't

6 CD2 ▶22 **PRONUNCIATION** Listen and practise. Copy the stress and weak form of *can*.

You can /kən/ watch TV programmes online.

7 a Read about mobile phones. Fill in the gaps with *can*, *can't*, *could* or *couldn't*.

Motorola launched the first mobile phone in 1983, but you ¹ _could_ (+) only use it in a car because it needed a big battery. A few years later you ² _____ (+) buy a mobile that you ³ _____ (+) take to work – but it was in a suitcase!

In the early nineties you ⁴ _____ (+) buy a small mobile for $200, but you ⁵ _____ (−) send texts until 1995. The BlackBerry, launched in 1999, was one of the first phones you ⁶ _____ (+) use to go online. And you ⁷ _____ (−) buy a mobile with a camera in Europe until 2002.

These days most people ⁸ _____ (−) leave home without their mobile. You ⁹ _____ (+) use your phone to go online, make video calls and find your way with GPS. You ¹⁰ _____ (+) also download apps, watch TV programmes or play games. But a lot of people still ¹¹ _____ (−) remember to charge their phone or turn it off in the cinema!

b CD2 ▶23 Listen and check your answers.

8 a Write four sentences with *could* and *couldn't* about your first mobile.

I could send texts with my first mobile.
I couldn't make video calls.

b Work in pairs. Compare sentences. Are any the same?

Get ready … Get it right!

9 Make notes on what you can and can't do with these things.
- your mobile (and apps)   • your computer/laptop   • your TV

my mobile – I can make video calls, send texts, find restaurants …

10 a Work in pairs. Ask questions to find out what you can do with the things in **9**, but your partner can't do.

Can you make video calls on your mobile?   Yes, I can.

b Tell the class two things you found out about your partner's mobile, computer or TV.

51

6C REAL WORLD
The news

Real World talking about the news
Vocabulary verbs from news stories

QUICK REVIEW Past time phrases Work in pairs. Take turns to ask your partner when he/she last did these things: cook a meal, eat out, play tennis, go clubbing, read a good book, go to the cinema. Ask follow-up questions. A *When did you last cook a meal?* B *Two weeks ago.* A *What did you cook?*

The one o'clock news

1 Work in groups. Discuss these questions.
1. Where do you usually get your news – the internet, the TV, the radio or newspapers?
2. Do you watch or listen to the news every day? If so, at what time of day?
3. What's in the news at the moment?

2 a Work in pairs. Which of these verbs do you know? What are the Past Simple forms of the irregular verbs? Check in **VOCABULARY 6.4** p140.

REGULAR VERBS	IRREGULAR VERBS
damage sail	buy lose
die receive	find put
crash save	say tell

b **CD2 24** **PRONUNCIATION** Listen and practise all the verbs in **2a** and their Past Simple forms.

3 a Before you listen, check these words/phrases with your teacher.

a train   a hospital   a storm   a couple
missing at sea   the coast   a helicopter
a boat   an envelope

b Work in pairs. Look at photos A–D of some news stories. Which words are in each story, do you think?

4 a **CD2 25** Listen to the news and put photos A–D in order.

b Listen again and choose the correct answers.
1. a Over *16/60* people are in hospital after a train crash.
   b The train crashed in *London/Scotland*.
2. a There were storms in *Florida/California* last night.
   b *53/153* people died in the storms.
3. a Bill and Nancy Potter are *70/80* years old.
   b They are now *in Australia/missing at sea*.
4. a Joe Hall won over *£3/£13* million last night.
   b *Joe/His dog* chose the lottery numbers.

HELP WITH LISTENING Sentence stress (3)

5 a **CD2 25** Listen again to the first two sentences from the news. Notice the stressed words.

It's one o'clock and here's George Lucan with the news.
Over sixty people are in hospital after a train crash in Scotland this morning.

b Look at Audio Script **CD2 25** p159. Listen again and follow the stressed words.

Read all about it!

6 Look at the headlines on page 53 of two news reports from the next day. Which TV news stories are they about?

A B C D

52

NewsWorld

COUPLE FOUND AT SEA

Bill and Nancy Potter, the 80-year-old British couple who were missing at sea, are now safe. A helicopter found them a hundred miles from the Australian coast and took them to a hospital in Sydney.

"The weather was beautiful when we left New Zealand," said Nancy. "But when we were about a hundred and fifty miles from Sydney there was a terrible storm. There was a lot of damage to the boat. Things were really bad and we couldn't use the radio because that was damaged too. All we could do was wait for help. We were very happy to see the helicopter. Those people saved our lives."

The couple bought the boat two years ago. "We wanted to be the first 80-year-old couple to sail round the world," said Bill. "Nancy wants to try again next year, but I'm not so sure."

1

DOG WINS LOTTERY!

Wednesday night's lottery winner Joe Hall received a cheque for over £13 million yesterday at the supermarket where he works. His dog, Max, who chose the winning numbers, was there with him.

"I usually choose the numbers," said 28-year-old Joe. "But I never win anything. So this time I asked Max to choose the numbers for me – and I won over £13 million!"

But how did the dog choose the numbers? "I wrote the numbers 1 to 50 on envelopes and put a dog biscuit in each envelope," Joe explained. "I put the envelopes in different places in my house and told Max to find the biscuits. Then I wrote down the numbers from the first six envelopes he found – and now I'm a millionaire!"

Now Joe wants Max to find him a girlfriend!

2

REAL WORLD

7 a Work in two groups. Group A, read report 1 and answer questions 1–5. Group B, read report 2 and answer questions a–e.

1 Where did the helicopter find Bill and Nancy?
2 Which city are they in now?
3 Where were they when the storm started?
4 Why didn't they use their radio?
5 When did they buy their boat?

a What did Joe do yesterday?
b What did he write on the envelopes?
c Where did he put them?
d Why did the dog want to find the envelopes?
e What does Joe want his dog to do now?

b Work in pairs. Student A, ask your partner questions a–e. Student B, ask your partner questions 1–5.

What happened?

8 a VIDEO 6 CD2 26 Watch or listen to four conversations about the news. Which news story is each conversation about?

b Watch or listen again. Match sentences 1–6 to responses a–f.

1 Over thirteen million pounds.
2 His dog chose the numbers for him!
3 Over sixty people are in hospital.
4 Did you hear about the storms in Florida?
5 Their boat was damaged in a storm.
6 Yes, a helicopter found them yesterday.

a Oh no, that's terrible.
b Really?
c You're joking!
d Oh, dear. Are they OK?
e Oh, that's good.
f Yes, isn't it awful?

REAL WORLD Talking about the news

9 a Fill in the gaps in the questions and responses with these words.

| was | happened | about | hear |

1 A Did you _____ about that train crash?
   B No, where _____ it?
2 A Did you read _____ the eighty-year-old couple and their boat?
   B No, what _____ ?

b Write responses a–f in **8b** in the table.

good news	bad news	surprising news
		Really?

c Check in REAL WORLD 6.1 p141.

10 CD2 27 PRONUNCIATION Listen and practise the questions and responses in **9a** and **9b**. Copy the stress and intonation.

Did you hear about that train crash?
No, where was it?

11 Work in pairs. Student A p106. Student B p111.

VOCABULARY 6D AND SKILLS — Mario Man

Vocabulary articles: *a*, *an* and *the*
Skills reading: a fact file; listening: a radio programme

QUICK REVIEW Irregular verbs Work in pairs. What can you remember about the four news stories from 6C? Compare ideas with another pair. Then check on p52 and p53.

1 Work in groups. Discuss these questions.

1. Do you play video games? If so, discuss questions a–d. If not, discuss questions e–h.
   a What games do you play?
   b How often do you play?
   c When and where do you play?
   d What's your favourite game?
   e Why don't you play video games?
   f Do your friends or family play them?
   g Did you play when you were young?
   h Do you know any video games?
2. Do you think video games are a good or a bad thing? Why?/Why not?

2 a Before you read, check these words with your teacher.

> a designer   art
> an award   a hero
> a villain   a princess
> a prince

b Read about Shigeru Miyamoto. Answer the questions.

1. What's Shigeru's job?
2. Who does he work for?
3. Where was he born?
4. Where did he study?
5. Is he married?
6. What was his wife's job at Nintendo?
7. Does he play a lot of video games?
8. Who is his favourite video game character?

3 CD2 ▶28 Listen to the beginning of a radio programme about Shigeru Miyamoto. Fill in gaps 1–7 in the fact file.

Shigeru Miyamoto
FACT FILE

Occupation
World-famous video game designer. Works for Nintendo. People call him the father of video games.

Born
Kyoto, Japan, November 16th [1]_____ .

Education
Studied art at Kanazawa College of Art from 1970 to [2]_____ .

Awards
Between 1998 and 2010 he won awards in the USA, the UK, [3]_____ and Spain.

Family life
Married with two children, a boy and a girl. Met his wife, Yasuko, when she was a manager at Nintendo in Japan.

Interesting facts
Doesn't play video games very often. Usually goes to work by [4]_____ . Can write with both hands, but usually uses his left hand. Can play the guitar and write [5]_____ .

Once said
"They say video games are [6]_____ for you. But that's what they said about rock 'n' roll."

The video games
Shigeru designed the first Mario Brothers game in [7]_____ and Mario is his favourite video game character.

All Mario Bros. video games have **a story**. **The story** always has **a hero**, **a princess** and **a villain**. **The villain** wants to marry **the princess**, so he takes her to **a place** where **the hero** can't find her. But **the hero** always finds **the place** and saves **the princess** from **the villain**. And that's **the end** of the game.

HELP WITH VOCABULARY
Articles: *a*, *an* and *the*

4 a Look at the words in bold in these sentences. Then complete the rules with *a* or *the*.

People call him **the father** of video games.
The story always has **a hero**, **a princess** and **a villain**.
The villain wants to marry **the princess**.

1 We use _____ when we know which thing, person, place, etc. because there is only one.
2 We use _____ or *an* to talk about things or people for the first time.
3 We use _____ to talk about a person or a thing for the second, third, fourth, etc. time.

TIP • We use *the* in some fixed phrases: at **the** weekend, in **the** evening, go to **the** cinema, etc.

b Check in VOCABULARY 6.5 > p140.

5 Work in pairs. Look at the words in bold in the last paragraph of the fact file. Match the words in bold to rules 1–3 in **4a**.

6 a Read about a new video game. Fill in the gaps with *a*, *an* and *the*.

I bought ¹ *a* new video game at ² _____ weekend. ³ _____ game is about ⁴ _____ beautiful princess. One day ⁵ _____ princess goes for ⁶ _____ walk. She meets ⁷ _____ old man and ⁸ _____ beautiful white dog. ⁹ _____ old man takes ¹⁰ _____ princess away because he wants to marry her. But ¹¹ _____ dog saves ¹² _____ princess from ¹³ _____ old man. Then at ¹⁴ _____ end of ¹⁵ _____ game, you find out that ¹⁶ _____ dog is really ¹⁷ _____ prince.

b Work in pairs. Compare answers.

7 a Choose the correct word.
1 Did you have *a/the* big lunch yesterday?
2 Is there *a/the* park near your home?
3 Did you go to *a/the* capital city of another country last year?
4 Do you often go to *a/the* cinema at *a/the* weekend?
5 What was *a/the* last film you saw?
6 Is there *a/the* TV programme you watch every week?

b Work in pairs. Ask and answer the questions. Ask follow-up questions if possible.

HELP WITH PRONUNCIATION
Past Simple of regular verbs

1 a CD2 29 Listen to these regular verbs and their Past Simple forms. Notice how we say the *-ed* endings.

1 watch → watch**ed** /t/   ask → ask**ed** /t/
2 stay → stay**ed** /d/   enjoy → enjoy**ed** /d/
3 start → start**ed** /ɪd/   want → want**ed** /ɪd/

TIP • When a regular verb ends in /t/ or /d/, *-ed* is pronounced /ɪd/.

b Listen again and practise.

2 a Work in pairs. Which Past Simple form has an /ɪd/ ending?
1 moved   loved   (wanted)
2 downloaded   liked   played
3 lived   crashed   chatted
4 listened   hated   worked
5 recorded   travelled   finished
6 walked   visited   phoned

b CD2 30 Listen and check. Listen again and practise.

3 Work in pairs. Take turns to say a verb from **1a** or **2a**. Your partner says the Past Simple form.

continue2learn

■ **Vocabulary, Grammar and Real World**
  ■ **Extra Practice 6 and Progress Portfolio 6** p120
  ■ **Language Summary 6** p140
  ■ **6A–D** Workbook p30

■ **Reading and Writing**
  ■ **Portfolio 6** Text me! Workbook p74
  Reading entertainment adjectives
  Writing messages (2); a text message

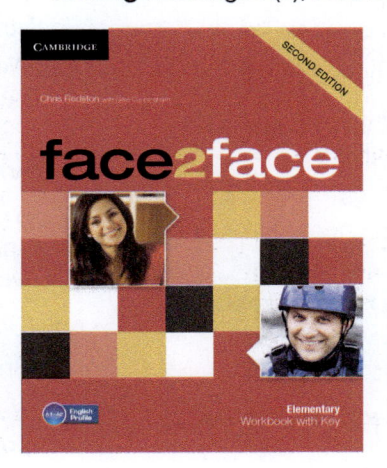

7A Where I live

Vocabulary places in a town
Grammar there is/there are

QUICK REVIEW Verbs Work in pairs. Can you write one verb for each letter of the alphabet? *A = ask, B = buy, C = come,* etc. Compare verbs with another pair. Which pair has the most verbs?

Vocabulary
Places in a town

1 a Work in pairs. Which of these words do you know? Then do the exercise in Language Summary **VOCABULARY 7.1 p142**.

> a building   a house   a flat
> a square   a market   a station
> a bus station   a park   a museum
> a theatre   a cinema   a hotel   a café
> a shop   a restaurant   a bar
> a pub   an airport   a beach   a road

b Look again at the pictures on p142. Take turns to cover the words and test your partner.

What's picture n?   *It's a hotel.*

Listening and Speaking

2 a Look at photos 1–3. Which is: a big city, a small town, a village? Which things from **1a** can you see in the photos?

b **CD2 32** Listen to conversations A–C. Match them to the photos and the things the people talk about 1–3.
1 where he/she lives now
2 where his/her grandparents live
3 where he/she went last weekend

3 a Work in pairs. Which conversation talks about these things?
1 beautiful old buildings
2 a flat near a beach
3 a great place to go out at night
4 a place two hours from an airport
5 pubs that have very good food
6 a good place to go for walks

b Listen again. Check your answers.

1 *Eyeries*

2 *Brisbane*

HELP WITH LISTENING Weak forms (3): prepositions
- Remember: we often say small words (*do, does, you, was, were, can,* etc.) with a schwa /ə/. These are called weak forms.

4 a **CD2 33** Listen to these sentences from conversations A and B. Notice how we say the prepositions in pink. Are these words stressed?

We lived there **for** /fə/ 12 years and then we moved **to** /tə/ London.
I stayed **at** /ət/ home all weekend.
It's about two hours **from** /frəm/ Cork airport.
And all **of** /əv/ the houses are different colours!

b Look at Audio Script **CD2 32** p160. Listen to conversations A and B again. Notice how we say the prepositions and the other weak forms in pink.

5 a Work in groups. Which place would you like to visit: Eyeries, Brisbane or Burford? Why?

b Compare answers with the class. Which place is the most popular?

Burford

HELP WITH GRAMMAR there is/there are

6 **a** Fill in the gaps in the tables with *'s*, *is*, *are*, *isn't* or *aren't*.

	singular
POSITIVE (+)	There _____ a nice beach.
NEGATIVE (–)	There _____ a station.
QUESTIONS (?)	_____ there a hotel?
SHORT ANSWERS	Yes, there _____ ./No, there _____ .

	plural
POSITIVE (+)	There _____ lots of things to do.
NEGATIVE (–)	There _____ any restaurants.
QUESTIONS (?)	_____ there any good pubs?
SHORT ANSWERS	Yes, there _____ ./No, there _____ .

TIP • We use *any* in negatives and questions with *there are*.

b What is the Past Simple of *there is* and *there are*?

c Check in **GRAMMAR 7.1** p144.

7 **a** Look at these sentences about Burford. Fill in the gaps with *There's*, *There are*, *There isn't* or *There aren't*.

1 (✓) *There are* lots of good shops.
2 (✗) *There isn't* a station.
3 (✓) _____ a market every weekend.
4 (✗) _____ any five-star hotels.
5 (✗) _____ a theatre.
6 (✓) _____ lots of nice cafés.
7 (✓) _____ an interesting museum.
8 (✗) _____ an airport near the town.

b **CD2 ▶ 34 PRONUNCIATION** Listen and practise the sentences in **7a**. Notice how we say *there's* /ðeəz/ and *there are* /ðeərə/.

8 **a** Look at the table. Complete questions 1–8 with *Is there* or *Are there*.

places near my home	me	my partner
1 _____ a station?		
2 _____ any shops?		
3 _____ a hotel?		
4 _____ a market?		
5 _____ any good restaurants?		
6 _____ a park?		
7 _____ a cinema or a theatre?		
8 _____ any nice cafés?		

b Think about places near your home. Put *yes* or *no* in the *me* column.

c **CD2 ▶ 35 PRONUNCIATION** Listen and practise the questions in **8a** and the short answers.

Is there a station?   *Are there any shops?*

d Work in pairs. Ask and answer the questions in **8a**. Write *yes* or *no* in the *my partner* column. Continue the conversation if possible.

Is there a station near your home?

Yes, there is. It's about ten minutes away.

Get ready ... Get it right!

9 Choose your favourite town, city or village in your country (not the one you're in now). Tick the things in the box that are in this place and cross out the things that aren't.

My favourite place is: _____

beautiful/famous buildings   big/small parks
a market   a square   an airport   a beach
old/new houses   interesting shops
a museum   a theatre   a cinema   a station
cheap/expensive restaurants
nice cafés, bars or pubs   good hotels

10 **a** Work in groups. Tell the other students about your favourite place.

There are lots of beautiful buildings and two big parks.

b Choose one of your group's places that you would like to visit. Tell the class why you want to go there.

7B A new home

Vocabulary rooms and things in a house
Grammar How much ... ? and How many ... ?; some, any, a

QUICK REVIEW *there is/there are* Work in groups. Talk about the good and bad things about the town or city you're in now. Use *there is*, *there are*, *there isn't*, and *there aren't*.

Vocabulary Rooms and things in a house

1 Read the advert and look at the plan of the flat. Match the words in bold to A–E on the plan.

2 Match these things in a house to 1–20 on the plan.

> furniture *1*   a double bed *10*   a single bed
> a fridge   a coffee table   a bath   a shower
> a cooker   a toilet   a sink   a desk   a plant
> a sofa   an armchair   a washing machine
> a washbasin   a table   a chair   a cupboard
> a shelf

3 Look again at the advert and the plan of the flat. Answer these questions.
1 How much space is there? *80m²*
2 What's the postcode of the flat?
3 How many bedrooms are there?
4 How much is the rent?
5 How many chairs are there in the kitchen?
6 How many plants are there?
7 How much furniture is there in the living room? Make a list.

Description | Map & Schools | Street View | LOGIN

Park Road M13 7ED

Large flat (80m²) for rent in city centre. On quiet street near station and park. Large **kitchen**, **living room**, **bathroom**, two **bedrooms**, small **balcony**. No garden.

Rent: £800 per month

HELP WITH GRAMMAR
How much ... ? and How many ... ?

4 a Which of these nouns are countable (C)? Which are uncountable (U)?

> table *C*   bedroom   furniture   people
> money   chair   space   time   plant

b Look again at the questions in **3**. Then complete the rules with *How much ... ?* or *How many ... ?*.
- We use _____ with plural countable nouns.
- We use _____ with uncountable nouns.

c Check in GRAMMAR 7.2 p144.

Listening and Speaking

6 a CD2 37 John and his wife, Becky, want to find a flat. Listen to their conversation with the estate agent. Put the things they talk about in order.

a the furniture 1   c the kitchen   e the rent
b the bathroom   d the bedrooms   f shops

b Listen again. Are these sentences true (T) or false (F)?

1 There's some furniture in the flat. T
2 There's a TV in the flat.
3 The estate agent says there are two big bedrooms.
4 John and Becky haven't got any children.
5 The estate agent says there isn't a cooker.
6 There aren't any shops near the flat.
7 John and Becky don't want to see the flat.

HELP WITH GRAMMAR *some, any, a*

7 a Fill in the gaps in the table with *some, any* or *a*.

	singular countable nouns	plural countable nouns	uncountable nouns
+	There's *a* cooker.	There are *some* chairs.	We'd like _____ information.
–	There isn't _____ TV.	We haven't got _____ children.	I haven't got *any* money.
?	Has it got _____ shower?	Are there _____ shops?	Is there _____ furniture?

b When do we use *some* and *any*?

c Check in GRAMMAR 7.3 p144.

8 CD2 38 PRONUNCIATION Listen and practise the sentences in **7a**. Notice the way we say *some*.

There's a cooker. There are some /səm/ chairs.

9 a John and Becky now live in the flat. Read their phone conversation. Fill in the gaps with *some, any* or *a*.

BECKY Hi. I'm at the supermarket. Have we got ¹ *any* bread?
JOHN Yes, we've got ² _____ bread, but we haven't got ³ _____ butter.
B OK. So we need ⁴ _____ butter. Is there ⁵ _____ milk?
J No, there isn't. And we need ⁶ _____ meat and ⁷ _____ eggs.
B Right. Have we got ⁸ _____ fruit?
J We've got ⁹ _____ big bag of oranges, but we haven't got ¹⁰ _____ apples.
B OK, I'll get ¹¹ _____ more fruit. And ¹² _____ cheese.
J And can you get ¹³ _____ big bottle of water too?
B Yes, OK. See you later. Bye.

b CD2 39 Listen and check.

Get ready ... Get it right!

10 Work in two groups. Group A p106. Group B p111.

5 a Fill in the gaps with *How much* or *How many*.

HOME SWEET HOME

1 *How many* people live in your home?
2 _____ rooms are there?
3 _____ furniture is there in your living room?
4 _____ TVs are there in your home?
5 _____ time do you spend watching TV every day?
6 _____ pictures are there in your bedroom?
7 _____ time do you spend cleaning the house every week?

b CD2 36 PRONUNCIATION Listen and check. Listen again and practise. Copy the stress.

How many people live in your home?

c Work in pairs. Ask and answer the questions in **5a**. Are any of your partner's answers surprising?

7C REAL WORLD — At the shops

Real World what sales assistants say; what customers say
Vocabulary shops; things to buy

QUICK REVIEW Rooms and things in a house What's your favourite room in your home? Work in pairs. Tell your partner five things about your favourite room. Use *There's a …* , *There are some …* , *There isn't a …* , *There aren't any …* .

I love shopping!

1 a Work in pairs. Which of these words do you know? Check in **VOCABULARY 7.3** p142.

> a bookshop   a clothes shop
> a shoe shop   a supermarket
> a kiosk   a newsagent's
> a department store   a post office
> a bank   a chemist's   a butcher's
> a baker's

b Work in the same pairs. Think of two things you can buy or do in each place.

> You can buy books and birthday cards in a bookshop.

2 Work in groups. Discuss these questions.
1 Do you like shopping? Why?/Why not?
2 What do you like or hate buying? Why?
3 Which shops do you go to every week? What do you buy there?
4 What's your favourite shop? Why?

3 a Tick the words you know. Then do the exercise in **VOCABULARY 7.4** p143.

> stamps   a map   a suitcase
> tissues   aspirin   a lamp
> postcards   a cake   a guide book
> a newspaper   cigarettes   chocolate

b Work in new pairs. Think of two places where you can buy the things in **3a**.

> You can buy stamps in a post office or a newsagent's.

Can I help you?

4 **VIDEO 7** **CD2 40** Look at the photos. Paul and Clare are at the shops. Watch or listen to their conversations. Answer these questions.

	Paul	Clare
1 Which shop is he/she in?		
2 What does he/she buy?		
3 How much does he/she spend?		

HELP WITH LISTENING What sales assistants say

5 a Read these things that sales assistants say. Check new words with your teacher.

CONVERSATION 1
a Here's your change and your receipt.
b Anything else?
c Can I help you?
d Yes, they're over there.
e Would you like a bag?

CONVERSATION 2
f Would you like anything else?
g Your pin number, please.
h That's £17.50, please.
i Do you need any help?
j They're on the second floor.

b **VIDEO 7** **CD2 40** Watch or listen again. Put sentences a–j in **5a** in the order you hear them (1–10).

REAL WORLD What customers say

6 a Fill in the gaps with the phrases in the boxes.

> ~~Have you got~~   Do you sell   I'll have   Can I have

SAYING WHAT YOU WANT

Have you got any guide books for London?
_____ four stamps for Europe, please?
_____ suitcases?
_____ this one, please.

> your help   that's all   Here you
> How much is   How much are

ASKING ABOUT PRICES　　**OTHER USEFUL PHRASES**

_____ this map?　　No, _____, thanks.
_____ these lamps?　　_____ are.
　　　　　　　　　　　　　　　Thanks for _____.

TIPS • We use *one* in place of a singular noun:
A *Would you like **a bag**?* B *No, thanks. I've got **one**.*

• We use *ones* in place of a plural noun:
A *How much are these **lamps**?* B *The big **ones** are £25.*

b Check in **REAL WORLD 7.2** p144.

7 CD2 41 PRONUNCIATION Listen and practise the sentences in **6a**.

Have you got any guide books for London?

8 a Clare is now on the second floor of the department store. Read the conversation and choose the correct words.

SALES ASSISTANT Do you [1]*have/(need)* any help?
CLARE Yes, please. I'd like to buy a suitcase.
SA Yes, they're over [2]*their/there*.
C Oh, yes. How much [3]*is/are* they?
SA The big [4]*one/ones* are £55 and the small [5]*one/ones* are £40.
C OK. [6]*I/I'll* have this small [7]*one/ones*, please.
SA Sure. [8]*Do/Would* you like anything else?
C No, that's [9]*every/all*, thanks.
SA OK, [10]*that/that's* £40, please.
C [11]*Here you are/Here are you*.
SA Thank you. Your [12]*pin number/number pin*, please. Right, here's your suitcase and your [13]*change/receipt*. Have a nice day.
C You too. Bye.
SA Goodbye.

b Work in pairs. Practise the conversation. Take turns to be the sales assistant.

9 a Work in new pairs. Write a conversation in a department store.

b Practise the conversation until you can remember it.

c Work in groups of four. Take turns to say your conversations. Listen to the other pair's conversation. What does the customer buy and how much does he/she spend?

VOCABULARY 7D AND SKILLS > What to wear

Vocabulary clothes; colours; plural nouns
Skills reading: a magazine article

QUICK REVIEW Shops Write a list of shops. Work in pairs and compare lists. Who has more words? Tell your partner the last time you went to shops on your list. What did you buy there? *I went to a supermarket two days ago. I bought … .*

1 Work in pairs. Which of these words do you know? Then do the exercise in **VOCABULARY 7.5** **p143**.

trousers	shorts	jeans	a dress	shoes
a suit	a skirt	a jumper	trainers	a jacket
a hat	a tie	boots	socks	a T-shirt
a top	a coat	a cap	a shirt	

2 Match these words to colours 1–12.

| white 4 | black | red | blue | yellow | grey | pink |
| brown | orange | purple | dark green | light green |

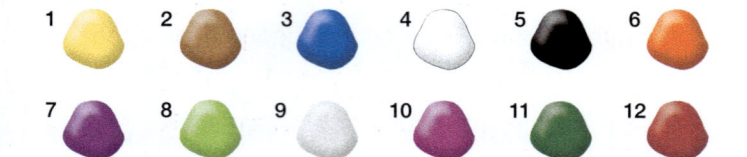

3 a Write lists for you.
1 clothes and colours I usually wear
2 clothes and colours I sometimes wear
3 clothes and colours I never wear

b Work in groups. Tell other students about the clothes and colours you wear.

> I usually wear a suit in the week.
> I sometimes wear jeans.
> I never wear pink.

HELP WITH VOCABULARY Plural nouns

4 a Some nouns look plural, but they mean 'one thing'. Look at these examples.

*Those **jeans** are nice.*   (= 1 thing)
*Where are my **shoes**?*   (= 2 things)

b Which of these nouns can mean 'one thing'? Which can be singular?

| jeans | shoes | socks | shorts |
| boots | trousers | trainers | |

TIP • We can use *a pair of …* with both types of plural noun: *I've got **a pair of** red jeans/shoes.*

5 a Fill in the gaps with *some*, *any* or *a*.
1 I haven't got _____ white shirts.
2 I've got _____ black jeans.
3 I need _____ new pair of trainers.
4 I haven't got _____ blue suit.
5 I want to buy _____ brown shoes.
6 I haven't got _____ shorts.
7 I've got _____ clothes that I never wear.

b Which sentences are true for you? Compare with a partner.

6 a Before you read, check these phrases with your teacher.

| designer clothes | fashion magazines |
| try on | send back |

b Read the article. Match paragraphs 1–3 to the people in the photos.

Me and my clothes

Do you think what you wear is important? We talked to three people from different countries to find out what they think about clothes, shopping, the internet – and, of course, shoes!

1 I like looking good and I spend a lot of money on clothes and shoes. I'm a sales manager for a software company, so what I wear at work is important. I do a lot of shopping online because it's quick and easy. And if you don't like something, you can send it back. I buy a lot of shirts and I love designer clothes. They're expensive, but they look great. Yes, what I wear is important to me – and to my girlfriend!

2 I don't like shopping for clothes and I don't think what people wear is very important. When I go shopping, I only buy the clothes I need and that's all. The last time I went clothes shopping was about two months ago. I bought a nice blue jumper and five pairs of socks! I usually wear the same thing every day – jeans, a T-shirt and trainers. And I really hate buying shoes – I've only got three pairs!

3 Oh, I really love clothes! I read all the fashion magazines and I watch programmes about clothes on TV. And I love buying shoes – I've got about fifty pairs at home! And I love shopping with my friends. We go into town every Saturday and look at all the new clothes. I never buy clothes online because you can't try them on before you buy them. Next weekend I want to buy a dress for a party – and some new shoes, of course!

7 a Read the article again. Fill in the gaps with *Ronnie*, *Catherine* or *Samantha*.

1 _Samantha_ has a lot of shoes.
2 _____ doesn't buy clothes very often.
3 _____ buys clothes to look good at work.
4 _____ buys a lot of clothes online.
5 _____ never buys clothes online.
6 _____ doesn't have many pairs of shoes.
7 _____ likes reading about clothes.
8 _____ wears the same thing every day.
9 _____ likes buying designer clothes.

b Work in pairs. Compare answers.

8 Work in groups. Discuss these questions.

1 Which person from the article is similar to you? Why?
2 Do you like shopping for clothes? Why?/Why not?
3 What's your favourite clothes shop? What do you usually buy there?
4 Do you buy clothes online? Why?/Why not?

Catherine from the UK

Samantha from Australia

Ronnie from the USA

HELP WITH PRONUNCIATION
/ɔː/ and /ɜː/

1 CD2 42 Listen to these sounds and words. Listen again and practise.

/ɔː/ sh**or**ts w**a**lk f**our**   /ɜː/ sh**ir**t w**or**k g**ir**l

2 a Work in pairs. Look at the letters in bold. Write the words in the table.

| ~~Thursday~~ | ~~strawberry~~ | tall | word | August |
| birthday | person | bought | divorced | skirt |

/ɔː/ sh**or**ts	/ɜː/ sh**ir**t
strawberry	Thursday

b CD2 43 Listen and check. Listen again and practise.

3 a Work in pairs. Look at the letters in bold in these words. Are the sounds the same (S) or different (D)?

1 d**au**ghter p**oor** S
2 b**or**ing f**ur**niture
3 T**ur**kish G**er**man
4 m**or**ning **al**ways
5 th**ir**ty s**ur**name
6 sp**or**t **ear**ly
7 d**ir**ty w**a**ter
8 f**ir**st b**ur**ger
9 t**all** fl**oor**
10 **aw**ful b**or**ing

b CD2 44 Listen and check. Listen again and practise.

continue2learn

■ **Vocabulary, Grammar and Real World**
  ■ **Extra Practice 7 and Progress Portfolio 7** p121
  ■ **Language Summary 7** p142
  ■ **7A–D** Workbook p35

■ **Reading and Writing**
  Portfolio 7 Renting a flat Workbook p76
  Reading adverts for places to live
  Writing paragraphs (2); a letter to a friend

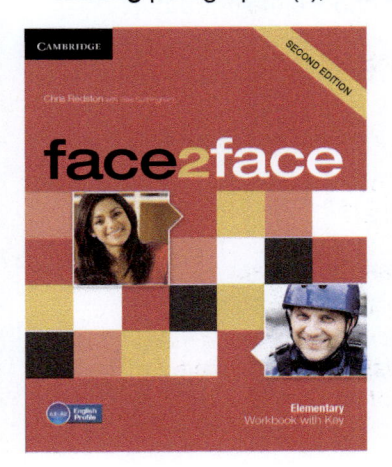

63

8A The meeting

Vocabulary work
Grammar Present Continuous: positive and negative, questions and short answers

QUICK REVIEW Clothes Write all the clothes you know. Work in pairs and compare lists. Then tell your partner about your favourite clothes: *I've got a really nice black jacket. I bought it in Milan.*

Vocabulary Work

1 a Work in pairs. Which of these words do you know? Then do the exercise in **VOCABULARY 8.1** ▶ p145.

> a customer   a report   notes
> a letter   a message   a contract
> a company   a meeting   a conference

b Work on your own. Which word/phrase does not go with the verb?
1 **write** a customer/a report/a letter
2 **answer** the phone/notes/an email
3 **take** contracts/messages/notes
4 **sign** a contract/a letter/a meeting
5 **work** for a company/in an office/a report
6 **go to** a meeting/a contract/a conference
7 **write to** a contract/a customer/a company

c Work in pairs. Compare answers. Then take turns to test your partner.

> letters   You write letters and sign letters.

Listening and Speaking

2 a Look at pictures 1 and 2. It's 9.50 a.m. Where are the people?

b [CD2 45] Listen to the conversation. What is Frank's problem?

c Listen again and choose the correct answers.
1 Frank isn't at work because the *bus/train* was late.
2 The meeting with the Tamada brothers is at *ten/eleven* o'clock.
3 Frank wants Janet to *start the meeting/wait for him*.
4 The contract is *Frank's/Janet's*.
5 Adriana is *in the office/at home*.
6 Janet wants Liz to *take notes in the meeting/finish some reports*.

Frank   *Liz*   *Janet*

3 a Who says these sentences – Frank, Janet or Liz?
1 I'm waiting for a taxi. *Frank*
2 They're sitting in your office.
3 They aren't looking very happy.
4 She's working at home today.
5 I'm not doing anything important at the moment.
6 Danny isn't doing anything.

b Work in pairs. Compare answers.

HELP WITH GRAMMAR
Present Continuous: positive and negative

4 a Are the sentences in **3a** about now or every day?

b We use *be* + verb+*ing* to make the Present Continuous. Fill in the gaps with *'m, 're, aren't, 's* or *isn't*.

POSITIVE (+)		NEGATIVE (–)	
I ____		I ____ not	
you/we/they ____	verb+*ing*	you/we/they ____	verb+*ing*
he/she/it ____		he/she/it ____	

c Write the -*ing* form of these verbs.

> play *playing*   make   study   sit
> look   go   run   write   live   stop

d Check in **GRAMMAR 8.1** ▶ p146.

64

5 CD2 ▶46 **PRONUNCIATION** Listen and practise the sentences in **3a**. Copy the stress.

I'm waiting for a taxi.

6 a Look at picture 3. Liz is talking to Danny. It's 9.55 a.m. Put the verbs in the Present Continuous.

LIZ Danny, are you busy?
DANNY Well, er, I ¹ _'m writing_ (write) a letter.
LIZ Can you take notes at the meeting, please?
DANNY Why me? Look, Bob ² _____ (read) the newspaper. Ask him.
LIZ He ³ _____ (not read) the newspaper. He ⁴ _____ (study) the business pages.
DANNY Well, I ⁵ _____ (wait) for a phone call from New York.
LIZ They ⁶ _____ (not work) in New York now, Danny. It's 5.00 a.m. there!
DANNY OK, OK, I ⁷ _____ (go) now. Which room?

b CD2 ▶47 Listen and check your answers.

7 Work in pairs. It's 10.05 a.m. What are these people doing now, do you think?

1 Janet   3 Danny
2 The Tamada brothers   4 Frank

I think Janet's having a meeting.

8 CD2 ▶48 It's now 10.15 a.m. Frank is phoning Liz. Listen and answer the questions.

1 Where is Frank calling from?
2 Is the taxi moving?
3 Are they having the meeting now?
4 What is Danny doing?
5 What is Frank doing at the end of the phone call?

HELP WITH GRAMMAR Present Continuous: questions and short answers

9 a Write questions 3 and 4 from **8** in the table.

question word	auxiliary	subject	verb+*ing*	
Where	is	Frank	calling	from?
	Is	the taxi	moving?	

b Write positive and negative short answers for these questions.

1 Am I working here today?
  Yes, _you are_./No, _____.
2 Is Janet answering her phone?
  Yes, _____./No, _____.
3 Are they having the meeting now?
  Yes, _____./No, _____.

c Check in **GRAMMAR 8.2** ▶ p146.

10 CD2 ▶49 Who signs the contract, do you think – Janet or Frank? Listen and check.

11 a It's now 6.30 p.m. Frank is talking to his wife, Karen, on the phone. Make questions in the Present Continuous.

FRANK Hi! It's me.
KAREN Hello, love. ¹you / work / late this evening?
       Are you working late this evening?
FRANK No, I'm having a drink with Liz. I signed the Tamada contract today.
KAREN Oh, that's fantastic! ²you / have / a nice time ?
FRANK Yes, thanks. ³What / you / do ?
KAREN I'm making dinner.
FRANK ⁴the kids / do / their homework ?
KAREN Er ... no, they're not.
FRANK ⁵What / they / do ?
KAREN They're watching TV.

b CD2 ▶50 Listen and check.

c CD2 ▶51 **PRONUNCIATION** Listen and practise the questions in **11a**. Copy the stress.

Are you working late this evening?

Get ready ... Get it right!

12 Work in two groups. Group A p107. Group B p112.

8B It's snowing!

Vocabulary types of transport; travelling verbs and phrases
Grammar Present Simple or Present Continuous

QUICK REVIEW Present Continuous Write six actions (*play tennis*, *watch TV*, etc.). Work in pairs. Take turns to mime the actions to your partner. He/She guesses what you are doing: **A** *Are you playing tennis?* **B** *Yes, I am.*

Vocabulary and Speaking
Types of transport

1 a Work in pairs. Which words do you know? Check new words in **VOCABULARY 8.2** p145.

> a car   a plane   a train   a taxi   a bus
> a tram   a bike   a scooter   a boat
> a motorbike   a ferry   a coach

b Put the words into two groups: public transport and private transport. Some words can go in both groups.

c Work in pairs. Compare groups. Are they the same?

2 a Match phrases 1–7 to a–g. Check in **VOCABULARY 8.3** p145.

1 go by car	a cycle
2 go by bike	b take the bus/coach
3 go by plane	c walk
4 go on foot	d take the ferry/boat
5 go by bus/coach	e fly
6 go by ferry/boat	f drive
7 go by train/tube/tram	g take the train/tube/tram

b Work in groups. Talk about how you travel:
1 to work/school/university
2 to the centre of your town/city
3 to other places in your country
4 to parties
5 when you're on holiday

Listening and Speaking

3 a Before you listen, check these words/phrases with your teacher.

> snow   a traffic jam   a journey   a normal day

b Look at the news website and the photo. What is happening in London?

NewsWorld
www.newsworld.com/London

London in the Snow
Traffic Jams All Over City

Heavy snow continues to fall in central London this morning as people try to get to work.

Travel news and updates

---

4 a **CD2 52** Listen to a news report. Fill in the table.

	how he/she usually travels to work	how he/she is travelling to work today
first man	*by train*	
woman		
second man		

b Listen again and answer these questions.
1 Are there any trains today?
2 What time does the first man usually start work?
3 How long is the woman's journey to work on a normal day?
4 When did she leave home?
5 Where is the second man from?
6 Do they have the same traffic problems in his country?

HELP WITH LISTENING Linking (2)

• Remember: we often link consonant sounds at the end of a word with vowel sounds at the beginning of the next word.

5 a **CD2 53** Listen and notice the linking.

YOU EXPECT TO HEAR	YOU USUALLY HEAR
I start at eight.	I start_at_eight.
And it's eight thirty now.	And_it's_eight thirty now.

b Look at Audio Script **CD2 52** p161. Listen again and notice the consonant-vowel links.

7 a Read what some other people are doing on the same day. Put the verbs in the Present Simple or Present Continuous.

MADDY I'm an accountant and I ¹ _work_ (work) for a bank. I usually ² _____ (work) in the city, but today I ³ _____ (work) at home because of the snow. At the moment I ⁴ _____ (sit) in the kitchen and I ⁵ _____ (write) emails on my laptop. I ⁶ _____ (not work) at home very often, so I'm happy it ⁷ _____ (snow) today!

EVE On Mondays we usually ⁸ _____ (drive) to Wimbledon and ⁹ _____ (visit) some friends. But we ¹⁰ _____ (stay) at home today because of the snow. At the moment my husband, Lenny, ¹¹ _____ (answer) his emails and I ¹² _____ (watch) the news. Normally I ¹³ _____ (not watch) TV in the day, but I want to know about the weather.

b CD2 ▶ 54 Listen and check your answers.

8 a Make questions about the people in **7a**. Fill in the gaps with *do, does, is, are* and the correct form of the verb in brackets.

1 What _does_ Maddy _do_ ? (do)
2 _____ she _____ in the city today? (work)
3 What _____ she _____ at the moment? (do)
4 _____ she _____ at home very often? (work)
5 What _____ Lenny and Eve usually _____ on Mondays? (do)
6 What _____ they _____ today? (do)
7 _____ Eve normally _____ TV in the day? (watch)
8 Why _____ she _____ it today? (watch)

b CD2 ▶ 55 **PRONUNCIATION** Listen and check. Listen again and practise.

c Work in pairs. Ask and answer the questions.

> What does Maddy do?   She's an accountant.

HELP WITH GRAMMAR
Present Simple or Present Continuous

6 a Look at this sentence. Then complete the rules with *Present Simple* or *Present Continuous*.

I usually go by train, but I'm taking the bus today.

- We use the _____ to talk about things that happen every day/week/month, etc.
- We use the _____ to talk about things that are happening now.

b Do we usually use the Present Simple (PS) or the Present Continuous (PC) with these words/phrases?

usually *PS*	now
today	sometimes
always often	normally
at the moment	never
hardly ever	every day

c Check in **GRAMMAR 8.3** ▶ p146.

Get ready … Get it right!

9 Work in two groups. Group A p107. Group B p112.

67

8C REAL WORLD   On the phone

Real World talking on the phone

QUICK REVIEW Types of transport Write ten words for types of transport (*car*, *bus*, etc.). Work in pairs. Compare lists. Tell your partner which types of transport you used last week. Where did you go?

I'll get back to you

1 Emily is at work. Look at A–C and answer the questions.
1. What is Chris Morris's job?
2. Where can you see *Not Now*?
3. What is the postcode of Morris Computers?
4. In which month is the conference?
5. How many phone calls does Emily want to make?
6. What is Chris Morris's email address?
7. Who are the actors in *Not Now*?
8. Is Clare a friend or a customer, do you think?

HELP WITH LISTENING
Phone messages

2 a Look at these sentences from phone messages. Work in pairs. Try to fill in the gaps with these words.

~~voicemail~~   person   choose
back   message   press   try

a Hello, this is Alan Wick's *voicemail*.
b If you leave a message, I'll get _____ to you.
c I'm sorry, but the _____ you called is not available.
d Please leave your _____ after the tone.
e Please _____ one of the following three options.
f For all other enquiries, _____ zero.
g Please _____ later.

b CD2 ▶56 Listen to four messages. Check your answers to **2a**. What do you do after each message?
a end the call
b leave a message
c press a number on the phone

3 CD2 ▶57 Emily is making three phone calls. Listen and answer these questions.
1 When does Emily want to:
  a meet Alan Wick?
  b meet Clare?
  c go to the theatre?
2 How much are the theatre tickets?

A   *Emily*

To do – Wed 16th
* phone Chris Morris
* check contract
* call Alan Wick
* check date of March conference
* call theatre – prices?
* phone Clare – coffee later?

B
Morris Computers Ltd
Chris Morris
Business Manager
103 Dean Street
Manchester
M18 7FT
Tel: 0161 496 0723
email: c.morris@mc.co.uk

C
Not Now
by Lionel Mayers
starring Bill Marks and Kelly Bolton
"THE YEAR'S BEST COMEDY!"
The Evening News

The Queen's Theatre, Manchester
Box Office: 08081 570570
www.queenstheatremanchester.com

Can I call you back?

4 Work in pairs. Discuss these questions.

1. How many phone calls do you make or get on a normal day?
2. Do you always answer your phone at work or at home? If not, why not?
3. When was the last phone call you made? Who did you call? Why?

5 a VIDEO 8 CD2 58 Close your book. Watch or listen to two phone calls. What does Emily talk to Clare about? When can Emily talk to Chris Morris again?

b Work in pairs. Choose the correct words/phrases.

TIM Hello, 3DUK. Can I help you?
CLARE Hello, ¹*I want to*/*can I* speak to Emily, please?
TIM ²*Hold on*/*Stop* a moment, she's here.
EMILY Hello. Emily Wise.
CLARE Hi. ³*It's*/*I'm* Clare. I ⁴*got*/*had* your message.
EMILY Good. Do you want to go for a coffee after work?
CLARE Sure. Is six o'clock OK?
EMILY Yes, that's fine. Let's meet at Café Uno.
CLARE OK. See you there at six. Bye.
EMILY Bye.

CHRIS Hello?
EMILY Hello, ⁵*is that*/*are you* Chris Morris?
CHRIS ⁶*Speaking.*/*I am.*
EMILY ⁷*This is*/*I'm* Emily Wise from 3DUK.
CHRIS Hello, Emily. Look, I've got a conference call in a minute. Can I call you ⁸*back*/*again* in an hour?
EMILY Of course. Call me ⁹*on*/*by* my mobile.
CHRIS Right. ¹⁰*I'll call*/*I'm calling* you later.
EMILY Thanks a lot. Bye.
CHRIS Bye.

c Watch or listen again. Check your answers.

6 Close your books. Work in pairs. What can you remember about the two conversations?

REAL WORLD Talking on the phone

7 Write these headings in a–d in the table.

~~other useful phrases~~   calling people back
saying who you are   asking to speak to people

a _____	b _____
Hello, can I speak to (Emily), please?	This is (Emily Wise) from (3DUK).
Hello, is that (Chris Morris)?	Speaking.
	It's (Clare).
c _____	d *other useful phrases*
Can I call you back (in an hour)?	I got your message.
I'll call you later.	Call me on my mobile.
Can you call me back?	Hold on a moment.

REAL WORLD 8.1 ▶ p146

8 CD2 59 **PRONUNCIATION** Listen and practise the sentences in **7**. Copy the stress and intonation.

Hello, can I speak to Emily, please?

9 a Clare is making some phone calls. Fill in the gaps with parts of the phrases from **7**.

CLARE Hello, ¹ *is that* Simon Dale?
SIMON Speaking.
CLARE Hi, Simon. ² _____ Clare Ross.
SIMON Oh, hello, Clare. Look, I can't talk right now. ³ _____ you back?
CLARE Yes, of course. ⁴ _____ my mobile.
SIMON Right. I'll ⁵ _____ later. Bye.

CLARE Hi, Vicky. ⁶ _____ Clare.
VICKY Hi, Clare. How are you?
CLARE I'm fine, thanks. ⁷ _____ to Rob, please?
VICKY ⁸ _____ a moment, I'll get him.
ROB Hello, Clare. I ⁹ _____ your message. Let's meet at 8.30 outside the cinema.
CLARE OK, see you then. Bye.

b Work in pairs. Compare answers.

10 a Work in new pairs. Write a phone conversation.

b Swap conversations with another pair. Correct any mistakes.

c Practise the new conversation with your partner. Then role-play it for the other pair.

VOCABULARY 8D AND SKILLS > Life outdoors

Vocabulary indoor and outdoor activities; adjectives and adverbs
Skills reading: an advert, a formal letter

QUICK REVIEW Talking on the phone
Write all the phrases for talking on the phone you can remember. Work in pairs. Take turns to say your phrases. How many are the same?

1 a Tick the words/phrases you know. Then do the exercise in VOCABULARY 8.4 p145.

> swim   ski   surf   windsurf   sail   sing
> cook   drive   speak another language
> ride a horse   ride a motorbike
> play a musical instrument

b Work in pairs. Find four things that you can do, but your partner can't do. Use the words/phrases in **1a** or your own ideas.

> Can you swim?   Yes, I can./No, I can't.

2 Read the job advert. Would you like to do this job? Why?/Why not?

South Wales Adventure Centre

Course Leaders
We are looking for people to work as course leaders at our outdoor centre in Pembrokeshire, Wales. We offer holidays and weekend courses for adults and teenagers (including school groups from Europe).

We are looking for people who:
- like working with people of all ages
- enjoy outdoor activities
- are good at water sports
- can ride and enjoy working with horses
- are good at languages
- have a driving licence

Email welshadventure@iol.co.uk for an application form.
Experience and references required.

3 a Before you read, check these words/phrases with your teacher.

> excellent   popular   fluent
> work hard   careful

b Read the reference letter. Do you think Ray is a good person for the job?

c Read the reference and advert again. Find five reasons why Ray can do the job.

Devon Outdoor Centre
Woodside | Devon | PL3 1GZ
Tel: 01541 766902   email: d.outdoor@gomail.co.uk

23rd March

Dear Sir or Madam

Reference: Mr Ray Downing

I am writing to recommend Ray for the position of course leader with your company. He worked for our outdoor centre for four months last summer. He was a very **popular** course leader and he planned all his group's activities very **carefully**. He always worked very **hard** and made friends **easily** with people of all ages.

Ray loves all outdoor activities, particularly cycling and horse riding. He can sail very **well** and he's a **good** surfer and a **fast** swimmer. He speaks Spanish **fluently** and is an **excellent** driver. Ray also wrote a **wonderful** blog for the teenagers' course and all the children's parents really enjoyed reading it.

If you would like any further information, please contact me by phone or email.

Yours faithfully

Stella James

Stella James
Centre Manager

HELP WITH VOCABULARY Adjectives and adverbs

4 a Look at this sentence. Then complete the rules with *adverbs* or *adjectives*.

          adverb   adjective
He speaks Spanish **fluently** and is an **excellent** driver.

- We use _____ to describe nouns. They usually come **before** the noun.
- We use _____ like *well*, *carefully*, etc. to describe verbs. They usually come **after** the verb.

b Look at the words in bold in the letter. Which are adverbs and which are adjectives? Which verbs or nouns do they describe?

c Write the adverbs for these adjectives. What are the spelling rules? Which adverb is irregular?

1 fluent   2 easy   3 careful   4 good

d Check in VOCABULARY 8.5 p145. Learn the irregular adverbs.

Ray

5 Write the adverbs.
1 safe *safely*   4 slow   7 quiet
2 happy   5 beautiful   8 bad
3 fast   6 hard   9 noisy

6 a Choose the correct words.
1 I'm a *good/well* tennis player.
2 I usually sleep quite *bad/badly*.
3 I work very *hard/hardly*.
4 I'm a *bad/badly* driver.
5 I speak more than one language *fluent/fluently*.
6 I'm a very *well/good* cook.
7 I can sing *beautiful/beautifully*.

b Tick the true sentences. Change the other sentences to make them true for you.
I'm not a very good tennis player.
I usually sleep very well.

c Work in pairs and compare sentences. How many are the same?

7 a Choose three adjectives or adverbs from **4c** or **5**. Write a sentence about you for each word. Give the sentences to your teacher.

b Listen to your teacher read sentences about different students. Can you guess who he/she is talking about?

HELP WITH PRONUNCIATION
/ɪ/ and /iː/

1 CD2▶60 Listen to these sounds and words. Listen again and practise.
1 /ɪ/   l**i**ve   f**i**sh   b**i**scuits
2 /iː/   l**ea**ve   w**ee**k   p**eo**ple

2 a Work in pairs. Match the vowels in bold in these words with sounds 1 or 2 in **1**.

m**i**lk *1*	t**ee**th	h**i**s	h**e**'s	**i**ll	sk**i**
b**ea**ch	m**ee**ting	**e**xcited	thirt**ee**n
w**i**ndow	**i**nteresting	mach**i**ne	ch**i**cken

b CD2▶61 Listen and check. Listen again and practise.

3 a Work in new pairs. Look at the vowels in bold. Which vowel sound is different?
1 b**ea**ch   mach**i**ne   (w**i**ndow)
2 **e**ngineer   ass**i**stant   t**ea**cher
3 m**a**rket   b**ui**lding   thr**ee**
4 ch**ee**se   s**au**sage   m**ea**t
5 b**u**sy   m**e**ssage   **e**mail
6 t**e**rrible   cr**ow**ded   cl**ea**n
7 **E**nglish   Ch**i**nese   Braz**i**lian

b CD2▶62 Listen and check. Listen again and practise.

continue2learn

■ **Vocabulary, Grammar and Real World**
  ■ **Extra Practice 8 and Progress Portfolio 8** p122
  ■ **Language Summary 8** p145
  ■ **8A–D** Workbook p40

■ **Reading and Writing**
  ■ **Portfolio 8** Finding a job Workbook p78
  Reading job adverts
  Writing a formal letter

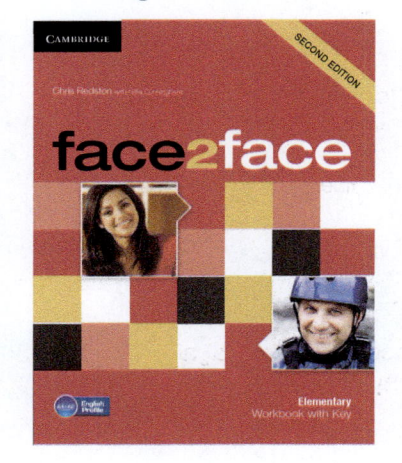

9A Holiday South Africa

Vocabulary holiday activities
Grammar infinitive of purpose

QUICK REVIEW Adjectives and adverbs Write six adjectives. Work in pairs. Take turns to say your adjectives. Your partner says the adverb and a sentence with that adverb: **A** *fluent* **B** *fluently*. *My sister can speak Russian fluently.*

Vocabulary and Speaking Holiday activities

1 a Work in pairs. Fill in the gaps with these verbs. Then check new words/phrases in **VOCABULARY 9.1** ▶ p147.

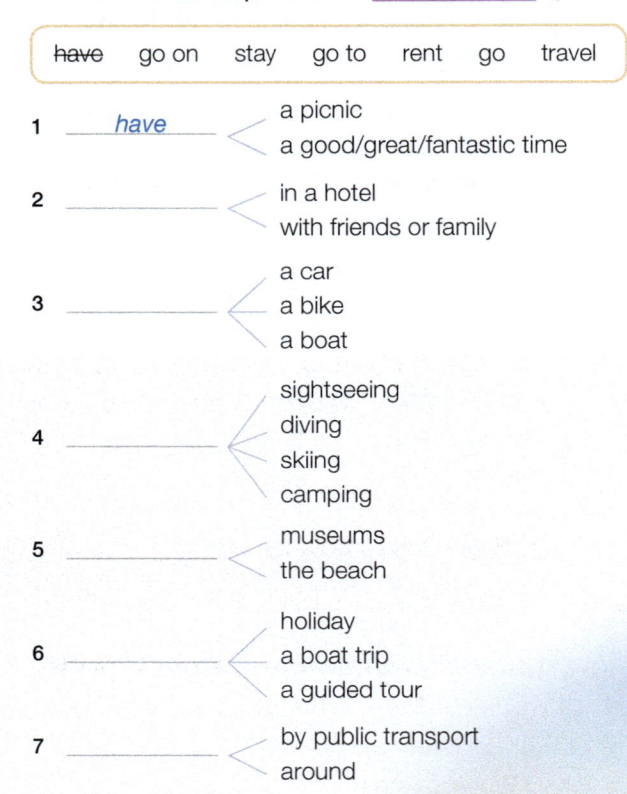

| ~~have~~ | go on | stay | go to | rent | go | travel |

1. *have* — a picnic / a good/great/fantastic time
2. _____ — in a hotel / with friends or family
3. _____ — a car / a bike / a boat
4. _____ — sightseeing / diving / skiing / camping
5. _____ — museums / the beach
6. _____ — holiday / a boat trip / a guided tour
7. _____ — by public transport / around

b Work in pairs. Which of the things in **1a** do you usually do on holiday?

2 a Make Past Simple questions with these words.
1. did / last / you / When / on / holiday / go ?
   When did you last go on holiday?
2. did / go / Where / you ?
3. a good time / you / Did / have ?
4. with / you / Who / go / did ?
5. do / did / there / What / you ?
6. did / stay / you / Where ?
7. you / travel / did / around / How ?
8. you / What else / do / did ?

b Work in pairs. Ask and answer the questions. Give more information if possible.

Listening and Speaking

3 a What do you know about Cape Town?

b Before you listen, check these words/phrases with your teacher.

| a tourist | a cable car | a wildlife park |
| an elephant | a prison | a cell | a whale |

c **CD3 ▶1** Jessica is asking her friend Andy about his last holiday. Listen and put photos A–D in order.

d Listen again. Are these sentences true (T) or false (F)?
1. Andy went to Cape Town for three weeks.
2. He went there with a friend from university.
3. They walked up Table Mountain.
4. They stayed in a hotel in Cape Town.
5. They rented a car for the first week.
6. They went on a boat trip on the last day of their holiday.

HELP WITH LISTENING Weak forms: review

- Remember: we often say words like *was*, *you*, *of*, etc. with a schwa /ə/. These are called weak forms.

4 a Work in pairs. Look at these sentences. Underline the words you hear as weak forms.

1 I went to Cape Town for two weeks.
2 Nigel, a friend from university.
3 And where did you stay?
4 I took lots of photos.
5 Yes, it was amazing.

b CD3 2 Listen and check.

c Look at Audio Script CD3 1 p162. Listen again and notice the weak forms of the words in pink.

HELP WITH GRAMMAR Infinitive of purpose

5 a Look at sentences 1 and 2. Do they have the same meaning?

1 We drove to a wildlife park to see some elephants.
2 We drove to a wildlife park because we wanted to see some elephants.

b Choose the correct words in the rule.

- To say why we do something, we often use the *infinitive/infinitive with to*.

TIP • We often answer *Why … ?* questions with the infinitive with *to*: **A** *Why did you go there?* **B** *To see some elephants.*

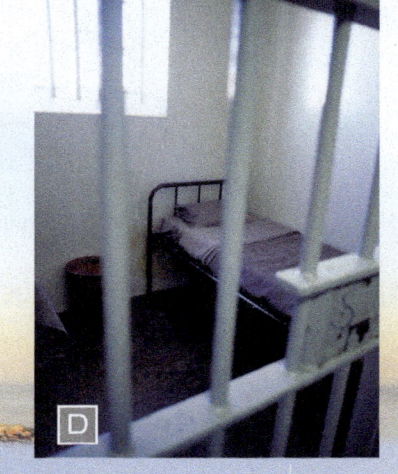

GRAMMAR 9.1 p148

6 CD3 3 **PRONUNCIATION** Listen and practise.

to see some elephants →
We drove to a wildlife park to see some elephants.

7 a Make sentences about why tourists go to these places. Use these verbs.

| ~~see~~ stay take learn see go (x2) |

Tourists go to:

1 Nevada / the Grand Canyon
   Tourists go to Nevada to see the Grand Canyon.
2 Hawaii / diving
3 Dubai / in amazing hotels
4 Agra / the Taj Mahal
5 Switzerland / skiing
6 Kenya / photos of animals
7 London / English

b Work in pairs. Ask your partner why tourists go to the places in **7a**.

Why do tourists go to Nevada?
To see the Grand Canyon.

8 a Complete these sentences. Use the infinitive with *to* and your own ideas. Write true sentences if possible.

1 I need some money …
2 I often go online …
3 I'm studying English …
4 Last weekend I went into town …
5 Last night I phoned my friend …
6 Yesterday I went to the supermarket …

b Work in pairs. Take turns to say your sentences. Ask follow-up questions if possible.

Get ready … Get it right!

9 Write four places you went to in the last four weeks (cities, countries, places, shops, etc.). Think *why* you went there.

Rome   France   my parents' house   the post office

10 a Work in pairs. Ask why your partner went to the places on his/her list. Ask follow-up questions.

Why did you go to Rome?
To visit my sister.
When did you go there?
A week ago.

b Tell the class about one place your partner went to.

A week ago Reza went to Rome to visit his sister.

9B A trip to Egypt

Vocabulary natural places
Grammar comparatives

QUICK REVIEW Adjectives Work in pairs. Write six adjectives that can describe places (*crowded*, *safe*, etc.). Take turns to say sentences about places you know. Use the adjectives on your list: *The town centre is very crowded on Saturdays.*

Vocabulary and Speaking
Natural places

1 a Tick the words you know. Then do the exercise in VOCABULARY 9.2 p147.

> the countryside   a mountain   a hill
> a forest   a wood   a river   an island
> a lake   the sea   the desert

b Think of three famous natural places in your country. Use vocabulary from **1a** and your own ideas.

c Work in groups. Tell other students about the natural places you chose.

> There's a beautiful lake in Hungary called Lake Balaton.

Reading

2 a Before you read, check these words/phrases with your teacher.

> the Pyramids   a mosque
> go snorkelling   a coral reef   a camel

b Read a holiday brochure about two holiday places in Egypt. Choose one place for a holiday. Tell another student why you chose it.

c Read about the places again. Find three things you can do in each place.

3 Read these sentences. Which sentence is false?

a The Sels Hotel is **smaller** than the Shokran Hotel.
b Cairo is **hotter** than Sharm El Sheikh.
c Cairo is probably **noisier**.
d Cairo is **more crowded** than Sharm El Sheikh.
e The holiday in Cairo is **more expensive**.

Accommodation
Shokran Hotel ★★★ (126 rooms)
Cost per week (including flight): €1,490
Average temperature (April–May): 30°C

Cairo

Egypt's busy capital city is a wonderful place to visit. Most people come to Cairo to see the Pyramids at Giza and the famous Egyptian Museum. You can also go on a guided tour of Old Cairo to see the beautiful mosques and old buildings, or go shopping in the famous Khan al-Khalili market.
In the evening you can enjoy traditional Egyptian food in restaurants all over the city, or you can go on a boat trip and have dinner on the River Nile. Come to Cairo – and have the holiday of a lifetime!

HELP WITH GRAMMAR Comparatives

4 a Look at the comparatives in bold in **3**. Then complete the rules.

- Most 1-syllable adjectives (*small*, *old*) → add *-er* .
- 1-syllable adjectives ending in consonant + vowel + consonant (*hot*, *big*, etc.) → double the last consonant and add ____ .
- 2-syllable adjectives ending in -y (*noisy*, *happy*, etc.) → change the -y to ____ and add ____ .
- Other 2- and 3-syllable adjectives (*crowded*, *expensive*, etc.) → put ____ before the adjective.
- The comparatives for *good* and *bad* are irregular: good → better, bad → worse.

b Look at sentences a, b and d in **3**. Which word do we often use after the comparative?

c Check in GRAMMAR 9.2 p148.

Sharm El Sheikh

People come to Sharm El Sheikh from all over the world to go diving and snorkelling in the Red Sea – the beautiful coral reefs and colourful fish are amazing! You can also rent a motorbike and go into the desert to see the red mountains, or maybe go on a camel ride instead. And at the end of the day you can enjoy fresh seafood in one of Sharm El Sheikh's excellent restaurants and then go clubbing with your friends. Whatever you want from your holiday, it's here in Sharm El Sheikh!

Accommodation
Sels Hotel ★★★★ (39 rooms)
Cost per week (including flight): €1,670
Average temperature (April–May): 26°C

5 Write the comparatives.
1. safe *safer*
2. clean
3. boring
4. big
5. dirty
6. good
7. dangerous
8. fast
9. bad
10. easy
11. difficult
12. lucky

Listening and Speaking

6 a CD3 4 Listen to Patrick and Juliet planning a holiday in Egypt. Where does each person want to go? Find one reason why they want to go there.

b Fill in the gaps with the comparative form of the adjectives in brackets. Use *than* if necessary.
1. Sharm's *more beautiful than* Cairo. (beautiful)
2. Cairo's _____ . (interesting)
3. Sharm looks _____ Cairo. (nice)
4. Cairo's _____ Sharm. (busy)
5. The hotel in Cairo is _____ . (cheap)
6. Cairo's _____ Sharm. (good)
7. Sharm's probably _____ . (safe)
8. Sharm's _____ with young people. (popular)

c Work in pairs. Compare sentences. Who says each sentence in **6b** – Patrick or Juliet?

d Listen again and check.

7 CD3 5 **PRONUNCIATION** Listen and practise the sentences in **6b**. Copy the stress and weak form of *than*.
Shărm's mŏre beăutiful than /ðən/ Cairo.

8 CD3 6 Where do you think Patrick and Juliet went on holiday? Listen and check.

Get ready … Get it right!

9 Write five sentences comparing two friends or two people in your family. Use these words/phrases or your own ideas.

young	old	beautiful	tall	short	friendly
happy	busy	rich	famous	popular	
a good/boring/interesting job	a big/small/nice house
a difficult/easy/busy/interesting life

Carlos is younger than Diego.
Diego's got a more interesting job.

10 a Work in pairs. Tell your partner about the people you chose in **9**. Give more information if possible.

Carlos is younger than Diego.
Carlos is 27 and Diego is 30.

b Tell the class two things about the people your partner chose.

9C REAL WORLD — A day out

Real World deciding what to do
Vocabulary animals

QUICK REVIEW Natural places Write all the words for natural places that you know (*a mountain*, etc.). Work in pairs. Compare lists. Then tell your partner about the last time you went to two of the places on your list.

Two places to go

1 a Work in pairs. Which of these animals do you know? Then do the exercise in **VOCABULARY 9.3** p147.

> a lion   a chicken   a tiger   a cow
> a monkey a sheep   a wolf   a rabbit
> a mouse   a snake   a bird   a gorilla

b Put the animals from **1a** into these groups. Some animals can go in more than one group.
1 wild animals
2 farm animals
3 pets

c Work in pairs. Compare groups. Are they the same?

d Work in the same pairs. Which other animals do you know? Add them to your groups.

2 a Read about two places in the UK where people go for a day out. Which place is more interesting, do you think? Why?

b Read the articles again. Answer the questions.

LONGLEAT
1 How do you travel around the Safari Park?
2 Which animals can you see there?
3 Can you visit Longleat House?
4 Where does the gorilla live?

REGENT'S PARK
5 When did London Zoo first open?
6 Is the theatre open in October?
7 How many places to eat are there in the park?
8 Where can you hire boats from?

c Work in pairs. Compare answers.

LONGLEAT

Longleat is a fantastic day out for all the family. You can drive around the Safari Park and see hundreds of animals in the wild. There are monkeys, wolves, lions and tigers in the park, so don't forget to close your car windows!

You can also go on a guided tour of Longleat House, built in the 16th century, or just have lunch in the beautiful gardens. And then in the afternoon you can go on an exciting safari boat trip – look out for the gorilla that lives on an island in the middle of the lake!

Longleat is open every day from February to November. You can buy tickets online at www.longleat.co.uk.

What would you like to do?

3 a **VIDEO 9** **CD3 7** Watch or listen to the Wilson family planning a day out. Put the places they talk about in order. Where do they decide to go?

a Longleat   c a theatre   e London Zoo
b Regent's Park   d the beach *1*   f school

b Listen again. Are these sentences true (T) or false (F)?
1 The Wilson family went to the beach last weekend.
2 Josh's parents want to go to Regent's Park.
3 Josh's sister works at a restaurant every weekend.
4 Josh doesn't want to go to Longleat.
5 His friends went to Longleat two weeks ago.
6 He went to London Zoo last year.
7 He can't take a friend with him on Saturday.

WHAT'S ON IN REGENT'S PARK

LONDON ZOO
This world-famous zoo first opened in 1828 and is now home to 12,000 animals. You can see tigers, camels, snakes, colourful birds and lots more – and don't forget to visit the exciting rainforest area. For more information, go to www.zsl.org.

THE OPEN AIR THEATRE
The theatre is open from May to September. One of the plays this season is Shakespeare's *A Midsummer Night's Dream*. You can book tickets at www.openairtheatre.org.

EVENTS IN THE PARK
There are sometimes free concerts in the afternoons and guided bird walks at the weekend. See www.royalparks.gov.uk for more details of what's on this week.

FOOD AND DRINK
There are six excellent cafés and restaurants in Regent's Park. The Boathouse Café is a popular place for lunch, and the Garden Café is a great place for a meal before going to the open air theatre.

BOAT HIRE
You can hire boats on the lake from March to October from the Boathouse Café.

REAL WORLD Deciding what to do

4 a Look at these questions and answers. We use them when we're deciding what to do.

asking people what they want to do	saying what you want to do
What **would you like** to do?	**I'd like** (to go to the beach).
Where **do you want** to go?	**I want** (to go to Longleat).
Would you like (to go to London)?	Yes, that's a good idea.
Do you want (to go to Regent's Park)?	Not really. **I'd rather** (stay at home).

TIPS • *Would like* is more polite than *want*.
• We use *I'd rather* to say *I want to do this more than something else*.

b Complete the rules with *would/'d like*, *want* and *would/'d rather*.
- After _____ we use the infinitive (*go*, *do*, etc.).
- After _____ and _____ we use the infinitive with *to* (*to go*, *to do*, etc.).

REAL WORLD 9.1 ▶ p148

5 CD3 ▶ 8 **PRONUNCIATION** Listen and practise the sentences in **4a**. Copy the stress.

What would you /wʊdʒə/ like to do?

I'd /aɪd/ like to go to the beach.

6 a Work in pairs, A and B. Take turns to ask your partner what he/she would like to do.

> Would you like to go to the cinema?
>
> I'd rather watch a DVD.

1	A	go to the cinema?	B	watch a DVD
2	B	go for a walk?	A	✓
3	A	play tennis?	B	go swimming
4	B	watch TV?	A	go out
5	A	go shopping?	B	✓
6	B	go out for a meal?	A	go out for a drink

b Take turns to make and respond to three more suggestions.

7 a Choose a place near where you are now for a day out. Think of three reasons why you want to go there.

b Work in groups of three. Decide what to do for your day out. Talk about these things.

> which place   when to go   what you can do there
> where and when to meet   how to get there

> Where would you like to go?
>
> I'd like to go to …
>
> I'd rather go to …

c Tell the class about your group's day out.

REAL WORLD

VOCABULARY 9D AND SKILLS > Time for a change

Vocabulary verb patterns (*like doing*, *would like to do*, etc.)
Skills reading: a magazine article

QUICK REVIEW Comparatives Write eight adjectives. Work in pairs. Take turns to say your adjectives. Your partner says a sentence using the comparative form: A *Tall.* B *My sister is taller than me.*

1 Work in groups. Discuss these questions.
1. Do you live in a city or in the country?
2. Do you like where you live? Why?/Why not?
3. Would you like to move house? If yes, where to? Why?

2 Work in the same groups. Which of these sentences do you agree with? Give reasons if possible.
1. People have an easier life in the country.
2. It's more difficult to find jobs in the country.
3. It's cheaper to live in the country than the city.
4. Public transport is better in the city.
5. Life in the city is more interesting.
6. The city is more dangerous for young people.

3 a Work in pairs. Look at the photos of the people. Who agrees with the sentences in **2**, do you think – Neil or Barry?

b Read the article and check your answers.

4 a Read the article again and answer the questions.
1. When did the Price family decide to move house?
2. Why does Neil want to move to the country?
3. How often does Neil see his children?
4. Do all the Price family want to move to the country?
5. Was it easy for Barry to find a job in the city?
6. Has he got a car?
7. Does he sleep well, do you think?
8. Where does he want to live in the future?

b Work in pairs. Compare answers.

The Grass Is Always Greener

They say that the grass is always greener on the other side of the fence. But can moving house really solve your problems? We asked two people from different parts of the UK why they decided to change the way they live.

Neil Price

A month ago I got a job as a National Park manager, so we decided to sell our house in the city and move to the country. We want to have an easier life and I'd like to spend more time with my family. I really enjoy spending time with my two children, but I only see them on Sundays at the moment. I work six days a week because you need to have a lot of money to live in the city. Everything's more expensive here, especially if you have children. But the kids aren't very happy about moving. They love living in the city, but my wife and I think the country is safer for them. Of course, teenagers like going out on their own, but it can be quite dangerous around here, especially at night.

Barry Robson

I moved to the city two years ago because I needed to get a job. I stopped looking for work in the country because there weren't any jobs, but when I moved here I found one in the first week. I enjoy living in the city because there are more things to do in your free time – life in the country can be quite boring. Also public transport is a lot better in the city, so I don't need to have a car. But houses are more expensive, so generally the cost of living is about the same. Sometimes I hate living in the city – it's dirty, crowded and noisy at night – and I'd like to go back to the country one day. When I'm old, I'd love to have a little place in the mountains where it's really quiet.

HELP WITH VOCABULARY Verb patterns
(*like doing*, *would like to do*, etc.)

5 a Look at these sentences. What verb form comes after *like*? What verb form comes after *'d like*?

*Teenagers like **going** out on their own.*
*I'd like **to go** back to the country one day.*

b Find these verbs in the article. What verb form comes after them? Write the verbs in the table.

> decide   want   enjoy   need   love
> stop   hate   would/'d love

+ verb+*ing*	+ infinitive with *to*
like	would/'d like

c Check in **VOCABULARY 9.4** p148.

6 a Fill in the gaps with the correct form of the verb in brackets.

1. I like _reading_ fashion magazines. (read)
2. My sister hates _____ early. (get up)
3. I want _____ some new clothes. (buy)
4. My son loves _____ video games. (play)
5. I need _____ a new job. (find)
6. I'd like _____ this evening. (go out)
7. Last night Tim decided _____ his job. (leave)
8. I'd love _____ to Australia. (go)
9. My parents enjoy _____ new places. (visit)
10. I stopped _____ three years ago. (smoke)

b Work in pairs. Compare answers.

7 a Fill in the gaps with the correct form of these verbs.

> ~~live~~   watch   be   go to   travel   buy

1. I'd like _to live_ in the USA.
2. I like _____ by train.
3. I like _____ the cinema.
4. I'd like _____ a new computer.
5. I like _____ football on TV.
6. I'd like _____ famous!

b Make questions with *you* from the sentences in **7a**. Then write two more questions, one with *like* and one with *would like*.

Would you like to live in the USA?

c Work in pairs. Ask and answer the questions. Give reasons if possible.

HELP WITH PRONUNCIATION
Silent letters

1 a CD3 9 In some words we don't pronounce every letter. Listen to these words. Notice the silent letters in brackets ( ).

> lis(t)en   cam(e)ra   dau(gh)ter   su(i)tcase
> int(e)resting   si(gh)tseeing   (k)now
> gran(d)father   choc(o)late   fru(i)t

b Listen again and practise.

2 a Put brackets ( ) round the silent letters in these words.

1. (w)rite
2. island
3. friend
4. vegetables
5. building
6. two
7. sandwich
8. hour
9. bread
10. different
11. white
12. half

b Work in pairs. Compare answers.

c CD3 10 Listen and practise the words.

3 a CD3 11 Listen and write the words. Be careful of the silent letters!

1. wrote

b Work in pairs. Compare your spelling. Put brackets ( ) round the silent letter in each word.

c Check your spelling in Audio Script CD3 11 p163.

continue2learn

Vocabulary, Grammar and Real World
- **Extra Practice 9 and Progress Portfolio 9** p123
- **Language Summary 9** p147
- **9A–D** Workbook p45

Reading and Writing
- **Portfolio 9** Places to go Workbook p80
  Reading tourist information
  Writing describing places: paragraphs (3); phrases with and without *the*

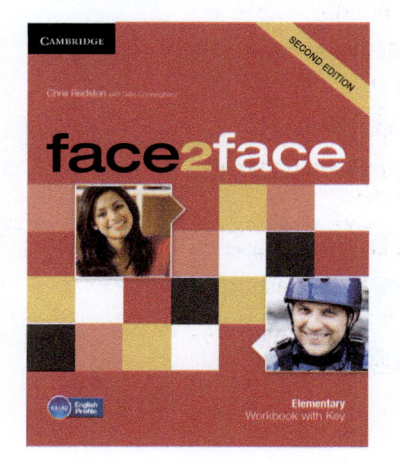

79

10A Stay fit and healthy

Vocabulary verb phrases; frequency expressions
Grammar imperatives; should/shouldn't

QUICK REVIEW: Verb patterns Work in pairs. Take turns to say something that you: love doing, would like to do tomorrow, enjoy doing at the weekend, need to do soon, hate doing, would love to do in the future. Continue the conversations if possible.

Vocabulary and Speaking Verb phrases

1 a Work in pairs. Match the verbs in A to the words/phrases in B. Check new words/phrases in **VOCABULARY 10.1** p149.

A	B
get	the windows/the car
spend	fit/stressed
carry	time/money
wash	the shopping/the bags
take	a bath/a shower
have	a bus/a train
do	the lift/the escalator
get on/off	the housework/some exercise

b Work in pairs. Take turns to test your partner.

    fit   get fit

2 a Write the name of one person you know who:
- walks to work
- watches TV a lot
- does a lot of sport
- gets stressed easily

b Work in pairs. Tell your partner about the people in **2a**. Ask follow-up questions.

Reading and Speaking

3 a Before you read, check these words with your teacher.

    a member   a survey   a calorie   a mile   healthy

b Read the first paragraph of the article. Then choose the best headline.
- Cheaper Gym Membership For All
- Get Fit For Free
- City People Don't Exercise

c Read the rest of the article. Match tips 1–8 to pictures a–h.

d Work in groups. Discuss these questions.
1 Which do you think is the best tip? Why?
2 Do you do any of these things now? If so, which ones?
3 Which would you like to do in the future?

Everyone wants to look good and get fit, so many of us go to a gym. In the UK there are over 6,000 gyms and 7 million gym members. That's a lot of exercise – or is it? A typical gym member spends £372 a year, but people spend £200 million every year on gym membership they don't use. So here are our top tips for getting fit without spending any money.

1 Walk up and down stairs. Don't take lifts. If there aren't any stairs and there's an escalator, walk up or down the escalator. Walking up an escalator uses ten calories, walking down uses four.

2 Get off the bus one stop earlier. You use about 80 calories for every mile you walk.

3 Walk around when you are talking on the phone. You use six calories **every minute**.

4 Wash the car. Don't use a car wash. Washing the car for 30 minutes uses 100 calories.

5 Do the housework faster than normal. You use four extra calories every minute.

6 Don't drive to the supermarket once a week. Walk to the shops three times a week and carry your shopping home. This can use 100 calories every mile.

7 Don't have a bath, have a shower instead. It saves water and you use one more calorie every three minutes.

8 Go for a run **twice a week**. You can use 150–200 calories a mile – and it's a lot cheaper than a gym!

HELP WITH GRAMMAR Imperatives

4 We often use imperatives to give strong advice. Look at these sentences and answer the questions.

Walk up and down stairs. Don't take lifts.

1 Is the positive imperative the same as the infinitive?
2 How do we make the negative imperative?

GRAMMAR 10.1 ▶ p150

5 a Write five more tips on how to stay fit and healthy.

Don't watch TV every night. Eat a lot of fruit.

b Work in groups. Compare sentences and choose your top five tips. Then tell the class what they are.

HELP WITH VOCABULARY
Frequency expressions

6 Look at the frequency expressions in bold in the article. Then fill in the gaps.

once	a day		
	a _____		day
three times	a month	every	week
four times	a year		month
			year

TIP • We use *How often … ?* to ask about frequency:
A *How often do you go to the gym?* B *Twice a week.*

VOCABULARY 10.2 ▶ p149

7 a Underline all the frequency expressions in the article. Then compare answers in pairs.

b Work in the same pairs. Ask your partner how often he/she does these things.

1 go for a walk?
2 go swimming?
3 have a holiday?
4 get very stressed?
5 eat vegetables?
6 eat fish?

> How often do you go for a walk?

> Oh, about once a week.

Listening

8 a CD3 ▶ 12 Look at the photo. Mrs Lee is at the doctor's. Listen to their conversation. Is she fit and healthy? Why?/Why not?

b Listen again and answer the questions.

1 How much does Mrs Lee weigh? *Seventy kilos.*
2 How often does she walk to school with the children?
3 When did she start going to the gym?
4 How often does she go to the gym?
5 What does she usually eat?
6 What advice did the doctor give her?

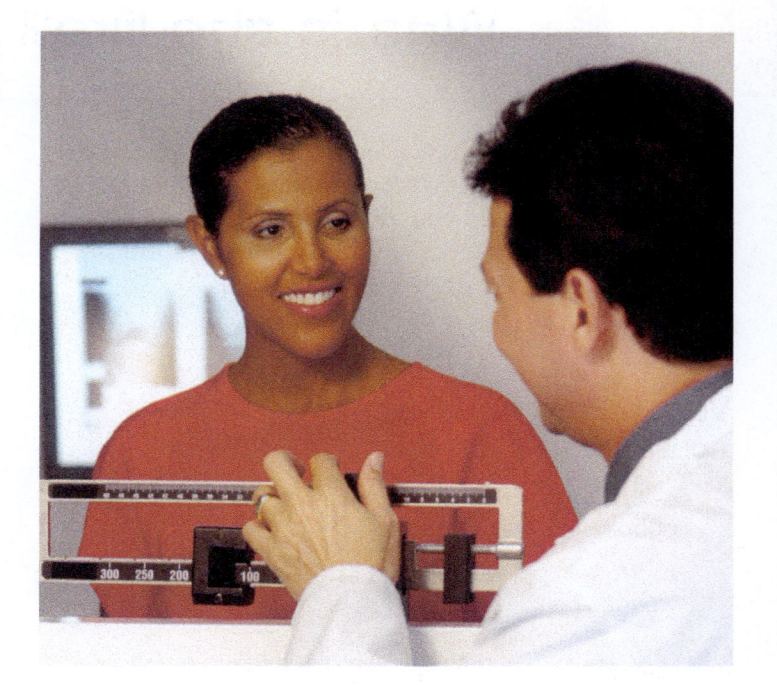

HELP WITH GRAMMAR should/shouldn't

9 We use *should* and *shouldn't* to give advice. Look at these sentences and choose the correct words in the rules.

*You **should** do some exercise three times a week.*

*You **shouldn't** eat so many pizzas and biscuits.*

- We use *should* to say something is a *good/bad* thing to do.
- We use *shouldn't* to say something is a *good/bad* thing to do.
- After *should* and *shouldn't* we use the *infinitive/ infinitive with to*.

GRAMMAR 10.2 ▶ p150

10 a The doctor gave Mrs Lee some more advice. Fill in the gaps with *should* or *shouldn't*.

1 You _____ go swimming every week.
2 You _____ eat big meals in the evening.
3 You _____ eat more salads.
4 You _____ drive to work every day.
5 You _____ walk to work twice a week.
6 You _____ sit and watch TV every evening.

b CD3 ▶ 13 PRONUNCIATION Listen and check. Then listen again and practise. Copy the stress.

You should go swimming every week.

Get ready … Get it right!

11 Work in groups of three. Student A p108. Student B p113. Student C p114.

10B What's she like?

Vocabulary appearance; character
Grammar questions with *like*

QUICK REVIEW *should/shouldn't; clothes* Write all the clothes you know. Work in pairs and compare lists. What clothes do you think people should and shouldn't wear when they go to: a wedding, a job interview, a birthday party?

Vocabulary and Speaking
Appearance

1 **a** Look at photos A–D for one minute. Remember the people and their clothes!

b Work in pairs. Close your book. What are the people wearing?

2 **a** Work in new pairs. Which of these words/phrases do you know? Check new words in **VOCABULARY 10.3** p149.

A
young   middle-aged   old
tall   short
thin   slim   fat   overweight
beautiful   good-looking   attractive
white   black   Asian
bald

B
blue/brown/green eyes
long/short hair
dark/fair/blonde/grey hair
a beard   a moustache

b Which group of words do we use with *have got*? Which do we use with *be*?

3 **a** Write a description of one person in photos A–D. Don't write his/her name.

b Work in pairs. Read your partner's description. Who is it? Is the description correct?

Listening

4 **a** **CD3 14** Leo and Tina want someone to advertise *Break*, a new chocolate bar. Listen and put the people they talk about in order.

b Listen again. How do Leo and Tina describe each person? Make notes.

c Work in pairs. Compare your answers. Who do Leo and Tina choose for the *Break* poster, do you think? Why?

d **CD3 15** Listen to the end of the conversation. Who did they choose? Why?

Vocabulary and Speaking
Character

5 **a** Tick the sentences that are true for you.
1 I work very hard.
2 I don't like working.
3 I like doing things to help other people.
4 I make people laugh a lot.
5 I usually think about myself, not other people.
6 I'm friendly and I like meeting new people.
7 When I promise to do something, I always do it.
8 It's difficult for me to talk to new people.
9 I like giving people money and presents.

b Work in pairs. Compare your answers. How many are the same?

A — Lily
B — Jake
C — Pete
D — Zoë

6 a Match these adjectives to the sentences in **5a**. Check in VOCABULARY 10.4 p149.

hard-working 1   generous   kind   funny
selfish   outgoing   lazy   reliable   shy

b Work in groups. Use the adjectives in **6a** to describe members of your family.

Listening and Speaking

7 CD3 16 Listen to Leo and Tina three weeks later. Match 1–3 to a–c. Who is Leo's new girlfriend?

1 What's she like?
2 What does she like doing?
3 What does she look like?

a She's tall and slim, and she's got long dark hair.
b She likes clubbing and going to restaurants.
c She's friendly and outgoing. And she's very beautiful.

HELP WITH GRAMMAR Questions with *like*

8 Complete the rules with questions 1–3 in **7**.

- We use _____ to ask for a general description. The answer can include character and physical appearance.
- We use _____ to ask about physical appearance only.
- We use _____ to ask what people enjoy doing in their free time.

TIP • *How is he/she?* asks about health, not personality:
A *How's your mum?* **B** *She's fine, thanks.*

GRAMMAR 10.3 p150

HELP WITH LISTENING Sentence stress (3)

9 a CD3 17 Listen and notice the stressed words.

What's she like?
What does she like doing?
What does she look like?

b Look at Audio Script CD3 16 p163. Listen again and follow the stress.

10 a Write the questions for these answers.

1 She's tall, attractive and friendly. *What's she like?*
2 She's quite short and has got dark hair.
3 He's selfish and lazy, but really good-looking!
4 She likes swimming and cycling.
5 He's not very tall and he's bald.
6 They're both quite shy.

b CD3 18 PRONUNCIATION Listen and check. Listen again and practise. Copy the stress.

Get ready … Get it right!

11 Write the names of three friends on a piece of paper. Think how you can describe their character, appearance and the things they enjoy doing. Don't write this information.

12 a Work in pairs and swap papers. Take turns to ask and answer the questions in **7** about your partner's friends.

b Choose one of your partner's friends that you would like to meet. Tell the class why you chose that person.

10C REAL WORLD — I feel ill

Real World talking about health
Vocabulary health problems; treatment

QUICK REVIEW Describing people's appearance and character
Think of two famous people. Make notes on how to describe them. You can talk about their appearance, character, job, age, nationality, etc. Work in pairs. Take turns to describe the people, but don't say their names. Guess the people your partner describes.

What's the matter?

1 Match the sentences to the people A–H.

1 I've got a stomach ache. *B*
2 I feel sick.
3 I've got a headache.
4 I've got a cold.
5 I've got a cough.
6 My back hurts.
7 I've got a temperature.
8 I've got a sore throat.

2 a Work in pairs. Write these words in the table. Check in VOCABULARY 10.5 p149.

| ~~a stomach ache~~ ~~ill~~ ~~back~~ terrible a headache |
| arm toothache sick a sore throat foot |
| a cold better a cough leg a temperature |

I've got …	a stomach ache
I feel …	ill
my … hurts	back

TIP • We can say *I've got **a** stomach ache/toothache* or *I've got stomach ache/toothache*, but not ~~I've got headache~~.

b CD3 19 PRONUNCIATION Listen and practise.

Get well soon

3 a Work in pairs. Match these words/phrases to the verbs. Check in VOCABULARY 10.6 p150.

| ~~to bed~~ ~~at home~~ ~~the day off~~ some painkillers |
| home to the doctor some cough medicine |
| in bed to the dentist some antibiotics |

go	stay	take
to bed	at home	the day off

b Work in groups. Look at the words/phrases in **2a** and **3a** again. What do you usually do when you're ill?

When I've got a cold I usually stay in bed.

I usually take some aspirin.

Rachel   Simon   Tim   Emily

4 **a** VIDEO 10 CD3 20 Watch or listen to two conversations. What's wrong with Simon and Emily? Are they going to the meeting?

b Watch or listen again. Who says these things – Rachel (R) or Tim (T)?

1 Are you OK? R
2 Are you alright?
3 What's the matter?
4 What's wrong?
5 Why don't you go home?
6 You shouldn't go to work today.
7 You should go to the doctor.
8 I hope you get better soon.
9 Take the day off.
10 Get well soon.

REAL WORLD
Talking about health

5 Cover **4b**. Then fill in the gaps in the table with the words in the boxes.

| ~~OK~~ | matter | better | Get | off | should |
| alright | What's | dear | hope | shouldn't | don't |

asking about someone's health	expressing sympathy	giving advice
Are you ¹OK ?	Oh, ⁵_____ .	Why ⁹_____ you go home?
Are you ²_____ ?	I ⁶_____ you get ⁷_____ soon.	You ¹⁰_____ go to work today.
³_____ wrong?	⁸_____ well soon.	You ¹¹_____ go to the doctor.
What's the ⁴_____ ?		Take the day ¹²_____ .

REAL WORLD 10.1 ▶ p150

HELP WITH LISTENING
Being sympathetic

6 **a** CD3 21 Listen to this question said twice. The first is not sympathetic. The second is sympathetic.

What's the matter?

b CD3 22 Which person sounds sympathetic, a or b?

1 Are you OK?   (a)   b
2 Are you alright?   a   b
3 What's wrong?   a   b
4 What's the matter?   a   b
5 Oh, dear.   a   b
6 I hope you get better soon. a   b

7 CD3 23 PRONUNCIATION Listen and practise the sentences in **5**. Copy the intonation.

Are you OK?

8 Work in pairs. Look at Audio and Video Script VIDEO 10 CD3 20 p163. Choose conversation 1 or 2. Underline all the phrases from **5**. Then practise the conversation with your partner. Change roles and practise the conversation again.

9 **a** Choose an illness from **2a**. Have conversations with other students. Take turns to be sympathetic and give advice.

b Tell the class about your illness. What advice did students give you? Was it good advice, do you think?

85

VOCABULARY 10D AND SKILLS > Winter blues

Vocabulary seasons; weather; word building
Skills reading: a magazine article

QUICK REVIEW Health problems and treatment Work in pairs. Take turns to mime illnesses to your partner. Don't speak! He/She guesses what's wrong and gives advice.

1 a Match the seasons to pictures A–D. Then check in VOCABULARY 10.7 p150.

winter   summer   autumn   spring

b Work in pairs. Which is your favourite season? Why?

2 a Before you read, check these words with your teacher.

depressed   a scientist   a box   bright   light   sad

b Read the first paragraph of the article. Why does the woman have a light on her desk?

c Read the whole article. Answer these questions.
1. What happened to Herb Kern in winter?
2. What did some scientists make for him?
3. Why do people get SAD?
4. Do men get SAD more than women?
5. How do you know if people have SAD?
6. In which countries is SAD common?
7. How long should you use a light box every day?

d Work in pairs. Compare answers.

3 Work in the same pairs. Discuss these questions.
1. Do you feel depressed in winter? Why?/Why not?
2. What activities do you usually do in winter?

If you're SAD, see the light!

A lot of people feel depressed in winter – but there's an easy way to fight those winter blues.

In the 1970s, an American engineer called Herb Kern noticed that in spring and summer he was happy and had a lot of energy, but every winter he became depressed and lazy. He thought it was because there wasn't much daylight in the winter and asked some scientists to make a 'light box'. He put the box on his desk and after a few days he felt a lot better. In 1982 the scientists gave his illness a name – Seasonal Affective Disorder, or SAD.

People get SAD in autumn and winter, when the days are shorter and there is less daylight. It is more common in women than in men. People with SAD usually sleep a lot and feel tired all the time. They also eat a lot of sweet food and feel depressed. In the UK about 5% of people have SAD and it is common in other countries like the USA, Sweden and Ireland. The best treatment for this illness is bright light. People with SAD should use a light box for half an hour a day. Or you can go on holiday to a sunny country, of course!

4 a Work in pairs. Match these weather words to the pictures. Then check in **VOCABULARY 10.8** p150.

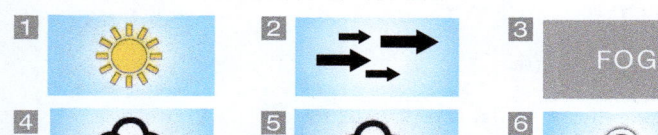

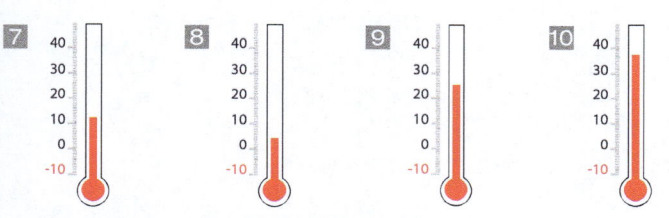

foggy 3 raining snowing
windy cloudy sunny

1 2 3 FOG
4 5 6

12° (degrees) 7 hot warm cold

7 8 9 10

b What's the weather like today?

5 Work in pairs. Student A p108. Student B p113.

HELP WITH VOCABULARY Word building

6 a Look at the table. Fill in the gaps. How do we make adjectives from nouns? How do we make nouns from adjectives?

noun	adjective	adjective	noun
sun	sunny	ill	illness
	windy		happiness
cloud		sad	
fog		fit	

b Check in **VOCABULARY 10.9** p150.

7 a Choose the correct words.
1. It was very sun/(sunny) yesterday.
2. There's a lot of cloud/cloudy today.
3. It was wind/windy last weekend.
4. We get a lot of fog/foggy where we live.
5. I always get the same ill/illness every winter.
6. I'm usually sad/sadness at the end of a holiday.
7. Some of my friends are very fit/fitness.
8. I think money is more important than happy/happiness.

b Tick the sentences that are true for where you live and for you.

c Work in pairs. Compare sentences. How many are the same?

HELP WITH PRONUNCIATION
The letter *a*

1 CD3 24 Listen and notice four ways we say the letter *a*. Listen again and practise.

/æ/ h**a**t b**a**nk   /eɪ/ l**a**zy he**a**dache
/ɑː/ b**a**th f**a**ther   /ə/ **a**go stom**a**ch

2 a Work in pairs. Write these words in the table.

~~rabbit~~ r**a**dio **a**nother contr**a**ct
answers g**a**mes eleph**a**nt f**a**mily
arm f**a**mous isl**a**nd d**a**nce

/æ/	h**a**t	rabbit
/ɑː/	b**a**th	
/eɪ/	l**a**zy	
/ə/	**a**go	

b CD3 25 Listen and check. Listen again and practise.

3 a CD3 26 Listen and practise these sentences.
1. I often have my laptop with me when I travel by taxi.
2. My hard-working father likes fast food and dancing.
3. Take a suitcase when you go on holiday by plane.
4. This is the address of the accountant's company.
5. The manager of our company has fast food every day.

b Work in pairs. Take turns to say the sentences.

continue2learn

■ **Vocabulary, Grammar and Real World**
- **Extra Practice 10 and Progress Portfolio 10** p124
- **Language Summary 10** p149
- **10A–D** Workbook p50

■ **Reading and Writing**
- **Portfolio 10** The advice page Workbook p82
  Reading letters asking for advice
  Writing pronouns and possessive adjectives; a letter of advice

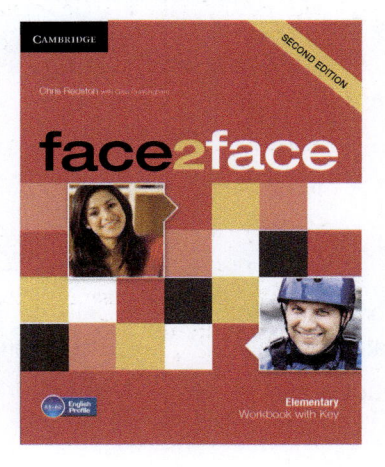

11A Happy New Year!

Vocabulary New Year's resolutions
Grammar *be going to* (1): positive, negative and *Wh-* questions

QUICK REVIEW The weather Work in pairs. Write all the weather words you know. Then use words on your list to describe the weather in your town or city: today, yesterday, last weekend, in December, in June.

Speaking and Vocabulary
New Year's resolutions

1 Work in pairs. Discuss these questions.
1 How do people in your country celebrate New Year?
2 Where were you last New Year's Eve? What did you do?
3 Do people in your country make New Year's resolutions? If so, what kind of resolutions?

2 a Look at New Year's resolutions 1–8. Then match these words/phrases to the verbs in bold. Check in **VOCABULARY 11.1** p151.

| fit | weight | smoking | house | less |
| fun | more exercise | chocolate cake | | |

1 **get** a new job/ *fit*
2 **work** hard/_____
3 **lose** three kilos/_____
4 **have** a holiday/_____
5 **do** a computer course/_____
6 **stop** working at weekends/_____
7 **move** to another country/_____
8 **not eat** sweet things/_____

b Work in pairs. Take turns to test your partner.

Listening and Speaking

3 CD3 27 Look at the photo of a New Year's Eve party. Listen to two conversations. Match the people to their New Year's resolutions A–E.

4 a Look at the people's New Year's resolutions. Fill in the gaps with words from **2a**.
1 I'm going to work *less* and have more *fun*.
2 I'm going to have a _____ this year.
3 I'm going to _____ to Australia.
4 I'm going to do a _____ .
5 We're going to get _____ .
6 Val's going to stop _____ .
7 David's going to _____ weight.
8 I'm going to do more _____ .
9 I'm not going to eat _____ things any more.

b CD3 27 Listen again and check.

HELP WITH GRAMMAR
be going to (1): positive and negative

5 a Look at the sentences in **4a**. Then choose the correct words in the rules.
- These sentences talk about the *past/present/future*.
- The people decided to do these things *before/when* they said them.
- We use *be going to* + infinitive for *future plans/ things we do every day*.

b Look at the sentences in the table. Then write sentences 7, 8 and 9 from **4a** in the table.

subject	be (+ *not*)	going to	infinitive	
We	're	going to	get	fit.
Val	's	going to	stop	smoking.

c Check in **GRAMMAR 11.1** p152.

HELP WITH GRAMMAR
be going to (1): Wh- questions

8 **a** Look at the questions in the table. Notice the word order.

question word	be	subject	going to	infinitive	
What	are	you	going to	do	next year?
Where	's	she	going to	live?	

b Write questions 1 and 2 in the table.
1 Where's he going to study?
2 When are they going to start getting fit?

c Check in **GRAMMAR 11.2** p152.

9 **a** Make questions with *you* and *be going to*.
1 What / do after class?
   What are you going to do after class?
2 How / get home today?
3 What / do next weekend?
4 What / have for dinner tonight?
5 Where / have lunch tomorrow?
6 When / do your English homework?

b **CD3 29** **PRONUNCIATION** Listen and practise the questions in **9a**. Copy the weak forms.
What are you /ələ/ going to /tə/ do after class?

c Work in pairs. Ask and answer the questions in **9a**.

Get ready … Get it right!

10 What are you going to do in the future? Write notes about your plans for: next week, next month, next year. Use the phrases in **2a** or your own ideas.

next week – have lunch with my sister

11 **a** Work in groups of four. Ask and answer questions about your plans. Give more information if possible. Are any of your plans the same?

> What are you going to do next week?

> On Monday I'm going to have lunch with a friend.

b Tell the class about people with the same plans as you.

David   Ed   Val

6 **CD3 28** **PRONUNCIATION** Listen and practise the sentences in **4a**. Copy the stress.

I'm going to /gəʊɪŋtə/ work less and have more fun.

7 **a** Fill in the gaps with the correct form of *be going to* and the verb in brackets.
1 I *'m going to look for* a new job. (look for)
2 He _____ working at weekends. (stop)
3 They _____ to the gym. (go)
4 I _____ any cigarettes. (not/buy)
5 She _____ her house. (sell)
6 We _____ every weekend. (not/eat out)
7 He _____ a new computer. (buy)
8 She _____ in the UK. (not/stay)

b Work in pairs. Match the sentences to the people at the party.

11B No more exams!

Vocabulary studying
Grammar *be going to* or *might*; *be going to* (2): *yes/no* questions and short answers

QUICK REVIEW *be going to* Work in pairs. Take turns to say three things you're going to do tomorrow. Ask follow-up questions if possible. Are you going to do the same things?

Melanie   *Jenny*   *Eric*

Vocabulary and Speaking Studying

1 Work in pairs. Fill in the gaps with these words/phrases. Then check in **VOCABULARY 11.2** p151.

> start   revise for   take   go to   some qualifications
> do   pass   fail   a degree   leave   a job

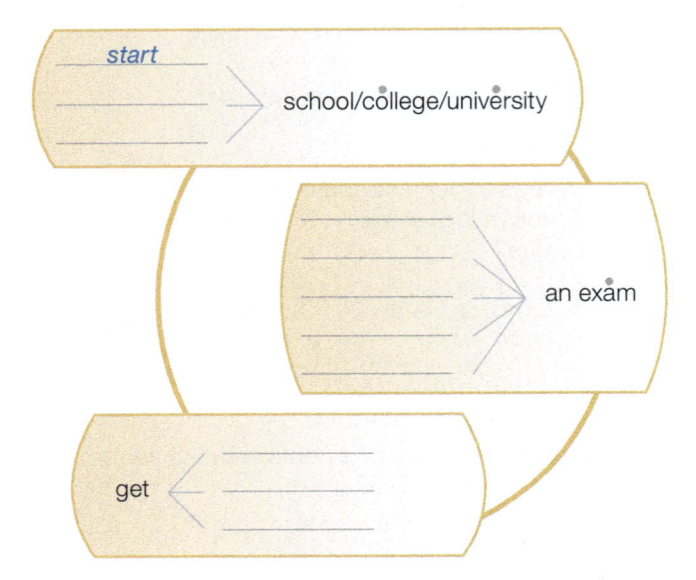

start → _____ school/college/university

_____ → an exam

_____ → get ←

2 Work in the same pairs. Discuss these questions.
1 Which things in **1** do people usually celebrate?
2 What was the last exam you took? Was it difficult?
3 Did you celebrate when you finished? If so, what did you do?

Listening and Speaking

3 a **CD3 30** Listen to Eric, Jenny and Melanie talking after their final university exam. Tick the things they talk about.

> the exam   a party   a film   a drink   a club
> a phone call   a concert   a meal   a job

b Listen again. Tick the true sentences. Correct the false ones.

　　　　　　　　　difficult
1 The exam was ~~easy~~.
2 Eric couldn't answer the last three questions.
3 There's a big party at Caroline's house this evening.
4 Eric wants to go home and sleep.
5 He's going to meet some friends this evening.
6 Jenny's going to phone her sister.

HELP WITH GRAMMAR be going to or might

4 a Look at these sentences. Then choose the correct words in the rules.

I'm going to meet some friends in town at seven.
I might go to the party or I might go out for a meal.

- We use *might/be going to* to say a future plan is decided.
- We use *might/be going to* to say something in the future is possible, but not decided.
- After *might* we use the *infinitive/infinitive with to*.

TIP • *Might* is the same for all subjects (*I, you, he*, etc.).

b Check in GRAMMAR 11.3 p152.

5 CD3 31 PRONUNCIATION Listen and practise sentences with *might*.

I might go to the party.

6 Look at Eric, Jenny and Melanie's plans for the summer. Fill in the gaps with the correct form of *be going to* or *might* and the verb in brackets. (✓) = decided, (✓✗) = not decided.

1 (✓) Eric _'s going to have_ a holiday. (have)
2 (✓) Jenny _____ a Spanish course. (do)
3 (✓✗) Melanie _____ camping. (go)
4 (✓) Eric _____ for his father. (not work)
5 (✓) Jenny and Sam _____ married. (get)
6 (✓✗) Melanie _____ friends in Scotland. (visit)
7 (✓✗) Eric _____ in a restaurant (work).

7 a Write three things you might do and three things you're going to do next month.

b Work in pairs. Take turns to say your sentences. Are any the same?

Listening and Speaking

HELP WITH LISTENING going to

8 a CD3 32 Listen and notice the two different ways we say *going to*. Both are correct.

a How are you going to /ɡəʊɪŋtə/ celebrate tonight?
b I'm going to /ɡənə/ meet some friends in town.

b CD3 33 Listen to these sentences. Which way do these people say *going to*, a or b?

	/ɡəʊɪŋtə/	/ɡənə/
1 Are you going to look for a job?	a	(b)
2 My cousin's going to teach English.	a	b
3 I'm going to do a business course.	a	b
4 How are you going to pay for it?	a	b
5 My parents are going to help me.	a	b
6 Are you going to sell your car?	a	b

9 CD3 34 Listen to Eric, Jenny and Melanie talk about their plans. Answer the questions.

1 Is Jenny going to look for a job? *Yes, she is.*
2 Are Jenny and Sam going to Italy next month?
3 Is Melanie going to teach English?
4 Is Eric going to do a computer course?
5 Are Eric's parents going to help him pay for the course?
6 Is Eric going to sell his car?

HELP WITH GRAMMAR be going to (2): yes/no questions and short answers

10 a Fill in the gaps with the correct part of the verb *be*.

1 A _Are_ you going to look for a job?
   B Yes, I _____./No, I _____ not.
2 A _____ he going to sell his car?
   B Yes, he _____./No, he _____.
3 A _____ his parents going to help him?
   B Yes, they _____./No, they _____.

TIP • We can also answer *yes/no* questions with (*Yes,*) *I might*: **A** Are you going to buy it? **B** I might.

b Check in GRAMMAR 11.4 p152.

11 Work in pairs. Student A p108. Student B p113.

Get ready ... Get it right!

12 Look at these possible plans. Make *yes/no* questions with *you* and the correct form of *be going to*.

- meet a friend after class
  Are you going to meet a friend after class?
- work next weekend
- study tonight
- stay at home tomorrow
- go away next weekend
- have a holiday in the next three months
- watch a DVD this evening
- buy some clothes next weekend
- take an exam this year

13 a Ask other students your questions. Try to find one person who is going to do each thing. Then ask two follow-up questions.

b Tell the class about another student's plans.

11C REAL WORLD Directions

Real World directions; asking for and giving directions

QUICK REVIEW Places in a town/city Write a list of places in a town or city (*a museum*, etc.). Work in pairs and compare lists. How many of these places are near where you are now?

Wayne   Daisy   Josh   Alison

Hill Place
- Three bedrooms (two double, one single). Sleeps 5.
- Kitchen and small garden.
- Living room with TV and DVD player.
- Shower room and separate toilet.
- 5 min walk to town centre.
- 10 min walk to beach.
- From £430 per week.

Benton House
- Three double bedrooms. Sleeps 6.
- Large kitchen and garden.
- Comfortable living room with DVD player and cable TV.
- Bathroom with separate shower.
- 10 min walk to town centre.
- Only 1 min from beach.
- From £480 per week.

Seaton Holiday Homes   01834 654389

Choosing a holiday home

1 a Look at the photo of the Wilson family. Then read the adverts for holiday homes in Seaton. Which place is better for the family's holiday, do you think? Why?

b Work in pairs. Say which holiday home you chose and why.

2 CD3 35 Listen to Alison phone Seaton Holiday Homes. When is the family's holiday? Which holiday home does she choose? Why?

It's on the left

3 Work in pairs. Which of these phrases do you know? Then do the exercise in REAL WORLD 11.1 p152.

> turn right   turn left   go over the bridge   go past the pub
> go along this road/street   it's on the/your left
> it's on the/your right   it's opposite   it's next to

4 a Read the email and look at the map. Draw the route from *You are here* to the holiday home.

b Work in pairs. Check your route. Which number is the holiday home on the map?

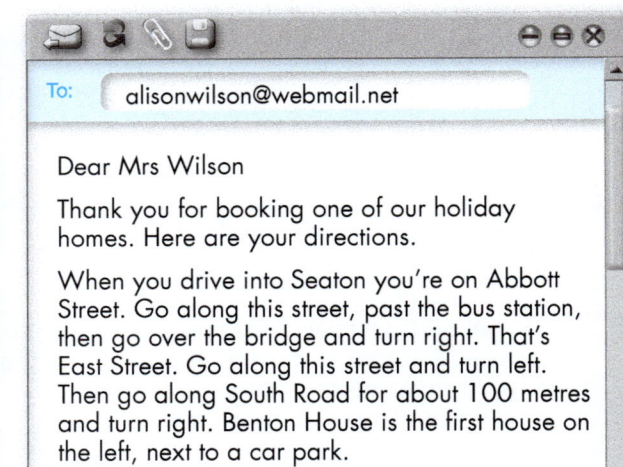

To: alisonwilson@webmail.net

Dear Mrs Wilson

Thank you for booking one of our holiday homes. Here are your directions.

When you drive into Seaton you're on Abbott Street. Go along this street, past the bus station, then go over the bridge and turn right. That's East Street. Go along this street and turn left. Then go along South Road for about 100 metres and turn right. Benton House is the first house on the left, next to a car park.

I hope you have a wonderful holiday.

Pauline Wells

---

5 CD3 36 Look at the map and listen. Start at *You are here*. Which four places do the directions take you to?

6 a VIDEO 11 CD3 37 The Wilson family are at the bus station. Close your book. Watch or listen to their conversations. Which places do they want to go to?

b Watch or listen again. Find the places on the map. What numbers are they?

REAL WORLD
Asking for and giving directions

7 a Fill in the gaps with these words.

> ~~Excuse~~   Where's   get   there

ASKING FOR DIRECTIONS

Excuse me. Is _____ (a newsagent's) near here?
Excuse me. _____ (the post office)?
Excuse me. How do I/we _____ to (the market)?

> ~~one~~   there   over   miss
> turn   on   past   next   It's

GIVING DIRECTIONS

There's *one* in (Berry Street).
Go along this road/street and _____ right/left.
Go _____ the pub.
Go _____ the bridge.
(The newsagent's) is _____ the/your right/left.
_____ opposite (the supermarket).
It's _____ to (the café).
It's over _____ .
You can't _____ it.

b Check in REAL WORLD 11.2 p152.

8 CD3 38 **PRONUNCIATION** Listen and practise the sentences in **7a**.

Excuse me. Is there a newsagent's near here?

9 a Fill in the gaps in these conversations with words from **7a**. They all start at *You are here* on the map.

1. A Excuse me. Is ¹ *there* a police station ² _____ here?
   B Yes, there's one ³ _____ Berry Street. Go ⁴ _____ this road and ⁵ _____ right. The police station is ⁶ _____ your left, next ⁷ _____ the baker's.
   A Thank you very much.

2. A Excuse me. How do I ⁸ _____ to the Park Hotel?
   B ⁹ _____ along this road and go ¹⁰ _____ the bridge. Go ¹¹ _____ the market and turn left. That's Russell Street. The Park Hotel is on ¹² _____ left. You ¹³ _____ miss it.
   A Thanks a lot.

3. A Excuse me. ¹⁴ _____ the museum?
   B It's ¹⁵ _____ there, opposite the station.
   A Oh yes, I can see it. Thanks.

b Work in pairs. Compare answers. Find the places on the map. What numbers are they?

c Work in the same pairs. Practise the conversations.

10 Work in pairs. Student A p105. Student B p110.

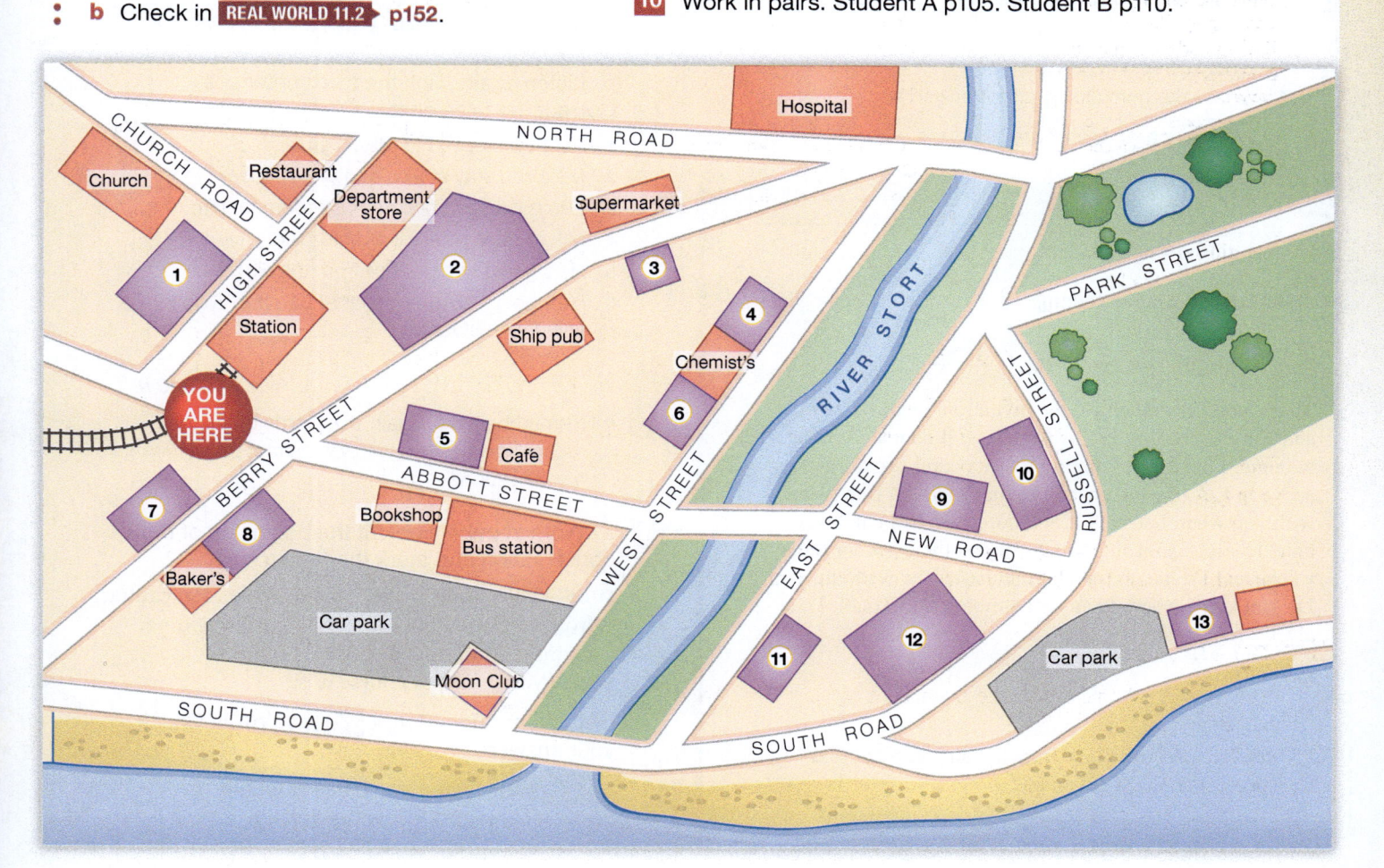

11D VOCABULARY AND SKILLS > An invitation

Vocabulary collocations
Skills reading: an email; listening: a phone conversation

QUICK REVIEW **Directions** Work in pairs. Write five places near where you are now that you both know. Take turns to give directions to two of the places. Your partner guesses the place. Start with: *Go out of the building and … .*

1 a Work on your own. Answer these questions.
1 When did you last go to a wedding or a party?
2 Where was it?
3 Whose wedding or party was it?
4 How many people were there?
5 What did you wear?
6 What did/didn't you like about the wedding or party?
7 What else do you remember about it?

b Work in pairs. Ask and answer the questions in **1a**. Give more information if possible.

2 a Read the email. Answer the questions.
1 Whose wedding is Mike going to?
2 When did he book his flight?
3 When is he going to arrive in L.A.?
4 Where does he want to stay?
5 What is he going to do after the wedding?

b Work in pairs. Compare answers.

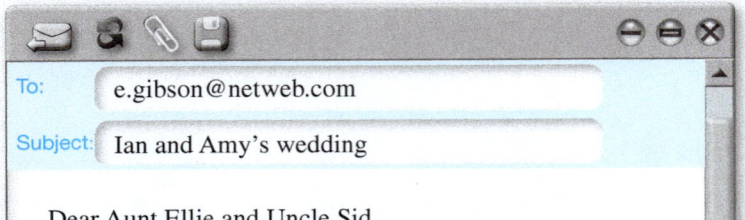

Mike

Ellie

3 a CD3 ▶39 Mike is phoning his aunt in L.A. Put these things in the order they talk about them.

a hotel   a motorbike   the wedding 1
Mike's email   a restaurant

b Listen again. Tick the true sentences. Correct the false ones.
1 Aunt Ellie replied to Mike's email.
2 Mike can stay at Ellie and Sid's house.
3 Ellie is going to book a hotel room for him.
4 Mike is going to rent a motorbike.
5 He's going to get a taxi from the airport.
6 He's going to have dinner at Ellie and Sid's favourite restaurant.

HELP WITH LISTENING Linking: review
• Remember: we usually link words that end in a consonant sound with words that begin with a vowel sound.

4 a Work in pairs. Look at the beginning of the conversation and mark the linking.
MIKE Hello, Aunt Ellie. This is Mike. I'm calling from England about Ian and Amy's wedding. Is this a good time to call?
ELLIE Mike! Yes, of course it is.

b Look at Audio Script CD3 ▶39 p165. Check your answers.

c CD3 ▶39 Listen again to the whole conversation and follow the linking.

To: e.gibson@netweb.com
Subject: Ian and Amy's wedding

Dear Aunt Ellie and Uncle Sid

Thank you very much for the invitation to cousin Ian and Amy's wedding in Los Angeles. Of course I'd love to come. I booked my flight yesterday and I'm going to arrive in L.A. three days before the wedding. Can I stay with you when I arrive? If not, don't worry. I can book a hotel room. Also, I'm going to stay in the USA for three weeks and I'd like to travel around after the wedding. Do you know where I can rent a motorbike? If not, I can always rent a car.

Lots of love

Mike

PS Can I get to your place from the airport by public transport, or should I get a taxi?

HELP WITH VOCABULARY Collocations

5 a Read the email again. Find two words or phrases that go with these verbs. Write them in the table.

book	stay	rent	get
	with (you)		

b Choose the correct verbs in these words/phrases.

1 stay/(rent) a flat
2 book/rent a train ticket
3 get/book married
4 get/rent home
5 book/stay a seat on a train
6 rent/book a house
7 get/stay in a hotel
8 rent/get divorced
9 stay/get at home
10 book/rent a table in a restaurant

c Check in VOCABULARY 11.3 ▶ p151.

6 Work in pairs. Take turns to test your partner on the collocations in **5a** and **5b**.

> a flight   book a flight

7 a Fill in the gaps with the correct form of *book*, *stay*, *rent* or *get*.

1 When did you last _stay_ with a friend?
2 Do you _____ flights or train tickets online?
3 How do you _____ home after class?
4 Where was the last hotel you _____ in?
5 Do you _____ your house or flat?
6 When did you last _____ a table at a restaurant?
7 What's a good age to _____ married?
8 Do you usually _____ a car when you go on holiday?

b Work in pairs. Ask and answer the questions. Ask follow-up questions if possible.

8 Two friends from another country want to visit you. Write them an email and answer their questions.

- Where can we stay?
- How can we get there from the airport?
- How can we travel around?
- What can we see and do?

HELP WITH PRONUNCIATION
/ʊ/ and /uː/

1 CD3 ▶40 Listen to these sounds and words. Listen again and practise.

/ʊ/ look put would   /uː/ room do fruit

2 a Work in pairs. Look at the vowels in bold. Write the words in the table.

> b̶o̶o̶k̶   b̶l̶u̶e̶   woman   June   should
> wood   suit   food   sugar   boots
> choose   good-looking

/ʊ/	look	book
/uː/	room	blue

b CD3 ▶41 Listen and check. Listen again and practise.

3 a Work in pairs. Look at the vowels in bold. Which vowel sound is different?

1 lose knew (look)
2 juice shoes wolf
3 too bookshop could
4 took school scooter
5 soup good wouldn't
6 cook butcher's move

b CD3 ▶42 Listen and check. Listen again and practise.

continue2learn

■ **Vocabulary, Grammar and Real World**
- **Extra Practice 11 and Progress Portfolio 11** p125
- **Language Summary 11** p151
- **11A–D** Workbook p55

■ **Reading and Writing**
- **Portfolio 11** A town by the sea Workbook p84
  Reading a tourist brochure; an email
  Writing common mistakes; a description of a town or city

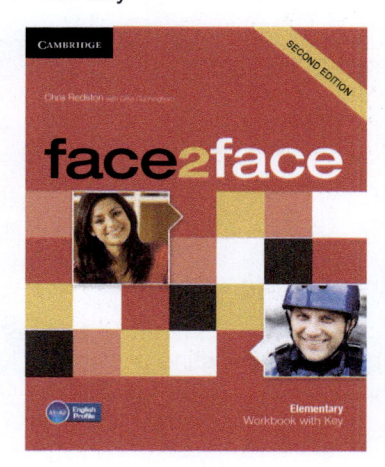

12A It's a world record

Vocabulary big and small numbers
Grammar superlatives

QUICK REVIEW Collocations Write words or phrases that go with these verbs: *book, stay, rent, get* (*book a flight, stay in a hotel,* etc.). Work in pairs. Compare lists. Take turns to make sentences with the phrases on your lists: *I stayed in a hotel last month.*

Vocabulary Big and small numbers

1 Work in pairs. Match the numbers to the words. Then check in VOCABULARY 12.1 p153.

0.2	1,000,000	2.45	850,000
32,470	127	2,300	50,000,000

1 nought point two *0.2*
2 two point four five
3 a hundred and twenty-seven
4 two thousand, three hundred
5 thirty-two thousand, four hundred and seventy
6 eight hundred and fifty thousand
7 a million
8 fifty million

2 a CD3 43 Listen and write the numbers.

b Work in pairs. Compare answers.

Reading

3 a Before you read, check these words with your teacher.

a bowl	a chilli	heavy
cost	a haircut	a litre

b Read the article. Match the world records 1–5 to pictures A–E.

4 a Read the article again. Fill in gaps a–h with this information.

73 hours	£8,000	$399
152 hours	35.6 kg	5,350 litres
one second	182 kg	

b CD3 44 Listen to the article. Check your answers.

c Which record is the most interesting or surprising, do you think?

RECORD BREAKERS

1 Sanjay Kumar Sinha taught the **longest** lesson in the world at a school in Bandra, India, in 2005. The lesson was a_____ and 37 minutes long and it was all about English grammar.

2 In July 2007, a group of people from the city of Durango, Mexico, made b_____ of soup – the **biggest** bowl of soup in the world. It had c_____ of chillis in it, so it was probably the world's **hottest** soup too!

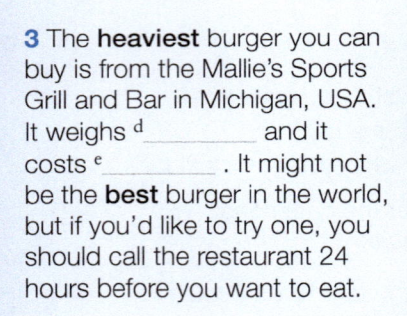

3 The **heaviest** burger you can buy is from the Mallie's Sports Grill and Bar in Michigan, USA. It weighs d_____ and it costs e_____. It might not be the **best** burger in the world, but if you'd like to try one, you should call the restaurant 24 hours before you want to eat.

4 The **shortest** film in the world is *Colin*, made by Marc Price, and it's just f_____ long. And the longest film is *Cinématon*, directed by Gérard Courant. It's g_____ long – so it might also be the world's **most boring** film.

5 Beverley Lateo, from Italy, had the world's **most expensive** haircut in October 2007. She paid h_____ for a visit to Stuart Philips Hair Salon in London – but she got a free lunch!

HELP WITH GRAMMAR Superlatives

5 a Look at the superlatives in bold in the article. Write them in the table.

adjective	comparative	superlative
long	longer	*longest*
short	shorter	
big	bigger	
hot	hotter	
heavy	heavier	
boring	more boring	
expensive	more expensive	
good	better	
bad	worse	*worst*

b Choose the correct words in these rules.
- We use *comparatives/superlatives* to compare two things.
- We use *comparatives/superlatives* to compare three or more things.

c Work in pairs. Look at the table in **5a** again. What are the rules for making superlatives? (Think about spelling and the number of syllables.)

d Check in GRAMMAR 12.1 ▶ p153 and read the TIPS.

6 a Write the superlatives.
1. rich *richest*
2. difficult
3. thin
4. happy
5. dirty
6. slow
7. safe
8. beautiful
9. bad
10. careful

b CD3 ▶ 45 PRONUNCIATION Listen and practise the superlatives in **6a**. Notice how we say *-est*.

richest /ˈrɪtʃɪst/

Reading, Listening and Speaking

7 a Work in groups. Read the World Quiz. Fill in the gaps with the superlative form of the adjectives in brackets. Then do the quiz.

b CD3 ▶ 46 Listen to Abby and Len do the quiz. Check your answers. How many answers did your group get right?

c Listen again. What do these numbers refer to?
- a $6,000
- b 57.8°
- c 8,000
- d 74.2 million
- e 6,650 km
- f 17,000

d Work in pairs. Compare answers.

The World Quiz

1. What's the world's _____ city? (expensive)
   a Moscow   b Tokyo   c Milan
2. Which of these countries is the _____ (hot)
   a Libya   b USA   c Australia
3. Which of these cities is the _____ ? (old)
   a Athens   b Rome   c Damascus
4. Which of these countries is the _____ with tourists? (popular)
   a Spain   b China   c France
5. Which is the _____ river in the world? (long)
   a The Nile   b The Amazon   c The Yangtze
6. Which is the world's _____ country? (crowded)
   a Bangladesh   b Singapore   c Monaco

HELP WITH LISTENING Sentence stress: review

8 a Work in pairs. Look at the beginning of Abby and Len's conversation. Decide which words are stressed.

ABBY Do you like doing quizzes, Len?
LEN Yes, I love them. Ask me the first question.
ABBY OK. What's the world's most expensive city?

b Look at Audio Script CD3 ▶ 46 p165. Check your answers.

c CD3 ▶ 46 Listen to the whole conversation again. Follow the sentence stress.

Get ready … Get it right!

9 Write six of these things on a piece of paper. Write one or two words, not complete sentences. Don't write the answers in order.
- the name of the oldest or youngest person in your family
- your oldest or most important possession
- the most interesting or most boring thing you did last weekend
- the latest or earliest you went to bed last week
- the best or worst present you got last birthday
- the best or worst film you saw last year

10 a Work in pairs. Swap papers. Take turns to ask questions about your partner's words. Ask follow-up questions.

Is Clara the youngest person in your family?
Yes, she is. She's two years old.

b Tell the class two things about your partner.

12B Have you ever ... ?

Vocabulary past participles
Grammar Present Perfect: positive and negative; *Have you ever ... ?* questions and short answers

QUICK REVIEW **Comparatives and superlatives** Write ten adjectives. Work in pairs. Say the adjectives. Your partner says the comparative and superlative: **A** *good* **B** *better, best*.

Speaking, Listening and Reading

1 Work in groups. Discuss these questions.
1 Do you know anyone who is self-employed? What do they do?
2 What are the good and bad things about being self-employed?
3 Would you like to be self-employed? Why?/Why not?

2 a CD3 47 Listen and read about three friends, Steve, Lucy and Guy. Do they like being self-employed?

b Tick the true sentences. Correct the false ones.
1 Steve went to Mexico two weeks ago.
2 He was in the Caribbean two months ago.
3 He wants to go to Australia on holiday.
4 Guy and Lucy were self-employed three years ago.
5 The Prime Minister came to their restaurant last month.
6 Guy and Lucy are going to Peru next year.

HELP WITH GRAMMAR
Present Perfect: positive and negative

3 a Look at sentences 1 and 2. Then answer questions **a** and **b**.
1 I'**ve been** to about forty countries. (Present Perfect)
2 Two weeks ago I **went** to Mexico. (Past Simple)

a In sentence 1, do we know when Steve went to these countries?
b In sentence 2, do we know when he went to Mexico?

b Complete these rules with *Present Perfect (PP)* or *Past Simple (PS)*.

- We use the _____ to talk about experiences in life until now. We don't say when they happened.
- We use the _____ if we say when something happened.

c Look at the examples of the Present Perfect in blue in the texts. Then complete the table with *'ve*, *'s*, *haven't* and *hasn't*.

POSITIVE (+)

I/you/we/they + _____ + past participle
he/she/it + _____ + past participle

NEGATIVE (–)

I/you/we/they + _____ + past participle
he/she/it + _____ + past participle

TIP • We can say *I haven't ...* or *I've never ...* :
I've never been to Australia.

d Check in GRAMMAR 12.2 p154. Read the rules for making past participles and the TIPS.

I love being a self-employed travel writer. I'**ve been** to about forty countries and I'**ve stayed** in some of the world's best hotels. I'**ve written** travel articles about lots of amazing places. Two weeks ago I went to Mexico and last month I spent five days in the Caribbean. But I **haven't been** to Australia. That's one country I'd love to go to – but for a holiday, not for work!

Steve White – travel writer

Vocabulary and Speaking
Past participles

4 a What are the past participles of these verbs? Check irregular past participles in the Irregular Verb List, p167. Which five verbs are regular?

1 be *been*   5 lose   9 study
2 cook   6 meet   10 visit
3 go   7 see   11 work
4 have   8 stay   12 write

b CD3 48 **PRONUNCIATION** Listen and practise the infinitive, Past Simple and past participle of the verbs in **4a**.

be, was/were, been

We've both had lots of other jobs. Three years ago Guy was a teacher and I worked in an office. But we'd rather be self-employed and we love having our own restaurant. We've met some really interesting people – last year the Prime Minister had dinner here! But it's hard work and Guy and I have never had a holiday together. We might go to Peru next year – Guy hasn't been to South America before.

Lucy and Guy Rogers – restaurant owners

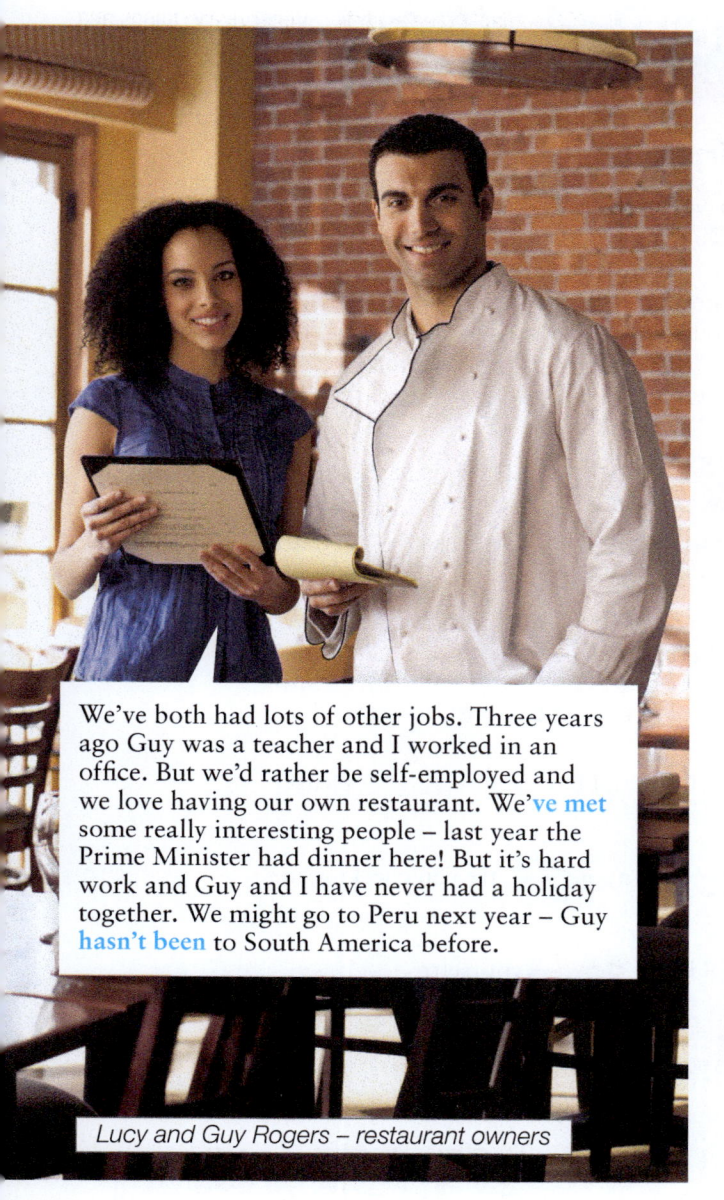

5 a Look at these phrases and write six sentences about your experiences. The sentences can be positive or negative.

- work in a restaurant
  I've worked in a restaurant.
- go to Canada
  I haven't been to Canada.
- meet someone from Ireland
- see a Japanese film
- stay in a five-star hotel
- cook a meal for someone's birthday
- work in an office
- study another foreign language
- lose something important

b Work in groups. Tell other students your sentences. How many are the same?

Listening and Speaking

6 a CD3 49 Listen to a conversation between Steve and Lucy. Where are they? What do they talk about?

b Listen again. Choose the correct words.
1 Steve has been to *Peru/Brazil*.
2 He went there about *two/three* years ago.
3 Lucy went to Australia *six/eight* years ago.
4 She travelled around Australia by *bus/car*.
5 Guy *has/hasn't* been to Australia.

HELP WITH GRAMMAR
Have you ever … ? questions and short answers

7 a Fill in the gaps in these questions and short answers with *have*, *haven't*, *did* or *didn't*.

A _____ you ever been to Peru?
B Yes, I _____ ./No, I _____ .
A _____ you have a good time?
B Yes, I _____ ./No, I _____ .

b Complete the rule with *Present Perfect (PP)* or *Past Simple (PS)*.

- We use the _____ to ask about people's experiences. If the answer is *yes*, we use the _____ to ask for (or give) more information.

TIP • *ever* + Present Perfect = any time in your life until now. We often use *ever* in questions.

c Check in GRAMMAR 12.3 p154.

8 CD3 50 PRONUNCIATION Listen and practise. Copy the stress.

Have you éver been to Perú?
Yés, I háve.

9 a Fill in the gaps. Put the verbs in brackets in the Present Perfect or Past Simple and complete the short answers.

1 A ¹ *Have* you ever *been* to France? (go)
  B Yes, I ² _____ . I ³ _____ there six years ago. (go)
  A Where ⁴ _____ you _____ ? (stay)
  B I ⁵ _____ a flat near Bordeaux. (rent)
2 A ⁶ _____ you ever _____ a diary? (write)
  B Yes, I ⁷ _____ . I ⁸ _____ one when I was a teenager. (write)
  A ⁹ _____ you _____ in it every day? (write)
  B No, I ¹⁰ _____ . Only when I ¹¹ _____ on holiday. (be)

b Work in pairs. Compare answers. Then practise the conversations.

Get ready … Get it right!

10 Work in two groups. Group A p108. Group B p113.

99

12C REAL WORLD > See you soon!

Real World at the airport; saying goodbye
Vocabulary things and places at an airport

QUICK REVIEW Past participles Write ten verbs. Work in pairs. Say the verbs to your partner. He/She says the Past Simple and the past participle: A *see* B *saw, seen*.

Travel experiences

1 a Fill in gaps 1–8 with the past participles of the verb in brackets. Check new past participles in the Irregular Verb List, p167.

Have you ever …

1 *missed* a plane? (miss)
2 _____ to another country by boat or ferry? (travel)
3 _____ on a long train or coach journey? (go)
4 _____ in a very small plane? (fly)
5 _____ at an airport or a station? (sleep)
6 _____ a really terrible journey? (have)
7 _____ ill on a plane? (be)
8 _____ or _____ in another country? (drive, cycle)

b Work in pairs. Ask and answer the questions. Ask follow-up questions if possible.

- Have you ever missed a plane?
- Yes, I have.
- When was that?
- About two years ago.

c Tell the class about your partner's travel experiences.

At the airport

2 Tick the words/phrases you know. Then do the exercise in **VOCABULARY 12.2** p153.

> a passport   a boarding pass   hand luggage   a ticket
> pack your bags   passengers   a flight number
> a gate   a check-in desk   a bag drop
> a window/a middle/an aisle seat   on time   delayed

3 a **VIDEO** 12.1 **CD3** 51 Daisy is at the airport. Watch or listen and answer the questions.

1 How many bags does she check in?
2 What is her seat number?
3 Has she got an aisle seat?
4 Is the flight delayed?

b Work in pairs. Look at the conversation. What does the man at the bag drop say to her?

> Hello, can I have your passport, please?

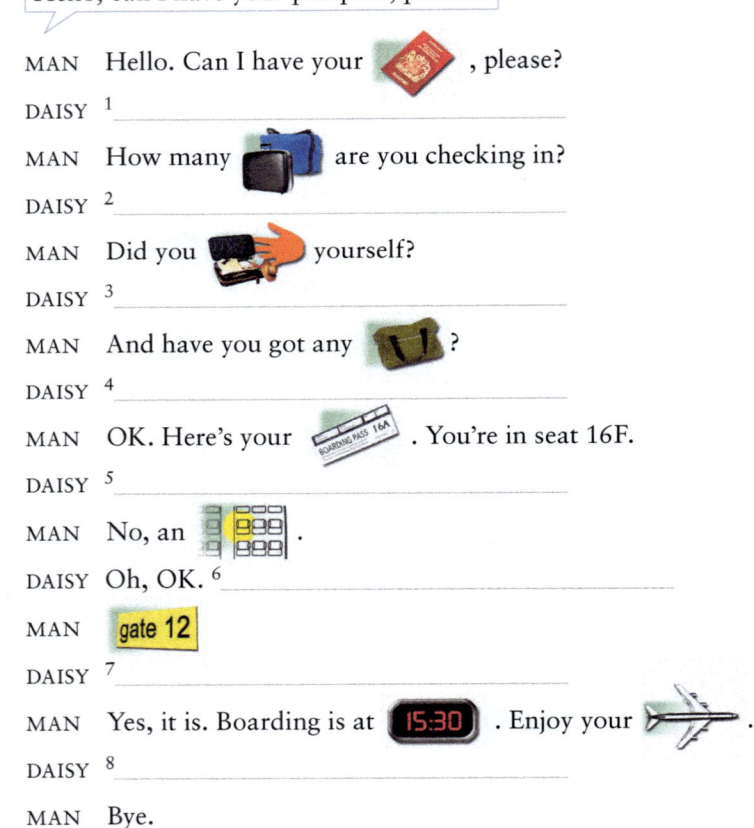

MAN   Hello. Can I have your [passport], please?
DAISY 1 _____
MAN   How many [bags] are you checking in?
DAISY 2 _____
MAN   Did you [pack] yourself?
DAISY 3 _____
MAN   And have you got any [hand luggage]?
DAISY 4 _____
MAN   OK. Here's your [boarding pass]. You're in seat 16F.
DAISY 5 _____
MAN   No, an [aisle seat].
DAISY Oh, OK. 6 _____
MAN   gate 12
DAISY 7 _____
MAN   Yes, it is. Boarding is at 15:30. Enjoy your [flight].
DAISY 8 _____
MAN   Bye.

4 a Fill in gaps 1–8 in **3b** with these sentences.

> Yes. Here you are.   One.   Is that a window seat?
> Yes, this bag.   Which gate is it?   Yes, I did.
> Is the flight on time?   Thanks. Bye.

b **VIDEO** 12.1 **CD3** 51 Watch or listen again. Check your answers.

5 a Work in pairs. Practise the conversation in **3b**. Take turns to be Daisy.

b Work in new pairs. Practise the conversation again. When you're Daisy, close your book.

REAL WORLD Saying goodbye

6 Fill in the gaps with these words/phrases.

| Don't forget | Have you got | See you | Have a |

1 _____	everything? your passport? your boarding pass?	Yes, I have, thanks.
2 _____	nice holiday. good time. good trip.	Thanks, I will.
3 _____ to send me/us	a text. an email. a postcard.	Yes, of course.
4 _____	in a month. soon. on the next course.	Yes, see you.

REAL WORLD 12.2 ▶ p154

7 CD3 ▶ 52 **PRONUNCIATION** Listen and practise the sentences in **6**.

Have you got everything?

8 a VIDEO ▶ 12.2 CD3 ▶ 53 Watch or listen to Daisy saying goodbye to her parents at the airport. Answer the questions.
1 Which country is she going to?
2 Who is she going to send a postcard to?
3 How long is she going away for?

b Watch or listen again. Tick the sentences in **6** that you hear.

9 a Work in pairs. Choose one of these situations and write a conversation.
1 Two friends are saying goodbye at the airport. One of them is going on holiday to Morocco for two weeks.
2 Two students are saying goodbye at the end of their course. Their new course starts in three months' time.

b Work in the same pairs. Practise your conversation until you can remember it.

c Work with another pair. Take turns to role-play your conversations.

HELP WITH PRONUNCIATION Vowel sounds: review

1 a Work in pairs. Look at the letters in bold. Match the words in boxes A, B and C with the same vowel sound.

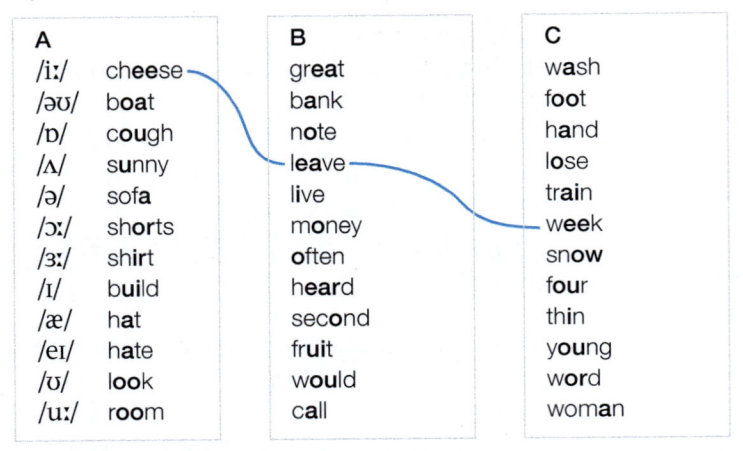

A		B	C
/iː/	cheese	great	wash
/əʊ/	boat	bank	foot
/ɒ/	cough	note	hand
/ʌ/	sunny	leave	lose
/ə/	sofa	live	train
/ɔː/	shorts	money	week
/ɜː/	shirt	often	snow
/ɪ/	build	heard	four
/æ/	hat	second	thin
/eɪ/	hate	fruit	young
/ʊ/	look	would	word
/uː/	room	call	woman

b CD3 ▶ 54 Listen and check. Listen again and practise.

c Work in groups of three: student A, student B, student C. Take turns to say words with the same vowel sounds in **1a**.

> cheese   leave   week

2 a Write one word with the same vowel sound as each group of three words in **1a**.

cheese, leave, week *seat*

b Work in pairs. Compare words. Are your partner's words correct?

continue2learn

■ **Vocabulary, Grammar and Real World**
  - **Extra Practice 12 and Progress Portfolio 12** p126
  - **Language Summary 12** p153
  - **12A–C** Workbook p60

■ **Reading and Writing**
  - **Portfolio 12** At the airport Workbook p86
    Reading airport signs; a postcard
    Writing useful phrases for a postcard

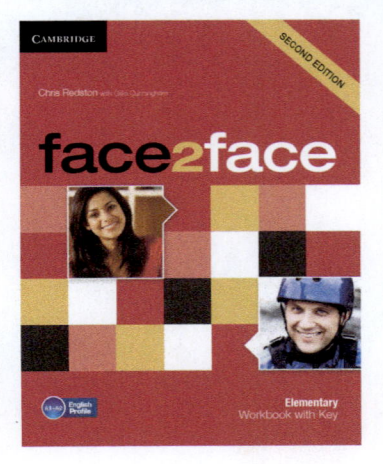

Work in groups of four. Read the rules. Then play the game!

Rules

You need: One counter for each student; one dice for each group.

How to play: Put your counters on **START**. Take turns to throw the dice, move your counter and read the instructions on the square. The first student to get to **FINISH** is the winner.

Grammar and **Vocabulary** **squares**: The first student to land on a Grammar or Vocabulary square answers question 1. If the other students think your answer is correct, you can stay on the square. If the answer is wrong, move back to the last square you were on. The second student to land on the same square answers question 2. If a third or fourth student lands on the same square, he/she can stay on the square without answering a question.

Talk about squares: If you land on a Talk about square, talk about the topic for 20 seconds. Another student can check the time. If you can't talk for 20 seconds, move back to the last square you were on. If a second or third student lands on the same square, he/she also talks about the same topic for 20 seconds.

End of Course Review

START

1. Make a question with *Where* for this answer.
1 His father was born in London.
2 My sister lives in Australia.

2. Say eight:
1 jobs
2 free time activities

3. Say the positive and negative short answers.
1 Were they at home last night?
2 Did he call you?

4. MOVE FORWARD THREE SQUARES

5. How do we say these numbers and prices?
1 376, 9,500, 0.8, £750,000
2 $250,000, 9.1, 524, 77,777

6. What is the Past Simple of these verbs?
1 become, find, meet, lose
2 leave, buy, write, put

7. Talk about your last holiday.

8. What are the opposites?
1 happy, excited, safe, awful
2 ill, slim, easy, different

9. Say the comparatives.
1 happy, bad, beautiful, short
2 good, boring, easy, thin

10. Make a sentence with these words.
1 Sunday / tennis / on / usually / I / play .
2 out / every / We / Thursday / eat .

11. Talk about what you did last weekend.

12. Correct this question.
1 What you going to do tomorrow?
2 Where you did go last month?

13. MOVE BACK TWO SQUARES

14. Make a sentence with these words.
1 go to / usually / I / bed / eleven / at .
2 We / our / ago / a year / bought / house

15. Say eight:
1 types of food
2 things you can wear

16. Talk about two people in your family.

17. Say the nationalities.
1 Turkey, Italy, Spain, the UK
2 China, France, the USA, Poland

18. Make questions with these words.
1 you / last / What / weekend / do / did ?
2 do / tonight / What / you / going to / are ?

19. MOVE FORWARD TWO SQUARES

20. Say six:
1 types of shop
2 weather words

21. Talk about your daily routine in the week.

22. Choose the correct word.
1 There are *some/any* chairs in the kitchen.
2 Is there *a/any* furniture?

23. What are the opposites?
1 quiet, friendly, clean, fast
2 interesting, tall, lucky, poor

24. MOVE FORWARD THREE SQUARES

25. Talk about what you do in your free time.

26. Do we use these words with the Present Simple or Present Continuous?
1 sometimes, at the moment, now
2 never, often, today

27. Talk about your house or flat.

28. MOVE BACK THREE SQUARES

29. Say the superlatives.
1 rich, hungry, excited, bad
2 good, long, dirty, crowded

30. Talk about things you can or can't do.

31. Say eight:
1 things in a house
2 family members

32. Make a sentence with these words.
1 going to / I'm / today / not / meet / him .
2 tonight / We / go to / might / the cinema .

33. Talk about what you're going to do next weekend.

34. Make adverbs from these adjectives:
1 fluent, bad, beautiful, fast
2 good, hard, happy, careful

35. Do we use *a* or *some* with these words?
1 meat, banana, tomato, cheese
2 milk, rice, sandwich, sausage

36. MOVE BACK THREE SQUARES

37. Say eight:
1 animals
2 types of transport

38. Make this sentence negative.
1 We went to the theatre last night.
2 They've got a new car.

FINISH

Pair and Group Work: Student/Group A

1A [11] p9

a Work with your partner. Ask questions about cards A, B and C. Write the names and countries. Don't look at your partner's cards.

Card A. What's her name?
How do you spell that?
Where's she from?

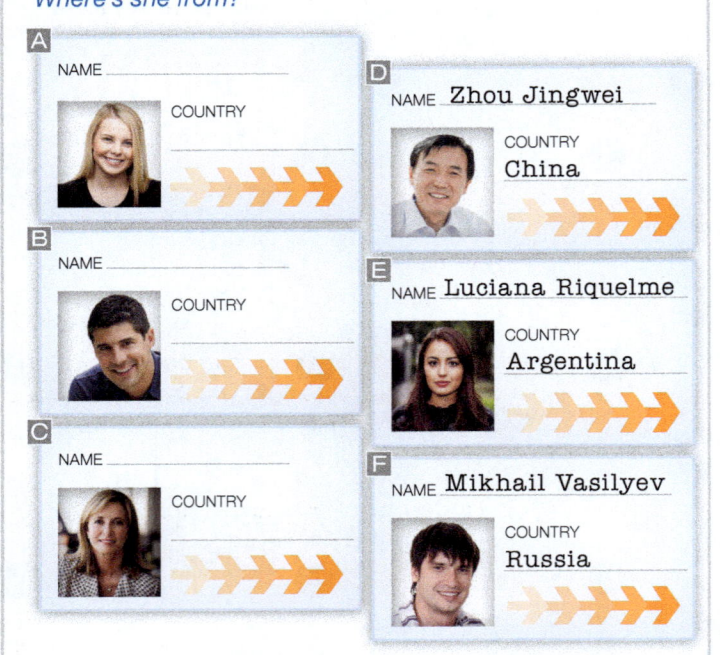

A NAME ___ COUNTRY ___
B NAME ___ COUNTRY ___
C NAME ___ COUNTRY ___

D NAME Zhou Jingwei COUNTRY China
E NAME Luciana Riquelme COUNTRY Argentina
F NAME Mikhail Vasilyev COUNTRY Russia

b Answer your partner's questions about cards D, E and F.

c Check your answers and spelling with your partner.

2A [13] p17

a Work on your own. Guess the things your partner has got, but don't talk to him/her. Put a tick (✓) or a cross (✗) in the *your guess* column.

	your guess	your partner's answer
mobile		
camera		
laptop		
car		
notebook		

b Look at the pictures. Write questions with *you*.

Have you got a mobile?

c Work with your partner. Ask and answer your questions. Put a tick or a cross in the *your partner's answer* column. Are your guesses correct?

d Work with a new partner. Tell him/her five things your first partner has/hasn't got.

1B [12] p11

a Work on your own. Look at the hotel conference list. Write *yes/no* questions to check the information in pink on the list (Mr = ↑ Mrs = ↑).

Is Mrs Ramos a teacher?

b Work with your partner. Take turns to ask your questions from **a**. Tick (✓) the correct information. Change the wrong information.

Is Mrs Ramos a teacher?
No, she isn't. She's a doctor.

c Compare answers with another student A.

Mrs Ramos isn't a teacher. She's a doctor.

Conference Guest List

name	job	nationality	room
Mrs Ramos	a teacher	Mexican	216
Mr Demir	a manager	Turkish	112
Mr Wong	an actor	Japanese	204
Mrs Ivanova	a teacher	Russian	307
Mr Fisher	a mechanic	Australian	209
Mrs Fisher	a lawyer		
Mr Bruni	a builder	Italian	108
Mrs Bruni	a musician		

Pair and Group Work: Student/Group A

2C 13 p21

a You are a customer. Choose one of these films. Buy two tickets from your partner. Fill in the times and the prices for your film. You start.

48 Hours	Time: _____ £ _____
Three Long Years	Time: _____ £ _____
Two Weeks on Sunday	Time: _____ £ _____

b You are a ticket seller. Look at the times and prices of the films at your cinema. Sell tickets to your partner. Your partner starts.

Today's films

60 Seconds	7.10
Nine Months	8.25
A Day in the Life	9.35
Adults £10.50	Children £8

c Do **a** and **b** again. Buy tickets for different films. Change the number and type of tickets you buy.

3B 10 p27

a Work on your own. Choose the correct words in phrases 1–5.

	name	name
1 watch TV *every/in* evening		
2 do sport *in/on* Saturdays		
3 go to bed after midnight *in/at* the week		
4 go to concerts *in/at* the weekends		
5 eat out *at/every* week		

b Make questions with *you* with phrases 1–5 in **a**.
1 *Do you watch TV every evening?*

c Ask other students in the class your questions. Try to find two people who answer *yes* for each question. Write their names in the table.

d Tell the class about the people in your table.
Kristina and Michiko watch TV every evening.

4B 9 p35

Jo is 29 and she's a lawyer. In her free time she watches TV, goes shopping and reads a lot. On Saturday evenings she usually goes to the cinema or eats out – she loves Chinese food. She doesn't like sport and she hates football. Her favourite music is rock and she also likes jazz. She likes animals but hasn't got any pets.

11C 10 p93

a Work on your own. Find these places on the map on p93. Don't tell your partner.

the cinema (2)   The Pizza Place (6)   a petrol station (11)

b Work with your partner. You are at *You are here* on the map. Ask for directions to these places: **a burger restaurant**, **the theatre**, **the school**. When you find the place, check the number on the map with your partner. Don't look at your partner's map. You start.

> Excuse me. Is there a burger restaurant near here?

5A 11 p41

a Work on your own. Write questions with *you* or *your* about when you were thirteen.

	you	your partner
1 / happy at school? *Were you happy at school?*		
2 Who / best friend?		
3 / good at languages?		
4 What / favourite food?		
5 What / favourite TV programme?		

b Write your answers in the *you* column.

c Work with your partner. Ask and answer your questions. Write your partner's answers in the table.

d Tell another student about you and your partner when you were thirteen.
I was happy at school when I was thirteen, but Paola wasn't.

Pair and Group Work: Student/Group A

6C 11 p53

a Work on your own. Read about the news stories. Check you understand all the words.

Big storm
Mexico
13 people died

Man who found 1 million dollars
under the kitchen floor
gave money to a hospital

Tourists missing in Africa
Sahara desert
lost for 2 weeks
other tourists found them – they're OK now

Man tries to post ma...
A woman who ...tioned about t... on Monday m... in the sleepy v... witness said th... man was in his...

b Work with your partner. Take turns to tell each other about the news stories. Use these phrases.

Did you hear/read about … ?   No, what happened?
No, where was it?   Oh, that's good.   Oh no, that's terrible.
Oh, dear. Are they OK?   You're joking!   Really?

4B 10 c p35

MARK I like Kim very much and we like a lot of the same things. We both go to the cinema a lot and we both really like animals. But she doesn't like the same music as me and she hasn't got a TV – I don't believe that! Yes, I'd like to see her again. She's very beautiful.

KIM Sorry, I don't like Mark very much. He talks about football and TV programmes all the time and I don't like watching TV. Also, we don't like the same music – and music's very important to me. I don't want a second date with him. Sorry.

7B 10 p59

a Work with a student from group A. Describe the picture. Use the phrases in bold.

There's a cat in the picture.
There's some fruit on the table.
There are nine eggs in the fridge.
There are some pizzas on the table.

b Make questions to ask a student from group B about his/her picture. Use the phrases in bold.

Is there a cat in the room?
Are there any eggs in the fridge?
How many bananas **are there**?
How much milk **is there**?

c Work with a student from group B. Don't look at your partner's picture. Ask and answer questions about the pictures. Find twelve differences.

d Work with your partner from group A. Compare answers.

Pair and Group Work: Student/Group A

8A 12 p65

a Work with a student from group A. Look at the picture. What are the people doing? What are they wearing?

> Kevin's talking on the phone.

> He's wearing a jacket, shirt and tie.

b Work with a student from group B. Don't look at his/her picture. Ask and answer questions. Find ten differences in the pictures.

> What's Kevin doing?

> What's he wearing?

c Work with a student from group A. Did you find the same differences?

8B 9 p67

a Work on your own. Write the questions (Q).

b Work with a student from group B. Look at the pictures. Take turns to ask and answer your questions. Write the answers (A). You start.

c Work with a student from group A. Compare answers.

USUALLY	TODAY	USUALLY	TODAY
1 What / Colin / usually / wear ? Q *What does Colin usually wear?* A _____	2	7	8 Where / Colin / work / this morning ? Q _____ A _____
3	4 How / Gabby / get / to work today ? Q _____ A _____	9 Where / Gabby and her friends / usually / have / lunch ? Q _____ A _____	10
5 What / the children / usually / do / in the morning ? Q _____ A _____	6	11	12 What / Colin / do / this afternoon ? Q _____ A _____

Pair and Group Work: Student/Group A

10A 11 p81

a You have these problems. Check you understand them. Then write one more problem.
1. I can't sleep at night.
2. I forgot my best friend's birthday.
3. I hate my job, but I need the money.
4. _____

b Work with students B and C. Take turns to ask for and give advice. Which piece of advice is the best, do you think?

> I can't sleep at night. What should I do?

> (I think) you should …

> Well, you shouldn't …

> Don't …

10D 5 p87

a Work with your partner. Ask and answer questions about the weather in these places. Fill in the gaps in the table. You start.

> What's the weather like in … today?

> It's … and it's … degrees.

	weather	°C
Amsterdam	🌧	6
Athens		
Bangkok	☀	31
Buenos Aires		
Chicago	➡➡	0
Helsinki		
London	🌨	2
Munich		
Paris	FOG	5
Rome		
San Francisco	☁	18
Sydney		

b Which places are: hot, warm, cold? Where's the best place to be today? Why?

11B 11 p91

a Look at what Eric, Melanie, Jenny and Sam are going to do next weekend. Take turns to ask and answer yes/no questions and fill in the gaps in the table.

> Is Eric going to visit his parents next weekend?

> ✓ Yes, he is.

> ✗ No, he isn't.

> ✓✗ He might.

	Eric	Melanie	Jenny and Sam
visit parents		✓	
go for a run	✓		✗
move house		✗	
watch lots of TV	✓✗		✗
go to a party		✗	
play tennis	✓		✓✗
stay in bed on Sunday		✓	

b Who is going to have: a lazy weekend, a busy weekend, an active weekend?

12B 10 p99

a Work with a student from group A. Write questions with *you* in the Present Perfect and follow-up questions in the Past Simple.

1. / go / on a boat trip?
   Have you ever been on a boat trip?
   Where / go?
   Where did you go?
2. / visit / the capital city of another country?
   Which city / visit?
3. / go / to a really good party?
   Whose party / be / it?
4. / meet / someone from the USA?
   Where / meet them?
5. / have / a pet?
   What / be / its name?

b Work with a student from group B. Ask and answer your questions. If the answer is *yes*, ask your follow-up question. Then ask two more questions if possible.

c Work with your partner from group A. Tell him/her about student B's life experiences.

Pair and Group Work: Student/Group B

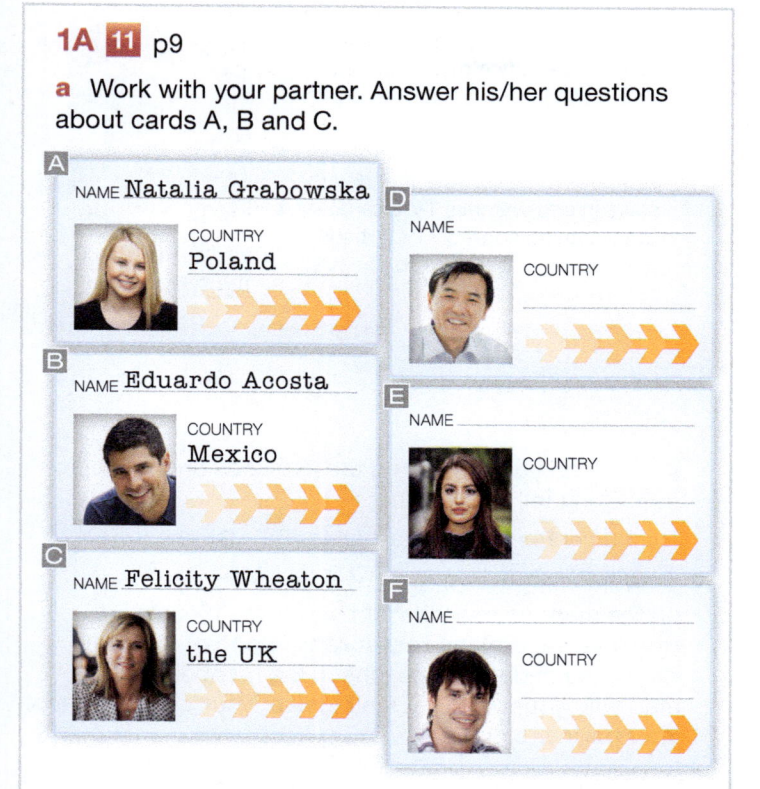

1A 11 p9

a Work with your partner. Answer his/her questions about cards A, B and C.

A NAME Natalia Grabowska COUNTRY Poland
B NAME Eduardo Acosta COUNTRY Mexico
C NAME Felicity Wheaton COUNTRY the UK
D NAME ___ COUNTRY ___
E NAME ___ COUNTRY ___
F NAME ___ COUNTRY ___

b Ask questions about cards D, E and F. Write the names and countries. Don't look at your partner's cards.

Card D. What's his name?
How do you spell that?
Where's he from?

c Check your answers and spelling with your partner.

2A 13 p17

a Work on your own. Guess the things your partner has got, but don't talk to him/her. Put a tick (✓) or a cross (✗) in the *your guess* column.

	your guess	your partner's answer
computer		
DVD player		
MP3 player		
radio		
bicycle		

b Look at the pictures. Write questions with *you*.
Have you got a computer?

c Work with your partner. Ask and answer your questions. Put a tick or a cross in the *your partner's answer* column. Are your guesses correct?

d Work with a new partner. Tell him/her five things your first partner has/hasn't got.

1B 12 p11

a Work on your own. Look at the hotel conference list. Write *yes/no* questions to check the information in pink on the list (Mr = 👨 Mrs = 👩).
Is Mr Demir a waiter?

b Work with your partner. Take turns to ask your questions from **a**. Tick (✓) the correct information. Change the wrong information.

> Is Mr Demir a waiter?
> No, he isn't. He's a manager.

c Compare answers with another student B.
Mr Demir isn't a waiter. He's a manager.

Conference Guest List

name	job	nationality	room
Mrs Ramos	a doctor	Spanish	216
Mr Demir	a waiter	Turkish	112
Mr Wong	a police officer	American	204
Mrs Ivanova	a waitress	Russian	317
Mr Fisher	a mechanic	British	209
Mrs Fisher	an accountant		
Mr Bruni	a builder	Italian	106
Mrs Bruni	an actress		

Pair and Group Work: Student/Group B

2C 13 p21

a You are a ticket seller. Look at the times and prices of the films at your cinema. Sell tickets to your partner. Your partner starts.

Today's films

48 Hours	7.20
Three Long Years	8.45
Two Weeks on Sunday	9.10
Adults £9.95	Children £7.35

b You are a customer. Choose one of these films. Buy two tickets from your partner. Fill in the times and the prices for your film. You start.

60 Seconds	Time: _____ £ _____
Nine Months	Time: _____ £ _____
A Day in the Life	Time: _____ £ _____

c Do a and b again. Buy tickets for different films. Change the number and type of tickets you buy.

3B 10 p27

a Work on your own. Choose the correct words in phrases 1–5.

		name	name
1	watch TV *in/on* the morning		
2	go shopping *every/in* Saturday		
3	go for a drink *at/on* Friday evenings		
4	go to the cinema *at/every* month		
5	work *at/in* the weekends		

b Make questions with *you* with phrases 1–5 in a.

1 *Do you watch TV in the morning?*

c Ask other students in the class your questions. Try to find two people who answer *yes* for each question. Write their names in the table.

d Tell the class about the people in your table.

Gabriela and Rudi watch TV in the morning.

4B 9 p35

Susie's 23 and she's a waitress. She really loves dance music but she doesn't like rock music. She doesn't go to restaurants very often but she loves fast food. On Saturday evenings she goes clubbing with friends or stays in and watches TV. She doesn't like watching sport on TV but she goes swimming a lot. And she has seven cats!

11C 10 p93

a Work on your own. Find these places on the map on p93. Don't tell your partner.

The Burger Bar (4)   the theatre (7)   the school (12)

b Work with your partner. You are at *You are here* on the map. Ask for directions to these places: **the cinema**, **a pizza restaurant**, **a petrol station**. When you find the place, check the number on the map with your partner. Don't look at your partner's map. Your partner starts.

Excuse me. How do I get to the cinema?

5A 11 p41

a Work on your own. Write questions with *you* or *your* about when you were thirteen.

		you	your partner
1	/ tall for your age? *Were you tall for your age?*		
2	Who / favourite teacher?		
3	/ good at sport?		
4	Who / favourite singer?		
5	Where / thirteenth birthday party?		

b Write your answers in the *you* column.

c Work with your partner. Ask and answer your questions. Write your partner's answers in the table.

d Tell another student about you and your partner when you were thirteen.

I was tall for my age when I was thirteen, but Johann wasn't.

Pair and Group Work: Student/Group B

6C 11 p53

a Work on your own. Read about the news stories. Check you understand all the words.

3 students lost in Brazil
Amazon jungle
lost for six days
helicopter found them
they're OK now

Plane crash
in Africa
over 80 people died

Man who won the lottery
dog ate ticket
gave dog to friend

**Planes at airpo...
why the...**

Tuesday morn:
a number of k
and have made
to the press at
"I see no reaso
said Mr Dawk

b Work with your partner. Take turns to tell each other about the news stories. Use these phrases.

Did you hear/read about … ?   No, what happened?
No, where was it?   Oh, that's good.   Oh no, that's terrible.
Oh, dear. Are they OK?   You're joking!   Really?

4B 10 c p35

MARK   Jo and I like some of the same things. We both like going to the cinema and eating Chinese food. But she talks about books and shopping *all* the time. We both like rock music, but she hates sport and I love it! No, I don't want to see her again. Sorry!

JO   I *really* like Mark. He's very different from me, but that's a good thing, I think. I hate football, but he loves it. And he plays video games all the time and he never reads books. But yes, I'd like a second date with him. Definitely. He's very nice.

7B 10 p59

a Work with a student from group B. Describe the picture. Use the phrases in bold.

There's a TV in the picture.
There's some fruit on the table.
There are six eggs in the fridge.
There are some chairs in the room.

b Make questions to ask a student from group A about his/her picture. Use the phrases in bold.

Is there a TV in the room?
Are there any eggs in the fridge?
How many apples **are there**?
How much water **is there**?

c Work with a student from group A. Don't look at your partner's picture. Ask and answer questions about the pictures. Find twelve differences.

d Work with your partner from group B. Compare answers.

Pair and Group Work: Student/Group B

8A 12 p65

a Work with a student from group B. Look at the picture. What are the people doing? What are the people wearing?

Kevin's sleeping.   *He's wearing a shirt and tie.*

b Work with a student from group A. Don't look at his/her picture. Ask and answer questions. Find ten differences in the pictures.

What's Kevin doing?

What's he wearing?

c Work with your partner from group B. Did you find the same differences?

8B 9 p67

a Work on your own. Write the questions (Q).

b Work with a student from group A. Look at the pictures. Take turns to ask and answer your questions. Write the answers (A). Your partner starts.

c Work with a student from group B. Compare answers.

USUALLY	TODAY	USUALLY	TODAY
1	2 What / Colin / wear / today ? Q *What's Colin wearing today?* A	7 Where / Colin / usually / work ? Q A	8
3 How / Gabby / usually / get / to work ? Q A	4	9	10 Where / Gabby and her friends / have / lunch today ? Q A
5	6 What / the children / do / this morning ? Q A	11 What / Colin / usually / do / in the afternoon ? Q A	12

Pair and Group Work: Student/Group B

10A 11 p81

a You have these problems. Check you understand them. Then write one more problem.
1. I want to practise my English more.
2. A friend bought me a present, but I hate it.
3. I need a holiday, but I haven't got any money.
4. _____

b Work with students A and C. Take turns to ask for and give advice. Which piece of advice is the best, do you think?

> I want to practise my English more. What should I do?

> (I think) you should …

> Well, you shouldn't …

> Don't …

10D 5 p87

a Work with your partner. Ask and answer questions about the weather in these places. Fill in the gaps in the table. Your partner starts.

> What's the weather like in … today?

> It's … and it's … degrees.

	weather	°C
Amsterdam		
Athens	FOG	17
Bangkok		
Buenos Aires	cloudy	30
Chicago		
Helsinki	snow	0
London		
Munich	windy	6
Paris		
Rome	rain	8
San Francisco		
Sydney	sunny	22

b Which places are: hot, warm, cold? Where's the best place to be today? Why?

11B 11 p91

a Look at what Eric, Melanie, Jenny and Sam are going to do next weekend. Take turns to ask and answer yes/no questions and fill in the gaps in the table.

> Is Melanie going to visit her parents next weekend?

> ✓ Yes, she is.
> ✗ No, she isn't.
> ✓✗ She might.

	Eric	Melanie	Jenny and Sam
visit parents	✗		✓✗
go for a run		✗	
move house	✗		✓
watch lots of TV		✓	
go to a party	✓		✓✗
play tennis		✗	
stay in bed on Sunday	✗		✗

b Who is going to have: a lazy weekend, a busy weekend, an active weekend?

12B 10 p99

a Work with a student from group B. Write questions with *you* in the Present Perfect and follow-up questions in the Past Simple.

1. / go / on holiday to a cold country?
   Have you ever been on holiday to a cold country?
   Where / go?
   Where did you go?
2. / learn / play a musical instrument?
   What instrument / learn?
3. / go / to a very expensive restaurant?
   What / eat?
4. / have / a really bad holiday?
   What problems / have?
5. / cook / a meal for more than six people?
   What / cook?

b Work with a student from group A. Ask and answer your questions. If the answer is *yes*, ask your follow-up question. Then ask two more questions if possible.

c Work with your partner from group B. Tell him/her about student A's life experiences.

113

Pair and Group Work: Other exercises

4B 10 c p35

MARK Susie's very nice. We both like the same things – watching TV and doing sport. Also, she has lots of cats and I really like cats. She doesn't like rock music very much, but that's OK. Yes, I'd like a second date with her. Yes, please!

SUSIE Mark? Yes, I like him. We both do a lot of sport. I like swimming and he likes football. And we both watch a lot of TV and DVDs, so that's a good thing. Do I want to see him again? Yes, why not? Maybe we can go clubbing next time.

10A 11 p81

a You have these problems. Check you understand them. Then write one more problem.
1 I can't find a job.
2 I need to find somewhere to live very quickly.
3 I want to learn more English vocabulary.
4 _____

b Work with students A and B. Take turns to ask for and give advice. Which piece of advice is the best, do you think?

I can't find a job. What should I do?

(I think) you should …

Well, you shouldn't …

Don't …

3D 2 b p30

Are you an early bird or a night owl?

1	a 1 point	b 2 points	c 3 points
2	a 2 points	b 1 point	c 3 points
3	a 3 points	b 1 point	c 2 points
4	a 3 points	b 2 points	c 1 point
5	a 2 points	b 1 point	c 3 points
6	a 1 point	b 2 points	c 3 points

6–9 points:
You're definitely an early bird. You probably get up very early and do lots of things before lunchtime. But you're probably not a good person to go to an all-night party with!

10–13 points:
You're not a night owl or an early bird – so you're probably an afternoon person! You probably get up early in the week and then sleep a lot at the weekend.

14–18 points:
You're definitely an night owl. You probably go out a lot in the evening and watch TV late at night. But you're probably not a good person to have breakfast with!

5B 11 p43

a Work on your own. Choose five to eight of these events in your life. Write the year/month when these things happened on a timeline.

- born
- brother/sister born
- start/leave school
- move to a new school
- start learning English
- go to your first concert/football match
- start/leave university
- meet your first girlfriend/boyfriend
- move to a different town/city
- meet your husband/wife
- start your first job/a new job
- get married
- have a child
- meet your best friend

b Work with your partner. Take turns to tell each other about your timeline. Ask questions to get more information.

c Tell another student three things about your partner's life.

BORN IN …   NOW

Extra Practice 1

Language Summary 1 p128

1A p8

1 a Find twelve countries (→↓).

R	E	B	R	A	Z	I	L	A
G	E	R	M	A	N	Y	R	R
U	P	S	E	D	F	P	U	G
K	I	T	A	L	Y	O	S	E
F	R	A	N	C	E	L	S	N
L	A	R	U	S	A	A	I	T
L	O	N	C	H	I	N	A	I
T	U	R	K	E	Y	D	W	N
A	U	S	T	R	A	L	I	A

b Write the nationalities.
Brazil → *Brazilian*

2 Fill in the gaps with *'m*, *'re*, *are* or *'s*.

- A What¹ *'s* your name?
- B My name² _____ Ali.
- A Where ³_____ you from?
- B I⁴ _____ from Egypt.
- A Where ⁵_____ they from?
- B They⁶ _____ from Australia.
- A What ⁷_____ their names?
- B His name⁸ _____ Jason and her name⁹ _____ Kylie.
- A Hi, Jo. How ¹⁰_____ you?
- B I¹¹ _____ fine, thanks. And you?
- A I¹² _____ OK, thanks.

3 Choose the correct words.

1. What's *you*/*your* name?
2. It's *she*/*her* dictionary.
3. *We*/*Our* 're Japanese.
4. *My*/*I* 'm from Turkey.
5. It's *he*/*his* computer.
6. *They're*/*Their* Spanish.
7. *You're*/*Your* in room C.
8. *It's*/*Its* an MP3 player.
9. What are *they*/*their* names?
10. *We*/*Our* names are Colin and Henry.
11. Where's *you*/*your* book?
12. *We*/*Our* 're students and Peter's *we*/*our* teacher.

1B p10

4 Fill in the gaps in these jobs with *a, e, i, o* or *u*. Then put *a* or *an* in the boxes.

1. [*a*] l *a* wy *e* r
2. [ ] d _ ct _ r
3. [ ] m _ s _ c _ _ n
4. [ ] w _ tr _ ss
5. [ ] _ cc _ _ nt _ nt
6. [ ] m _ n _ g _ r
7. [ ] _ ng _ n _ _ r
8. [ ] p _ l _ ce _ ff _ c _ r
9. [ ] m _ ch _ n _ c
10. [ ] cl _ _ n _ r
11. [ ] s _ l _ s _ _ ss _ st _ nt
12. [ ] t _ _ ch _ r

5 Make these sentences negative. Write correct sentences.

1. Julia Roberts is Polish.
   Julia Roberts isn't Polish. She's American.
2. Leonardo DiCaprio is an accountant.
3. David and Victoria Beckham are from Spain.
4. Pepsi and Coca-Cola are British companies.
5. Sydney is in the USA.
6. Ferraris are German cars.
7. Liverpool and Manchester are in Australia.

6 a Fill in the gaps in these questions with *Am*, *Are* or *Is*.

1. *Are* you a student?
2. _____ she an actress?
3. _____ they Argentinian?
4. _____ I in room 201?
5. _____ it an English hotel?
6. _____ he from Mexico?
7. _____ we in room B?
8. _____ you from London?

b Write positive and negative short answers for the questions in **6a**.

1. *Yes, I am. No, I'm not.*

1C p12

7 Write questions with *your* for these answers.

1. Jones. *What's your surname?*
2. It's Anna.
3. I'm British.
4. 67, West Road, London.
5. SE13 7GR.
6. My mobile number's 07954 362313.
7. It's 020 7946 0840.
8. jane22@webmail.com.

1D p14

8 Write the plurals.

1. a camera *cameras*
2. a surname
3. a watch
4. a dictionary
5. a dress
6. a pencil
7. a tooth
8. a woman
9. a man
10. an address

Progress Portfolio 1

Tick the things you can do in English.

- [ ] I can introduce people.
- [ ] I can say countries and nationalities.
- [ ] I can say and understand the numbers 0–100.
- [ ] I can talk about jobs.
- [ ] I can ask for, give and understand personal information (name, etc.).
- [ ] I can ask people to repeat things.

Extra Practice 2

Language Summary 2 p130

2A p16

1 Write the adjectives. Then write their opposites.

1	ewn	n ew	o ld
2	epahc	c_____	e_____
3	lamls	s_____	b_____
4	swol	s_____	f_____
5	lygu	u_____	b_____
6	ysea	e_____	d_____
7	uogny	y_____	o_____
8	dogo	g_____	b_____
9	leayr	e_____	l_____
10	ghrit	r_____	w_____

2 Choose the correct words.

1 She*'ve*/*'s* got an old bike.
2 We *haven't*/*hasn't* got a car.
3 They*'ve*/*'s* got a new DVD player.
4 Jo *haven't*/*hasn't* got a camera.
5 I*'ve*/*'s* got a new laptop.
6 He *haven't*/*hasn't* got an MP3 player.
7 They *haven't*/*hasn't* got a very big car.
8 You*'ve*/*'s* got a nice watch.
9 She *haven't*/*hasn't* got a pen.
10 We*'ve*/*'s* got a beautiful cat.

3 Fill in the gaps with *have*, *has*, *haven't* or *hasn't*.

1 A _Have_ you got a computer?
　B Yes, I have.
2 A _____ Mona got a laptop?
　B No, she _____ .
3 A _____ you got a dictionary?
　B Yes, I _____ .
4 A _____ they got a new DVD player?
　B No, they _____ .
5 A _____ he got a camera?
　B Yes, he _____ .
6 A _____ we got his address?
　B Yes, we _____ .
7 A _____ Bob got a car?
　B No, he _____ .
8 A _____ they got a big TV?
　B Yes, they _____ .

2B p18

4 Complete these sentences.

1 Your mother's son is …
　your brother
2 Your mother's daughter is …
3 Your son's children are …
4 Your mother's brother is …
5 Your father's sister is …
6 Your father's parents are …
7 Your mother's brother's daughter is …

5 Look at these sentences. Does *'s* mean *is*, *has* or possessive?

1 Jack**'s** got a camera. *'s = has*
2 She**'s** got an MP3 player.
3 Mark**'s** unemployed.
4 This is Ed**'s** baby.
5 She**'s** from Prague.
6 That**'s** Pam**'s** husband.

2C p20

6 a Put these times in order.

twenty to ten 1	five to ten
quarter past ten	ten past ten
quarter to ten	ten to ten
twenty-five past ten	half past ten

b Write the times in **6a** in a different way.

twenty to ten → nine forty

7 Read this conversation at a cinema. Fill in the gaps with these words.

~~Can~~	Here	course	Thanks
film	tickets	That's	starts
time	much		

A [1] _Can_ I have two [2] _____ for *24 Hours*, please?
B Yes, of [3] _____ .
A How [4] _____ is that?
B [5] _____ £18, please.
A [6] _____ you are. What [7] _____ is the film?
B It [8] _____ at six fifty.
A Right. [9] _____ a lot.
B You're welcome. Enjoy the [10] _____ .

2D p22

8 Look at pictures 1–6. Complete the words. Then fill in the gaps with these prepositions.

| ~~by~~ | under | in | behind |
| in front of | on | | |

1 The plant's _by_ the d _o o r_ .
2 The plant's _____ the b ____ .
3 The plant's _____ the d _____ .
4 The plant's _____ the s _____ .
5 The plant's _____ the b _____ .
6 The plant's _____ the c _____ t _____ .

Progress Portfolio 2

Tick the things you can do in English.

☐ I can use adjectives with *very* to describe things.
☐ I can talk about personal possessions.
☐ I can talk about families.
☐ I can talk about times and prices.
☐ I can find information in adverts for cinemas, etc.
☐ I can buy a ticket at the cinema.
☐ I can say where things are in a room.

Extra Practice 3

Language Summary 3 p132

3A p24

1 Read about Vince's day. Fill in the gaps with these verbs.

~~live~~	work	finish	start
go	leave	get	
get up	have (x2)		

1 I _live_ in Brighton.
2 I _____ at 7.00.
3 I _____ home at 8.30.
4 I _____ work at 9.00.
5 I _____ in a school.
6 I _____ lunch in a café.
7 I _____ work at 5.30.
8 I _____ home at 6.00.
9 I _____ dinner at home.
10 I _____ to bed at 11.30.

2 Complete these questions with *you* for the words/phrases in bold in **1**.

1 Where _do you live_ ?
2 What time _____ ?
3 When _____ ?
4 What time _____ ?
5 Where _____ ?
6 Where _____ ?
7 When _____ ?
8 What time _____ ?
9 Where _____ ?
10 When _____ ?

3B p26

3 Match a word/phrase in A to a word/phrase in B.

A	B
go	your family
visit	in
do	out
stay	sport
have	the cinema
go to	coffee with friends
go	concerts
watch	shopping
eat	friends
go to	a drink
phone	TV
go for	out

4 a Fill in the gaps with *in*, *on* or *at*.

1 I get up early _in_ the week.
2 They work _____ the weekend.
3 Gavin and Ruby eat out _____ Friday evenings.
4 My brother and I go to the cinema _____ Sundays.
5 Tom and Bob work _____ night.
6 I phone my mum and dad _____ the mornings.
7 My parents have lunch _____ one o'clock.
8 We do sport _____ the afternoon.
9 I phone my son _____ Saturdays.
10 I get up _____ half past six.

b Make the sentences in **4a** negative.

1 I don't get up early in the week.

3C p28

5 What do you say on these special days?

1 your sister's birthday
   Happy birthday!
2 a friend's wedding
3 1st January
4 the birth of a baby
5 a wedding anniversary

6 Complete the words in this conversation.

A What ¹s_hall_ we ²g_____ Maya for her birthday?
B What ³a_____ a new watch?
A No, I don't ⁴t_____ so. She's got a nice watch.
B Why ⁵d_____ we get her a radio?
A ⁶M_____ . But she's got an MP3 player.
B I know! ⁷L_____ get her a camera.
A Yes, ⁸t_____ a good ⁹i_____ . Where's your credit card?
B *My* credit card?!

3D p30

7 Make sentences with these words.

1 Sundays / work / I / usually / on .
   I usually work on Sundays.
2 I / in / never / the afternoon / sleep .
3 on / I / Saturday / at home / sometimes / 'm / evenings .
4 often / go out / friends / the week / in / I / with .
5 always / My / birthday / remember / friends / my .
6 New Year's Eve / on / hardly ever / are / at home / My parents .
7 tired / evenings / usually / 'm / on / very / Friday / I .

8 Choose the correct words.

1 Do you know *he*/(*him*)?
2 Is *she*/*her* a doctor?
3 They email *we*/*us* a lot.
4 How do you know *she*/*her*?
5 I don't understand *they*/*them*.
6 Why don't *they*/*them* phone *I*/*me*?

Progress Portfolio 3

Tick the things you can do in English.

☐ I can describe my daily routine.
☐ I can talk about my free time activities and say when I do them.
☐ I can ask people about their routines and free time.
☐ I can use phrases for special days.
☐ I can ask for, make and respond to suggestions.
☐ I can say how often I do things.

Extra Practice 4

Language Summary 4 p135

4A p32

1 Match the verbs to the words/phrases.

go	to music
go	running
listen	photos
take	swimming
go	tennis
play	to the radio
read	clubbing
listen	books or magazines
go	video games
play	sport on TV
go to	cycling
watch	the gym

2 a Add -s, -es or – to the verbs in these sentences.

1 My son watch *es* TV a lot.
2 Barry take__ good photos.
3 Paula go__ out on Saturdays.
4 Ian and Liz work__ at home.
5 My sister live__ in the USA.
6 Our class finish__ at 8.30.
7 Luke's parents like__ jazz.
8 Rob watch__ sport on TV.
9 We go__ out on Fridays.
10 She do__ a lot of sport.

b Make the sentences negative.

1 *My son doesn't watch TV a lot.*

4B p34

3 Look at the pictures. Fill in the gaps with the correct form of these words/phrases.

love	hate	really like
don't like	is/are OK
quite like	like

1 He *loves* cats.
2 We _____ cooking.
3 She _____ dogs.
4 I _____ jazz.
5 I think tennis _____ .
6 They _____ football.
7 He _____ shopping for clothes.

4 a Make questions with these words.

1 What / do / does / he ?
  What does he do?
2 work / does / Where / he ?
3 like / rock music / he / Does ?
4 What / she / on Friday nights / does / do ?
5 What / like / she / does / food ?
6 she / watch / Does / on TV / sport ?

b Fill in the gaps with the correct form of the verb in brackets and complete the short answers. Then match answers a–f to questions 1–6.

a He *teaches* English. (teach) 1
b She _____ clubbing. (go)
c She _____ Italian food. (like)
d He _____ in Spain. (work)
e Yes, she _____ . She _____ football and tennis. (love)
f No, he _____ . He _____ dance music and jazz. (like)

4C p36

5 Betty is in a restaurant. Fill in the gaps with these phrases.

to order	can I have
I'd like	Would you like (x3)
the bill	to drink
a glass of	that's all

WAITER Would you like ¹ *to order* now?
BETTY Yes, ² _____ the burger and chips, please.
W What would you like ³ _____ ?
B I'd like ⁴ _____ red wine, please.
W ⁵ _____ anything else?
B No, ⁶ _____ , thanks.
W ⁷ _____ a dessert?
B Yes, ⁸ _____ the apple pie, please?
W ⁹ _____ tea or coffee?
B No, thanks. Can I have ¹⁰ _____ , please?
W Certainly, madam.

4D p38

6 a Find fifteen words for food and drink. (→↓).

C	H	E	E	S	E	F	O	T
B	Y	T	O	A	S	T	F	O
A	E	F	R	U	I	T	I	M
N	E	G	G	S	L	K	S	A
A	B	R	E	A	D	E	H	T
N	T	E	A	G	M	X	A	O
A	P	P	L	E	R	I	C	E
M	E	A	T	S	L	L	W	S
M	I	L	K	O	K	J	A	M

b Which words are countable (C)? Which are uncountable (U)?

cheese U   *banana* C

7 Fill in the gaps with a, an or –.

1 Do you have – sugar?
2 Can I have _____ croissant?
3 I don't like _____ olives.
4 Would you like _____ biscuit?
5 I love _____ chicken soup.
6 I always have _____ egg sandwich for lunch.

Progress Portfolio 4

Tick the things you can do in English.

- [ ] I can talk about other people's routines and free time activities.
- [ ] I can say what I like and don't like.
- [ ] I can ask and answer questions about people I don't know.
- [ ] I can say and understand words for food and drink.
- [ ] I can order something to eat and drink in a restaurant.
- [ ] I can offer things to people.
- [ ] I can ask people for things.

Extra Practice 5

Language Summary 5 p138

5A p40

1 Write the opposites of these adjectives.

1 ill *well*
2 happy
3 hot
4 lucky
5 different
6 tall
7 friendly
8 boring
9 fantastic
10 quiet

2 Choose the correct words.

1 I *was*/were at home yesterday.
2 Jack and I *was/were* in Rome last week.
3 The film *was/were* amazing!
4 My uncle *was/were* a doctor.
5 I *wasn't/weren't* here last year.
6 He *wasn't/weren't* very well.
7 You *wasn't/weren't* here on Monday.
8 They *wasn't/weren't* born in the UK.

3 Make questions with these words.

1 were / night / you / Where / last ?
   Where were you last night?
2 they / at home / yesterday / Were / afternoon ?
3 the party / Was / son / your / at ?
4 at / were / 5 p.m. / you / Where ?
5 born / were / Where / you ?
6 they / When / born / were ?
7 in / he / Was / born / London ?

5B p42

4 a Choose the correct verbs.

1 *have*/write children
2 win/make a film
3 meet/study English
4 leave/meet school
5 make/become famous
6 become/write a book
7 win/meet a lot of money
8 move/leave house

b Write the Past Simple of the correct verbs in **4a**.

have → had

5 a Read about Beryl, Jason's grandmother. Fill in gaps 1–8 with the Past Simple of these verbs.

| ~~be~~ | meet (x2) | have |
| go | live | move | get |

I ¹ *was* born ᵃ**in 1954** and my family ² _____ ᵇ**in Liverpool**. In 1973 I ³ _____ my husband, Albert, at ᶜ**a party** and we ⁴ _____ married ᵈ**on May 1ˢᵗ 1975**. We ⁵ _____ our first child, Matt, ᵉ**in 1977**. Matt ⁶ _____ to ᶠ**Spain** on holiday in 1997 and ⁷ _____ ᵍ**his wife** there. They ⁸ _____ to Bristol ʰ**in 1999** and they have four children now.

b Make questions for the words/phrases a–h in bold.

a *When was Beryl born?*
b *Where did her family live?*

5C p44

6 Match the verbs to the phrases.

go	for the weekend
write	to a party
clean	an email
go away	the car
do	for a walk
have	with friends
stay	a great time
go	the washing

7 Choose the correct response in these conversations.

1 A I won £50,000 yesterday.
   B Oh, nice./*Wow!*
2 A Tim and I went to Venice last week.
   B What a shame./Really?
3 A I was ill last weekend.
   B Oh, dear./Oh, nice.
4 A I met the President of the USA last month.
   B You're joking!/Oh, dear.
5 A I stayed in all weekend.
   B Oh, right./What a shame.
6 A I went clubbing last night.
   B Oh, dear./Oh, nice.

5D p46

8 a Write the missing letters in these adjectives.

1 c *r* ow *d* ed
2 d _ rt _
3 ex _ _ t _ d
4 p _ _ r
5 dan _ er _ us
6 cl _ _ n
7 e _ pt _
8 r _ c _
9 b _ r _ d
10 s _ f _

b Match the opposite adjectives in **8a**.

crowded, empty

9 Choose the correct words.

1 Sorry, I can't come today. I'm *too*/quite busy.
2 Let's go to that restaurant. It's too/really nice.
3 He's a very/too important man.
4 Mike is always quite/too lucky.
5 Kim's husband is too/quite rich.
6 That film was too/quite long. I went to sleep after 5 hours!
7 This book is really/too interesting.

Progress Portfolio 5

Tick the things you can do in English.

- [ ] I can describe people and places.
- [ ] I can talk about things that happened in my life.
- [ ] I can ask questions about things other people did in the past.
- [ ] I can say and understand years.
- [ ] I can talk about what I did last weekend.
- [ ] I can respond to people's news and ask follow-up questions.

Extra Practice 6

Language Summary 6 p140

6A p48

1 Fill in the gaps with these words.

> ~~website~~   get   blog   emails
> online   download   chat
> WiFi   use   search engine

1 I don't have a favourite *website*.
2 Paul sends lots of _____ every day.
3 Did you _____ my email?
4 This café has _____.
5 I _____ the internet for my food shopping.
6 Do you always use the same _____?
7 My kids _____ a lot of videos and music.
8 I _____ to my sister online every day.
9 I often go _____ and read my friend's _____.

2 Fill in the gaps with *didn't*, *wasn't* or *weren't*.

1 I *didn't* go to bed late last night.
2 I _____ watch TV yesterday.
3 My parents _____ go to university.
4 I _____ at home last week.
5 My parents _____ born in the UK.
6 I _____ like my first school.
7 I _____ have a holiday last year.
8 I _____ late for work last week.

3 Fill in the gaps with the Past Simple of the verbs in brackets, *did* or *didn't*.

A [1] *Did* you *go out* yesterday evening? (go out)
B Yes, I [2] _____. I [3] _____ to see my sister. (go)
A What [4] _____ you _____? (do)
B We [5] _____ a DVD. (watch)
A [6] _____ you _____ it? (enjoy)
B No, I [7] _____. It [8] _____ terrible! (be)
A [9] _____ you _____ at your sister's? (stay)
B No I [10] _____. I [11] _____ home. (come)

6B p50

4 Choose the correct words.

1 I didn't *send*/*get* your text. Can you *send*/*get* it again?
2 Remember to *turn on*/*turn off* your phone before the film starts.
3 What was the last *app*/*GPS* you downloaded?
4 Which *programme*/*channel* is the football on?
5 I need a new *charge*/*battery* for my mobile.
6 Do you *charge*/*record* your phone every night?
7 Can you *turn on*/*turn off* the TV? My favourite *programme*/*channel* is on now.

5 Make sentences with these words.

1 ago / I / two / him / days / met .
   I met him two days ago.
2 born / He / eighteenth / the / in / century / was .
3 night / out / I / last / went .
4 days / arrived / She / ago / ten .
5 2011 / to Paris / My parents / in / went .
6 in / famous / was / the eighties / His father .

6 Choose the correct words.

1 Excuse me. *Can*/*Could* you make video calls on this mobile?
2 You *can't*/*couldn't* go online in 1970.
3 You *can*/*could* buy mobiles in the 1990s.
4 Sorry, we *can't*/*couldn't* come to your party next week.
5 Look! You *can*/*could* see my house from here.
6 He *can't*/*couldn't* go to work last week.
7 *Can*/*Could* you watch TV on your new mobile?
8 Two years ago you *can't*/*couldn't* buy these phones.
9 You *can*/*could* use Google in 1998.
10 Help! I *can't*/*couldn't* swim!

6C p52

7 Fill in the gaps with these words.

> ~~hear~~   read   where   joking
> died   what   Really   terrible

A Did you [1] *hear* about that plane crash?
B No, [2] _____ was it?
A In the USA. 310 people [3] _____.
B Oh no, that's [4] _____.
A Did you [5] _____ about the woman who won the lottery?
B No, [6] _____ happened?
A Her baby chose the numbers.
B [7] _____? You're [8] _____!

6D p54

8 Fill in the gaps with *a*, *an* or *the*.

1 I've got *an* old car.
2 I went to _____ cinema at _____ weekend.
3 What happens at _____ end of _____ game?
4 I'd like to buy _____ new hat.
5 This book is about _____ young doctor and _____ old woman. _____ doctor is rich, but _____ woman is very poor.

Progress Portfolio 6

Tick the things you can do in English.

☐ I can talk about the internet, my mobile phone and TV.
☐ I can say when things happened in the past.
☐ I can talk about things I can do in the present and could do in the past.
☐ I can understand simple news stories.
☐ I can talk about the news and respond to news stories.

Extra Practice 7

Language Summary 7 p142

7A p56

1 Find 12 places in a town or city. (→↓).

S	B	M	A	R	K	E	T
T	A	U	E	H	D	A	O
A	R	S	P	O	G	B	S
T	H	E	A	T	R	E	Q
I	O	U	R	E	W	A	U
O	U	M	K	L	L	C	A
N	S	F	L	A	T	H	R
Z	E	K	R	O	A	D	E

2 Read about Catford, in London. Fill in the gaps with *There's*, *There are*, *There isn't* or *There aren't*.

1 (✓) *There's* a theatre in Catford.
2 (✗) _____ a cinema.
3 (✓) _____ two stations.
4 (✗) _____ a square.
5 (✓) _____ a nice park.
6 (✗) _____ any museums.
7 (✓) _____ a lot of shops.
8 (✗) _____ any big hotels.

3 a Choose the correct words.

1 *Is*/*Are* there a theatre in Catford?
2 *Is*/*Are* there any big hotels?
3 *Is*/*Are* there a cinema?
4 *Is*/*Are* there any museums?
5 *Is*/*Are* there any shops?
6 *Is*/*Are* there a park?
7 *Is*/*Are* there a square?

b Look again at **2**. Write short answers for the questions in **3a**.

1 *Yes, there is.*

7B p58

4 Which word is the odd one out?

1 table   chair   *balcony*
2 cooker   bed   fridge
3 bathroom   kitchen   shower
4 sink   desk   washbasin
5 bath   toilet   living room
6 cupboard   sofa   armchair

5 Fill in the gaps with *some*, *any*, *a* or *an*.

A I'm hungry. Have you got ¹ *any* food?
B Yes, there's ² _____ bread and cheese. I can make you ³ _____ sandwich.
A Have you got ⁴ _____ tomatoes?
B No, I haven't, but I've got ⁵ _____ eggs. Would you like ⁶ _____ egg sandwich?
A Yes, that sounds nice.
B Would you like ⁷ _____ drink?
A Yes, ⁸ _____ milk, please. And have you got ⁹ _____ fruit? ¹⁰ _____ banana, maybe?
B There are ¹¹ _____ oranges, but there aren't ¹² _____ bananas.
A OK. I'll have ¹³ _____ orange.

7C p60

6 Write the vowels (*a, e, i, o, u*) in these shops.

1 a b *o o* ksh *o* p
2 a ch _ m _ st's
3 a sh _ _ sh _ p
4 a b _ k _ r's
5 a b _ nk
6 a k _ _ sk
7 a p _ st _ ff _ c _
8 a n _ ws _ g _ nt's
9 a b _ tch _ r's
10 a d _ p _ rtm _ nt st _ r _
11 a s _ p _ rm _ rk _ t
12 a cl _ th _ s sh _ p

7 Write the words for these things.

1 *a map*
2 _____
3 _____
4 _____
5 _____
6 _____
7 _____
8 _____

8 Fill in the gaps with these words.

~~Can~~	over	I'll	else
help	Have	that's
one	receipt	any

A Hello. ¹ *Can* I help you?
B Yes. ² _____ you got ³ _____ maps of London?
A Yes, they're ⁴ _____ there.
B Oh, yes. ⁵ _____ have this ⁶ _____, please.
A Anything ⁷ _____ ?
B No, ⁸ _____ all, thanks. Thanks for your ⁹ _____ .
A OK. Here's your ¹⁰ _____ .

7D p62

9 Write the colours and clothes.

1 *a pink jacket*
2 _____
3 _____
4 _____
5 _____
6 _____

Progress Portfolio 7

Tick the things you can do in English.

☐ I can describe my town and other places I know.
☐ I can describe my home and the things in it.
☐ I can ask about other people's towns and homes.
☐ I can buy things in a shop.
☐ I can talk about clothes.
☐ I can say colours.

Extra Practice 8

Language Summary 8 p145

8A p64

1 Fill in the gaps with these words.

> ~~phone~~   report   notes
> company   contract
> meeting   customers

1 Can you answer the _phone_, please?
2 I work for a _____ in Rome.
3 They signed the _____ yesterday.
4 I'm going to a _____ now.
5 Lisa, can you take _____ at the meeting, please?
6 I write to a lot of _____ every day.
7 Did you write this _____ ?

2 Put the verbs in the Present Continuous.

MUM   Jim, can you help me?
JIM   Sorry, Mum. I¹ _'m doing_ my homework. (do)
MUM   What² _____ your sister _____ ? (do)
JIM   She³ _____ _____ a shower. (have)
MUM   And what ⁴ _____ your brothers _____ ? (do)
JIM   They⁵ _____ _____ football. (play). But Dad ⁶ _____ _____ anything. (not do)
DAD   Yes, I am. I ⁷ _____ _____ the paper. (read)
MUM   Not any more!

8B p66

3 a Write these travelling verbs/phrases.

1 ylf — _fly_
2 leccy — _____
3 vired — _____
4 kawl — _____
5 og yb ratin — _____
6 og yb occah — _____
7 og yb buet — _____

b What is another way to say the verbs/phrases in **3a**?

fly → go by plane

4 a Put the verbs in the Present Simple or Present Continuous.

1 Where _does_ Ben _work_ ? (work)
2 What _____ Sue _____ at the moment? (do)
3 Which TV programmes _____ you _____ every week? (watch)
4 What _____ you _____ today? (wear)
5 Where _____ you usually _____ on Friday evenings? (go)
6 What _____ Dave and Rita _____ now? (do)
7 What time _____ your lesson usually _____ ? (finish)
8 What _____ Ben _____ at the moment? (do)

b Write the answers for questions 1–8 in **4a**.

1 work / in a bank
   He works in a bank.
2 take / the children to school
3 watch / sport on TV
4 wear / jeans and a T-shirt
5 usually / go / clubbing
6 have / lunch
7 usually / finish / at 4.30
8 walk / to work

8C p68

5 Read this phone conversation. Fill in the gaps with these words.

> ~~help you~~   Can I   Speaking
> It's   I got   I'll call   Hold on
> Is that   call you back   Call me

KEVIN   Hello. Can I ¹ _help you_ ?
BILL   Hello. ² _____ Kevin Doyle?
K   ³ _____ .
B   Hi, Kevin. ⁴ _____ Bill. ⁵ _____ speak to Jo, please?
K   ⁶ _____ a moment, I'll get her.
JO   Hello?
B   Hi, Jo. ⁷ _____ your message.
J   Oh, hi, Bill. I've got a meeting now. Can I ⁸ _____ ?
B   Sure. ⁹ _____ on my mobile.
J   OK. ¹⁰ _____ you later. Bye.

8D p70

6 Write words/phrases for these indoor and outdoor activities.

1 _drive_   4 _____
2 _____   5 _____
3 _____   6 _____

7 Choose the correct words.

A Tina's husband is a ¹(good)/ well cook.
B And he can play tennis really ²good/well.
A He also speaks three languages ³fluent/fluently.
B But he isn't a very ⁴careful/ carefully driver. I don't feel ⁵safe/ safely when he's driving.
A So there's one thing he does ⁶bad/badly!

Progress Portfolio 8

Tick the things you can do in English.

☐ I can talk about things people do at work.
☐ I can describe things that are happening now.
☐ I can talk about transport.
☐ I can understand simple phone messages.
☐ I can have a conversation on the phone.
☐ I can understand a simple letter.

Extra Practice 9

Language Summary 9 p147

9A p72

1 Choose the correct verbs.

1. have/(stay) with friends
2. travel/hire a car
3. go to/go the beach
4. stay/hire in a hotel
5. have/travel around
6. go on/go camping
7. hire/go skiing
8. go on/go a boat trip
9. hire/travel a bike
10. go/have a picnic
11. go on/go to holiday
12. have/go a good time

2 Complete these sentences with the infinitive of purpose. Use these verbs.

| ~~get~~ | watch | buy | tell |
| visit | study | chat | |

1. I went to the baker's *to get* some bread.
2. We stayed at home _____ the football.
3. I'm going to Valencia _____ Spanish.
4. I went to L.A. _____ a friend.
5. She often goes online _____ to her friends.
6. He's going to the supermarket _____ some biscuits.
7. Jack phoned his wife _____ her the good news.

9B p74

3 Write the letters in these natural places.

1. the s *e a*
2. a w _ _ d
3. an i _ l _ _ d
4. a f _ r _ _ t
5. a m _ _ nt _ _ n
6. a h _ _ l
7. a l _ k _
8. a r _ v _ _
9. the c o _ _ t _ y s _ _ e
10. the d _ s _ _ t

4 Write sentences with comparatives.

1. Russia / cold / Egypt
   Russia is colder than Egypt.
2. Stockholm / safe / New York
3. Mumbai / big / Paris
4. India / cheap / Australia
5. Tokyo / expensive / Bangkok
6. São Paolo / hot / Montreal
7. Beijing / crowded / Berlin
8. Spain / small / Argentina
9. Mexico City / busy / Quito
10. Public transport in London / good / public transport in Los Angeles

9C p76

5 Write the animals.

1. dirb — b*ird*
2. olni — l_____
3. aesnk — s_____
4. semou — m_____
5. nceckih — c_____
6. bratbi — r_____
7. woc — c_____
8. largoil — g_____
9. komyen — m_____
10. grite — t_____
11. ephse — s_____
12. lwfo — w_____

6 Read the conversation and choose the correct verb form.

A What do you want ¹do/(to do) tomorrow?
B I'd like ²go/to go shopping in town.
A We did that last weekend. I'd rather ³go/to go to the beach.
B OK, let's ⁴do/to do that. Where would you like ⁵go/to go?
A Can we ⁶go/to go to Angel Beach? It's really nice.
B Yes, good idea. Let's ⁷go to/go there. Do you want ⁸drive/to drive?
A No, I don't think so. I'd rather ⁹take/to take the train.
B OK. See you tomorrow.

9D p78

7 Fill in the gaps with the correct form of the verbs in brackets, verb+*ing* or the infinitive with *to*.

A Would you like ¹ *to go out* (go out) this evening?
B I'm sorry, I can't. I need ² _____ (finish) this report.
A I really enjoy ³ _____ (watch) *The Simpsons*.
B Oh, I stopped ⁴ _____ (watch) it years ago.
A I'd really love ⁵ _____ (go) to San Francisco.
B Yes, me too. But I really hate ⁶ _____ (fly)!
A Do you like ⁷ _____ (go) to the cinema?
B No, I don't, but I love ⁸ _____ (watch) DVDs.
A Last night I decided ⁹ _____ (leave) my job.
B Wow! What do you want ¹⁰ _____ (do) now?

Progress Portfolio 9

Tick the things you can do in English.

- [ ] I can talk about things I do on holiday.
- [ ] I can give reasons why I do things.
- [ ] I can describe and compare places I know.
- [ ] I can find important facts in tourist brochures.
- [ ] I can discuss and plan a day out.
- [ ] I can understand a simple magazine article.

Extra Practice 10

Language Summary 10 p149

10A p80

1 Choose the correct words.
1 I want to *get*/*have* fit.
2 Can you *carry*/*spend* the shopping, please?
3 How often do you *do*/*have* the housework?
4 I'd like to *have*/*spend* a bath.
5 I need to *do*/*spend* some exercise.
6 I don't like *taking*/*doing* lifts.
7 Joe's *washing*/*doing* the car.
8 Did you *spend*/*do* lots of money?
9 I *take*/*get* stressed at work.
10 He *got on*/*got off* the bus and walked home.

2 Fill in the gaps with these imperatives.

| ~~Don't eat~~ | Turn off | Call |
| Don't forget | Don't work | Tell |

1 *Don't eat* biscuits every day.
2 _____ him on his mobile.
3 _____ too hard.
4 _____ her to go away.
5 _____ the TV and go to bed.
6 _____ to send him a present.

3 Fill in the gaps in these frequency expressions.
1 once a week = *every* 7 days
2 every 6 hours = _____ a day
3 twice a year = _____ 6 months
4 12 times a year = _____ a month
5 every 12 hours = _____ a day

4 Look at these tips for a healthy life. Fill in the gaps with *should* or *shouldn't* and these verbs.

| ~~do~~ | work | drink |
| sleep | eat | walk |

1 You *should do* some exercise.
2 You _____ chips every day.
3 You _____ 7 days a week.
4 You _____ to the shops.
5 You _____ so much coffee.
6 You _____ for 7 or 8 hours every night.

10B p82

5 Write the vowels (*a, e, i, o, u*) in these words. Do they describe appearance (A) or character (C)?
1 *a* ttr *a* ct *i* v *e* A
2 l *a* zy C
3 b _ _ t _ f _ l
4 f _ nny
5 _ v _ rw _ _ ght
6 s _ lf _ sh
7 g _ n _ r _ _ s
8 sl _ m
9 k _ nd
10 th _ n
11 g _ _ d - l _ _ k _ ng
12 h _ rd - w _ rk _ ng

6 a Make questions with these words.
1 Who / Joe / is ? *Who is Joe?*
2 like / What / look / he / does ?
3 doing / he / like / does / What ?
4 he / 's / like / What ?

b Match questions 1–4 with answers a–d.
a He likes travelling.
b He's very kind and quite shy.
c He's my brother.
d He's tall and he's got fair hair.

10C p84

7 a Find 10 words for health problems and parts of the body (→↓).

C	O	L	D	T	G	A	Q
F	B	B	J	O	I	L	L
O	E	A	C	O	U	G	H
O	A	C	W	T	P	E	F
T	X	K	O	H	K	G	L
H	E	A	D	A	C	H	E
W	L	R	M	C	D	W	G
Q	S	M	I	H	A	L	P
S	I	C	K	E	M	W	E

b Match the words in **7a** to these phrases.
1 I've got (a) … *cold*
2 I feel …
3 my …. hurts

8 Fill in the gaps with these words.

~~wrong~~	ache	better	take
sore	don't	terrible	matter
shouldn't	dear	painkillers	

A What's [1] *wrong* ?
B I feel [2] _____ .
A Oh, [3] _____ . What's the [4] _____ ?
B I've got a stomach [5] _____ and a [6] _____ throat. Have you got any [7] _____ ?
A Sorry, no, but you [8] _____ be at work. Why [9] _____ you [10] _____ the day off?
B Yes, good idea.
A I hope you get [11] _____ soon.

10D p86

9 What's the weather like? Write sentences with *It's …* .

1 *It's cold.* 5 _____
2 _____ 6 _____
3 _____ 7 _____
4 _____ 8 _____

Progress Portfolio 10

Tick the things you can do in English.
☐ I can ask for and give advice.
☐ I can talk about people's appearance and character.
☐ I can talk about health.
☐ I can be sympathetic.
☐ I can talk about the weather.
☐ I can understand a simple magazine article.

Extra Practice 11

Language Summary 11 p151

11A p88

1 Fill in the gaps with these verbs.

~~have~~	move	work	get
do	lose	eat	stop

1. _have_ a holiday/fun
2. _____ a computer course/ more exercise
3. _____ chocolate cake/ sweet things
4. _____ a new job/fit
5. _____ hard/less
6. _____ working at weekends/ smoking
7. _____ house/to another country
8. _____ three kilos/weight

2 Fill in the gaps with the correct form of *be going to* and these verbs.

~~leave~~	watch	get
stay	buy	have

1. Ian (+) _'s going to leave_ his job.
2. I (+) _____ a new car.
3. Tina (–) _____ married in May.
4. We (–) _____ a holiday this year.
5. They (+) _____ in a hotel.
6. I (–) _____ TV tonight.

3 Make questions with these words.

1. going to / you / tomorrow evening / are / do / What ?
   What are you going to do tomorrow evening?
2. next year / a holiday / have / you / Are / going to ?
3. you / tomorrow afternoon / be / are / going to / Where ?
4. do / after class / going to / What / you / are ?
5. Are / study / going to / you / next year / English ?
6. your family / go / Where / going to / on holiday / 's ?

11B p90

4 Choose the correct verbs.

1. *do*/*get* an exam
2. *pass*/*get* a degree
3. *fail*/*start* college
4. *revise*/*take* for an exam
5. *go*/*pass* to university
6. *get*/*leave* school
7. *go*/*pass* an exam
8. *start*/*get* some qualifications
9. *fail*/*revise* an exam
10. *pass*/*get* a job
11. *go*/*take* an exam
12. *go to*/*pass* school

5 Read the email. Fill in the gaps with *might* or the correct form of *be going to*.

To: Alice Fisher

Hi Alice
I finished my exams today!
I ¹ _'m going to_ celebrate this evening, but I'm not sure what I want to do. I ² _____ have dinner with friends, or I ³ _____ go to a party. This weekend Trevor and I ⁴ _____ drive to Brighton – it's his sister's wedding on Saturday. On Sunday we ⁵ _____ go for a long walk or we ⁶ _____ go shopping in town. And of course we ⁷ _____ see *Hamlet* on Tuesday – I've got the tickets!

Love Henrietta

11C p92

6 Choose the correct words in these conversations.

A Excuse me. ¹*Where*/*How* do I get to the station?
B Go along this road and ²*turn*/*take* left. Then go ³*over*/*in* the bridge and turn right. ⁴*That's*/*It's* New Road. The station is on ⁵*my*/*your* left, ⁶*next*/*opposite* the hotel.
A Great, thank you very much.

A Excuse me. ⁷*Is*/*Are* there a supermarket near ⁸*there*/*here*?
B Yes, there's one ⁹*at*/*in* New Road. Go ¹⁰*along*/*over* this street and turn right. Go ¹¹*past*/*along* the chemist's and the supermarket is ¹²*in*/*on* the right. You ¹³*can't*/*don't* miss it.

A Excuse me. ¹⁴*Where's*/*What's* the post office?
B It's ¹⁵*under*/*over* there, ¹⁶*next*/*opposite* to the bank.
A Oh, yes. I ¹⁷*am*/*can* see it. Thanks a lot.

11D p94

7 Fill in the gaps with the correct form of *book*, *stay*, *rent* or *get*.

1. I need _to book_ a hotel room.
2. My brother _____ with us at the moment.
3. How do I _____ to your place?
4. He always _____ flights online.
5. Last year we _____ a house in Spain.
6. I love _____ in hotels.
7. We _____ home last night.
8. Are you going to _____ a car?

Progress Portfolio 11

Tick the things you can do in English.

- ☐ I can ask other people about their plans.
- ☐ I can talk about exams and studying.
- ☐ I can find information in holiday adverts.
- ☐ I can ask for, give and understand directions.
- ☐ I can understand a simple email.

Extra Practice 12

Language Summary 12 p153

12A p96

1 Write the numbers.
- a nought point four *0.4*
- b a hundred and thirty-two
- c seven million
- d six thousand seven hundred
- e three point seven six
- f five hundred thousand
- g forty-one thousand, three hundred and seventeen

2 Write the superlatives.
1. slim — *slimmest*
2. easy
3. boring
4. big
5. short
6. beautiful
7. crowded
8. difficult
9. funny
10. safe

3 Fill in the gaps with the comparative or superlative of the adjective in brackets. Use *the* with the superlative if necessary.
1. This is *the most expensive* hotel in the city. (expensive)
2. My sister is *younger* than me. (young)
3. I know a _____ restaurant than this one. (good)
4. What's _____ country in the world? (hot)
5. I'm _____ person in my family. (tall)
6. That's my son's _____ shirt. (expensive)
7. She's _____ person I know. (happy)
8. Where's _____ place to have lunch near here? (good)
9. Kath's _____ than her sister. (attractive)
10. That was _____ day of the holiday. (bad)
11. You look _____ than you were last year. (thin)
12. Which of these three bags is _____ ? (heavy)

12B p98

4 Write the past participles.
1. be — *been*
2. study
3. have
4. meet
5. stay
6. lose
7. see
8. write
9. visit
10. work
11. cook
12. go

5 Put the verbs in brackets in the Present Perfect or Past Simple and complete the short answers.

A ¹ *Have* you ever *been* to Ecuador? (go)
B No, I ² _____ , but I ³ _____ to Chile. (go)
A When ⁴ _____ you _____ there? (go)
B I ⁵ _____ in 2009. (go)
A ⁶ _____ you _____ a good time? (have)
B Yes. It ⁷ _____ fantastic! (be)
A ⁸ _____ you ever _____ as a waiter? (work)
B Yes, I ⁹ _____ . In the Station Hotel.
A ¹⁰ _____ you _____ it? (enjoy)
B No, it ¹¹ _____ hard work. (be)
A When ¹² _____ you _____ there? (work)
B In 2010, after I ¹³ _____ university. (leave)

12C p100

6 Read this conversation at an airport. Fill in the gaps with these words.

~~everything~~	will	in	have
See	boarding pass	time	
forget	text		

MUM Have you got ¹ *everything* ?
AMY Yes, I ² _____ , thanks.
DAD Have you got your ³ _____ ?
A Yes, Dad. Here it is.
M Well, have a good ⁴ _____ .
A Thanks, I ⁵ _____ .
D And don't ⁶ _____ to send us a ⁷ _____ when you get there.
A Yes, of course. ⁸ _____ you ⁹ _____ three weeks. Bye!

7 Do the puzzle. Find the message.

1. Did you have a good ... ?
2. 14C is an ... seat.
3. The opposite of *depart*.
4. On a plane you're a ... .
5. Pack your ... .
6. Have you got any hand ... ?
7. You can ... tickets online.
8. Can I have your ... , please?
9. 14A is a ... seat.
10. My plane leaves from ... 7.
11. Here's your ... pass.
12. Go to the ... desk.
13. You do this before you travel.

Progress Portfolio 12

Tick the things you can do in English.
- ☐ I can say big and small numbers.
- ☐ I can compare three or more things.
- ☐ I can talk about my experiences.
- ☐ I can ask other people about their experiences.
- ☐ I can ask and answer questions at the airport.
- ☐ I can say goodbye.

Language Summary Welcome

VOCABULARY

0.1 Numbers 0–20 3 p6

0 = zero	7 = seven	14 = fourteen
1 = one	8 = eight	15 = fifteen
2 = two	9 = nine	16 = sixteen
3 = three	10 = ten	17 = seventeen
4 = four	11 = eleven	18 = eighteen
5 = five	12 = twelve	19 = nineteen
6 = six	13 = thirteen	20 = twenty

0.2 The alphabet 5 p6

Aa Bb Cc Dd Ee Ff Gg Hh Ii
Jj Kk Ll Mm Nn Oo Pp Qq Rr
Ss Tt Uu Vv Ww Xx Yy Zz

TIP • ss = *double s*, A = *capital A*, a = *small a*

0.3 Things in the classroom 8 p7

a table
a chair 
a book 
a pencil 
a pen 
a dictionary 
a CD player 
a TV 
a DVD player 
a computer 

0.4 Days of the week 9 p7

Monday
Tuesday
Wednesday
Thursday
Friday
Saturday
Sunday

REAL WORLD

0.1 Introducing yourself 2 p6

Hello, my name's Hassan.
Hi, I'm Olga.
Nice to meet you.
You too.

0.2 Classroom instructions 4 p6

Open your book.
Look at the photo on page 11. 
Do exercise 6 on your own. 
Look at the board. 
Work in pairs. 
Work in groups. 
Fill in the gaps. 
Compare answers. 
Listen and check. 
Listen and practise. 
Match the words to the pictures. 
Ask and answer the questions. 

0.3 Names 6 p7

What's your name?
(My name's/It's) Deniz.

What's your first name?
It's Marcos.

What's your surname?
Fuentes.

How do you spell that?
F–U–E–N–T–E–S.

0.4 Saying goodbye 10 p7

Goodbye/Bye, Olga.
Goodbye/Bye. See you on Tuesday.
Yes, see you.

Language Summary 1

VOCABULARY

1.1 Countries, nationalities and languages
1A 3 p8

countries *I'm from …*	nationalities *I'm …*	languages *I speak …*
Brazil	Brazilian	Portuguese
Australia	Australian	English
Argentina	Argentinian	Spanish
the USA	American	English
Germany	German	German
Italy	Italian	Italian
Mexico	Mexican	Spanish
Russia	Russian	Russian
Egypt	Egyptian	Arabic
the UK	British	English
Spain	Spanish	Spanish
Poland	Polish	Polish
Turkey	Turkish	Turkish
China	Chinese	Chinese
Japan	Japanese	Japanese
France	French	French

1.2 Jobs **1B** 3 p10

Match the jobs to pictures a–p.

1	a	a manager /ˈmænɪdʒə/	9	a musician /mjuːˈzɪʃən/
2		a doctor	10	a teacher
3		an engineer	11	a student
4		a sales assistant	12	a housewife
5		a waiter/a waitress	13	an accountant
6		a cleaner	14	a lawyer /ˈlɔːjə/
7		a police officer	15	a builder
8		an actor/an actress	16	a mechanic

- In the Language Summaries we only show the main stress in words and phrases.
- You can check the phonemic symbols (/æ/, /dʒ/, etc.) on p167.

TIPS • We use *a* or *an* with jobs: *I'm a doctor.* not *I'm doctor.*

- We can also say *I'm unemployed.* not *I'm an unemployed.* and *I'm retired.* not *I'm a retired.*
- *What do you do?* = *What's your job?*

1.3 *a* and *an* **1B** 4 p10

- We use *a* with nouns that begin with a **consonant** sound. (The consonants are *b, c, d, f*, etc.): *I'm a student.*
- We use *an* with nouns that begin with a **vowel** sound. (The vowels are *a, e, i, o, u*): *He's an actor.*

TIP • We use *a* with nouns that begin with a /j/ sound: *a university* /juːnɪˈvɜːsɪti/.

1.4 Numbers 20–100 **1C** 1 p12

20 = twenty	26 = twenty-six	50 = fifty
21 = twenty-one	27 = twenty-seven	60 = sixty
22 = twenty-two	28 = twenty-eight	70 = seventy
23 = twenty-three	29 = twenty-nine	80 = eighty /ˈeɪti/
24 = twenty-four	30 = thirty /ˈθɜːti/	90 = ninety
25 = twenty-five	40 = forty	100 = a hundred

1.5 Personal possessions **1D** 1 p14

Do you remember these things? Check on p14.

a diary	an umbrella	a coat	a laptop
a wallet	a bag	a bike/bicycle	a dress
an MP3 player	shoes	a radio	an ID card
a mobile	a camera	a suitcase	false teeth
a watch			

TIP • We can say *a mobile*, *a phone* or *a mobile phone* (US: *a cell*, *a phone* or *a cell phone*).

1.6 Plurals **1D** 2 p14

singular	plural
	+ -s
a bag	bags
a wallet	wallets
a suitcase	suitcases
	+ -es
a watch	watches
a dress	dresses
	-y → -ies
a diary	diaries

singular	irregular plural
a man	men
a woman	women
a child	children
a person	people
a tooth	teeth

TIP • We also add *-es* to words ending in *-s, -sh, -x* and *-z*: *bus* → *buses*, etc.

1.7 this, that, these, those 1D 7 p15

	here ↓	there ↗
singular	this (umbrella)	that (camera)
plural	these (watches)	those (false teeth)

- *This, that, these, those* go **before** *be* in sentences: **Those** are my shoes.
- *This, that, these, those* go **after** *be* in questions: Is **that** your bag?

GRAMMAR

1.1 be (1): positive and Wh- questions 1A 6 p9

POSITIVE (+)

I'm from Spain. (= I am)
You're in room 6. (= you are)
He's from Italy. (= he is)
She's from Brazil. (= she is)
It's Carlos Moreno. (= it is)
We're from Australia. (= we are)
They're from the UK. (= they are)

WH- QUESTIONS (?)

Where are you from?
Where's he from?
Where's she from?
What's your name?
What are your names?
Where are they from?

TIPS • *you* and *your* are singular and plural.
- We can write *Where's, What's*, etc. but not ~~*Where're, What're*~~, etc.

1.2 Subject pronouns and possessive adjectives 1A 9 p9

subject pronouns	I	you	he	she	it	we	they
possessive adjectives	my	your	his	her	its	our	their

TIPS • We use *subject pronouns* with verbs: He's a doctor. We live in Paris.
- We use *possessive adjectives* with nouns: My name's Hanif. It's her bag.

1.3 be (2): negative, yes/no questions and short answers 1B 8 p11

NEGATIVE (–)

- We make negatives with *not*.

I'm not a teacher.
You/We/They aren't from the USA. (aren't = are not)
He/She/It isn't famous. (isn't = is not)

YES/NO QUESTIONS (?)	SHORT ANSWERS	
Am I late?	Yes, you are.	No, you aren't.
Are you from Spain?	Yes, I am.	No, I'm not.
Is he/she a musician?	Yes, he/she is.	No, he/she isn't.
Is it Japanese?	Yes, it is.	No, it isn't.
Are we in room 5?	Yes, we/you are.	No, we/you aren't.
Are you from New York?	Yes, we are.	No, we aren't.
Are they French?	Yes, they are.	No, they aren't.

TIPS • We can also make negatives and negative short answers with 's or 're + **not**: She's not famous. You're not from the USA. No, you're not. No, she's not, etc.
- We can't say ~~Yes, you're. Yes, I'm~~, etc.

REAL WORLD

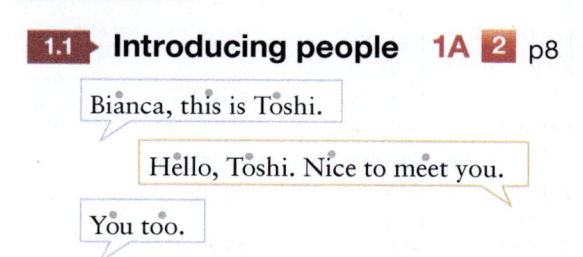

1.1 Introducing people 1A 2 p8

Bianca, this is Toshi.

Hello, Toshi. Nice to meet you.

You too.

TIP • When a person says *Nice to meet you.* we can say *You too., And you.* or *Nice to meet you too.*

1.2 Asking for personal details 1C 5 p13

What's your surname, please?
What's your first name?
What's your nationality?
What's your address?
What's your postcode?
What's your mobile number?
What's your home number?
What's your email address?

TIPS • We can say *surname* or *last name*.
- In phone numbers 0 = *oh* or *zero* and 11 = *double one*.
- We can say *What's your home number?* or *What's your landline (number)?*
- In email addresses we say: . = *dot*, @ = *at*, A = *capital A*.
- *postcode* (UK) = *zip code* (US)
- We say *How old are you?* to ask about age: **A** How old are you? **B** I'm fifty. not ~~I have fifty.~~ or ~~I'm fifty years.~~
- If you're not married, you can say you're **single**: **A** Are you married? **B** No, I'm single.
- We say *years old* for things: My bike's ten years old. not ~~My bike's ten.~~

1.3 Asking people to repeat things 1C 7 p13

I'm sorry?
Could you say that again, please?
Could you repeat that, please?

Language Summary 2

VOCABULARY

2.1 Adjectives (1)
2A 1 p16

Match the adjectives to pictures a–n.

1. new / old
2. good / bad
3. cheap / expensive
4. beautiful / ugly
5. easy / difficult
6. big / small
7. early / late
8. fast / slow
9. young / old
10. right / wrong
11. nice [m]
12. great
13. important
14. favourite

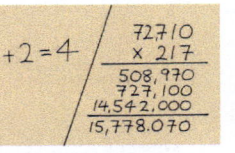

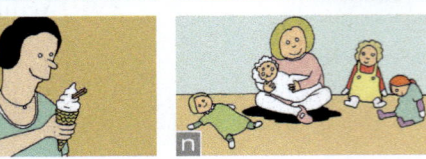

2.2 Adjective word order and *very*
2A 2 p16

- We put adjectives **after** the verb *be*: *She's **late**.*
- We put adjectives **before** a noun: *It's a **small** bag.*
- We put *very* **before** adjectives: *It's a **very** difficult question.*
- Adjectives **aren't** plural with plural nouns: *Those are my **new** shoes.*

2.3 Family **2B 2** p18

♂ male	♀ female	⚥ male and female
father (dad)	mother (mum)	parents
son /sʌn/	daughter /ˈdɔːtə/	children (kids)
brother /ˈbrʌðə/	sister	–
husband	wife (plural: wives)	–
grandfather	grandmother	grandparents
grandson	granddaughter	grandchildren
uncle	aunt /ɑːnt/	–
cousin /ˈkʌzən/	cousin	cousins

TIPS • *parents* = mother and father only; *relatives* = all the people in your family.
- *brothers* = men/boys only. We ask: *How many brothers and sisters have you got?*
- *a boyfriend/girlfriend* = a man/woman you have a romantic relationship with.
- We use **How many** (+ noun) to ask about a number: *How many children have you got?*
- *Dad*, *mum* and *kids* are informal words.

2.4 Time words **2C 1** p20

60 **seconds** = 1 **minute** /ˈmɪnɪt/   7 **days** = 1 **week**
60 **minutes** = 1 **hour**   12 **months** = 1 **year**
24 **hours** = 1 **day**

TIP • We say *two and a half hours* not *two hours and a half*.

2.5 Things in a house **2D 1** p22

Match the words to a–l in the picture.

1. a mirror
2. a desk
3. a sofa
4. a carpet
5. a door
6. a bookcase
7. a window
8. the floor
9. a plant
10. a coffee table
11. a lamp [h]
12. curtains

2.6 Prepositions of place 2D 2 p22

in   on   by

under   behind   in front of

GRAMMAR

2.1 have got: positive and negative 2A 5 p16

POSITIVE (+)	NEGATIVE (–)
I've got (= I have got)	I haven't got (= I have not got)
you've got	you haven't got
he's got (= he has got)	he hasn't got (= he has not got)
she's got	she hasn't got
it's got	it hasn't got
we've got	we haven't got
they've got	they haven't got

TIP • We use *any* with plural nouns in negatives: *He hasn't got any DVDs.*

2.2 have got: questions and short answers
2A 10 p17

YES/NO QUESTIONS (?)	SHORT ANSWERS	
Have I got any letters today?	Yes, you have.	No, you haven't.
Have you got a camera?	Yes, I have.	No, I haven't.
Has he got a DVD player?	Yes, he has.	No, he hasn't.
Has she got a DVD player?	Yes, she has.	No, she hasn't.
Has it got a DVD player?	Yes, it has.	No, it hasn't.
Have we got any CDs?	Yes, we/you have.	No, we/you haven't.
Have they got any cheap TVs?	Yes, they have.	No, they haven't.

TIPS • We use *any* with plural nouns in *yes/no* questions:
Have you got any DVDs?

• We don't use *got* in short answers:
Yes, I have. not *Yes, I have got.*

WH- QUESTIONS
What have you got in your bag?
What has he/she got in his/her bag?

2.3 Possessive 's 2B 5 p19

• We use a name + **'s** (*Pam's*, etc.) or a noun + **'s** (*husband's*, etc.) for the possessive:
Jill is Pam's sister.   My husband's name is Nick.

TIPS • For plural nouns, we write **s'**:
My parents' names are Mary and Ben.

• **'s** can mean the possessive, *is* or *has*:
Ben is Pam's father. ('s = possessive)
Jill's her sister. ('s = is)
She's got one brother. ('s = has)

• We use *Whose* to ask which person/people a thing belongs to: **A** *Whose mobile phone is it?* **B** *It's Nick's.*

REAL WORLD

2.1 Telling the time 2C 2 3 p20

one o'clock / one

five past two / two oh five

ten past three / three ten

quarter past four / four fifteen

twenty past five / five twenty

twenty-five past six / six twenty-five

half past seven / seven thirty

twenty-five to eight / seven thirty-five

twenty to nine / eight forty

quarter to ten / nine forty-five

ten to eleven / ten fifty

five to twelve / eleven fifty-five

TIPS • We can say *quarter past/to six* or *a quarter past/to six*. We don't say *fifteen past six*.

• For other times, we say *minutes*: *nineteen minutes past six* not *nineteen past six*.

2.2 Talking about the time 2C 5 p20

QUESTIONS ABOUT THE TIME

What time is it? — It's one o'clock.

What's the time, please? — It's about half past seven.

Excuse me. Have you got the time, please? — Yes, it's four fifteen.

PREPOSITIONS OF TIME

- We use **at** for times: *My English class is at ten.*
- We use **from** … **to** for length of time: *My son's class is from seven to nine thirty.*

TIP
- a.m. = 0.00–12.00   midday/noon = 12.00
- p.m. = 12.00–24.00   midnight = 24.00

2.3 Saying prices 2C 8 p21

£20 = twenty pounds
£7.50 = seven pounds fifty
40p = forty p /piː/
£29.99 = twenty-nine ninety-nine

€9 = nine euros /ˈjʊərəʊz/
€6.50 = six euros fifty
$35 = thirty-five dollars
50c = fifty cents /sents/

2.4 Buying tickets at the cinema 2C 11 p21

CUSTOMER

Can I have (two) tickets for (The Brothers), please?

(Two) tickets for (A New Day), please. One adult and one child.

How much is that?
How much are the tickets?

Here you are. What time is the film?

Right. Thanks a lot.
Thank you very much.

TICKET SELLER

Yes, of course.

That's (£23), please.
(£11.50) for adults and (£8.45) for children. So that's (£19.95), please.

It starts at (seven fifteen).
It starts in (two minutes).

You're welcome. Enjoy the film.

TIPS • We say *How much **is*** + *this*, *that* or a singular noun: *How much is that? How much is the exhibition?*

• We say *How much **are*** + *these*, *those* or a plural noun: *How much are these? How much are the tickets?*

Language Summary 3

VOCABULARY

3.1 Daily routines 3A 1 p24

Match the words/phrases to pictures a–o.

1. ☐ get up
2. ☐ go to bed
3. ☐ have breakfast /ˈbrekfəst/
4. ☐ have lunch
5. ☐ have dinner
6. ☐ start work /wɜːk/
7. ☐ start classes
8. ☐ finish work
9. ☐ finish classes
10. ☐ leave home
11. ☐ get home
12. [g] work
13. [h] study
14. ☐ sleep
15. ☐ live

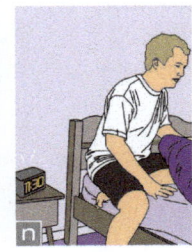

3.2 Free time activities (1) 3B 1 p26

Match the phrases to pictures a–l.

1. [f] stay in
2. [ ] go out (a lot)
3. [ ] eat out
4. [ ] go for a drink
5. [ ] go to the cinema
6. [ ] go to concerts
7. [ ] go shopping
8. [ ] phone friends/my family
9. [ ] visit friends/my family
10. [ ] have coffee with friends
11. [ ] do (a lot of) sport
12. [ ] watch (a lot of) TV/DVDs

TIPS • We say: *Do you want to go for a drink?* not *Do you want to drink something?*

• We can say **do** sport or **play** sport: *I play sport at the weekend.*

• We can say **a lot of** + noun or **lots of** + noun: *I do a lot of sport. I watch lots of DVDs.*

• *go to the cinema* (UK) = *go to the movies* (US)

3.3 Time phrases with *on*, *in*, *at*, *every* 3B 9 p27

on	in	at	every
+ day	+ part of the day	+ time	week
Saturday	the morning	nine o'clock	day
Mondays	the afternoon	half past three	month
Monday mornings	the evening	night	night
Sunday afternoon		the weekend	morning
	the week		Sunday afternoon

TIPS • We can use the singular or plural of days, parts of the day and *the weekend* to talk about routines: *I stay in on Monday/Mondays. I go out in the evening/evenings. I work at the weekend/weekends.*

• We don't use a plural with *every*: *every week* not *every weeks*.

• We say *in* the morning/afternoon/evening but *at* night.

3.4 Months 3C 3 p28

January July
February August
March September
April October
May November
June December

TIP • We use *in* with months: *My birthday's in December.*

3.5 Dates 3C 4 p28

1st	first	17th	seventeenth
2nd	second	18th	eighteenth
3rd	third	19th	nineteenth
4th	fourth	20th	twentieth
5th	fifth	21st	twenty-first
6th	sixth	22nd	twenty-second
7th	seventh	23rd	twenty-third
8th	eighth	24th	twenty-fourth
9th	ninth	25th	twenty-fifth
10th	tenth	26th	twenty-sixth
11th	eleventh	27th	twenty-seventh
12th	twelfth	28th	twenty-eighth
13th	thirteenth	29th	twenty-ninth
14th	fourteenth	30th	thirtieth
15th	fifteenth	31st	thirty-first
16th	sixteenth		

3.6 Frequency adverbs 3D 1 p30

always — usually — often — sometimes — hardly ever — never

100% ————————————————— 0%

3.7 Word order of frequency adverbs 3D 4 p30

• Frequency adverbs go **after** the verb *be*: *I'm **always** happy and I have a lot of energy.*

• Frequency adverbs go **before** other verbs: *I **sometimes** get up before 9 a.m.*

TIPS • We can use *always*, *usually* and *often* with negative verb forms: *I don't often eat out.*

• We can't use *sometimes*, *hardly ever* or *never* with negative verb forms: *We don't sometimes watch TV.*

GRAMMAR

3.1 Present Simple (1): positive (I/you/we/they) 3A 4 p24

- We use the Present Simple to talk about daily routines.
- The Present Simple positive is the same for *I*, *you*, *we* and *they*.

I **get up** at 4.30 in the morning.
You **get up** very early.
We **start** work at about 7.00.
They **have** an hour for lunch.

3.2 Present Simple (1): Wh- questions (I/you/we/they) 3A 9 p25

question word	auxiliary	subject	infinitive	
What time	do	you	get up	?
When	do	you	have	lunch?
When	do	you	finish	work?
What time	do	you	get	home?
Where	do	you	have	dinner?

TIP • Present Simple questions are the same for *I*, *you*, *we* and *they*: Who do **I** ask? When do **we** start classes? What time do **they** have lunch?

3.3 Present Simple (2): negative (I/you/we/they) 3B 4 p26

- In Present Simple negative sentences with *I*, *you*, *we* and *they* we use:
  subject + **don't** (= do not) + **infinitive**

subject	auxiliary	infinitive	
I	don't	go out	on Saturday evening.
You	don't	work	in this office.
We	don't	stay in	at the weekend.
They	don't	watch	TV in the day.

3.4 Present Simple (2): yes/no questions and short answers (I/you/we/they) 3B 6 p27

YES/NO QUESTIONS (?)				SHORT ANSWERS
auxiliary	subject	infinitive		
Do	you	eat out	a lot?	Yes, I do. / No, I don't.
Do	you	go	to concerts?	Yes, we do. / No, we don't.
Do	they	watch	TV a lot?	Yes, they do. / No, they don't.

3.5 Subject and object pronouns 3D 6 p31

subject pronouns	I	you	he	she	it	we	they
object pronouns	me	you	him	her	it	us	them

TIP • In positive and negative sentences, **subject pronouns** go **before** the verb and **object pronouns** go **after** the verb: *I often see **him** on Saturday. They don't usually call **her** in the morning.*

REAL WORLD

3.1 Phrases for special days 3C 2 p28

- a birthday /ˈbɜːθdeɪ/ — Happy birthday!
- a wedding / the birth of a new baby — Congratulations!
- a New Year's Eve party — Happy New Year!
- a wedding anniversary — Happy anniversary!

3.2 Talking about days and dates 3C 5 p28

- What day is it today? — It's Wednesday.
- What's the date today? — (It's) the fifth of March.
- What's the date tomorrow? — (It's) March the sixth.
- When's your birthday? — (It's on) June the third.

TIPS • We say: **the** fifth **of** March or March **the** fifth. We write: 5th March or March 5th.

- We use **on** with dates: *My birthday's on December 30th.*
- In the UK, 3.7.17 = 3rd July 2017 (day/month/year).
  In the USA, 3.7.17 = 7th March 2017 (month/day/year).

3.3 Suggestions 3C 9 p29

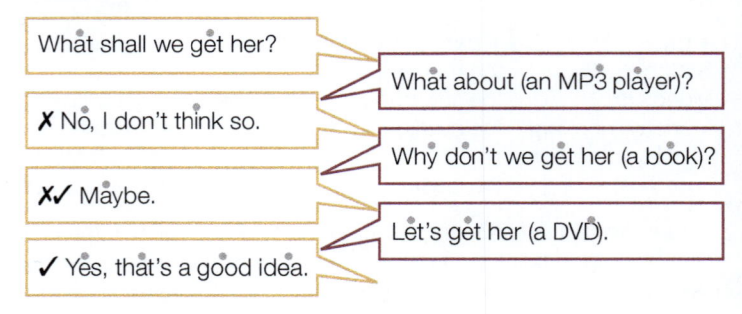

- What shall we get her?
- ✗ No, I don't think so.
- ✗✓ Maybe.
- ✓ Yes, that's a good idea.
- What about (an MP3 player)?
- Why don't we get her (a book)?
- Let's get her (a DVD).

TIPS • We can say **get** or **buy**: *What shall we get/buy her?*

- We use the infinitive after *What shall we ... ?* and *Let's ... : What shall we **do** tonight? Let's **go** to the cinema.*

Language Summary 4

VOCABULARY

4.1 Free time activities (2)
4A 1 p32

Match the phrases to pictures a–l.

1. ☐ take photos
2. ☐ go to the gym
3. ☐ watch sport on TV
4. ☐ play video games
5. ☐ play tennis
6. ☐ read books or magazines
7. ☐ go cycling
8. ☐ go swimming
9. ☐ go running
10. ☐ go clubbing
11. ☐ listen to music
12. ☐ listen to the radio

TIPS • We can say *play video games* or *play computer games*.
• *go cycling* (UK) = *go biking* (US)

4.2 Things you like and don't like **4B 1** p34

Match the words/phrases to pictures a–o.

1. ☐ reading
2. ☐ football
3. ☐ travelling
4. ☐ cats
5. ☐ shopping for clothes
6. ☐ video games
7. ☐ animals
8. ☐ dancing
9. ☐ cooking
10. ☐ dance music
11. ☐ rock music
12. ☐ jazz
13. ☐ Italian food
14. ☐ Chinese food
15. ☐ fast food

4.3 like/love/hate **4B 2** p34

- 😍 I love ...
- 😊 I really like ...
- 🙂 I like ...
- 😐 I quite like ...
- 😑 ... is/are OK.
- 🙁 I don't like ...
- 😠 I hate ...

4.4 Verb+ing **4B 3** p34

verb + verb+*ing*	verb + noun
I love **reading**.	I love **rock music**.
I really like **travelling**.	I like **books**.
I don't like **shopping** for clothes.	I quite like **Italian food**.
I hate **cooking**.	I don't like **video games**.

TIPS • We use *enjoy* + verb+*ing* to say we like doing something:
I enjoy travelling.

• We don't use *the* to talk about things we like/don't like in general:
I love books. (= books in general). *He doesn't like cats.* (= cats in general).

• We often use *very much* with *like*. We put it after the noun or verb+*ing*:
I like reading very much. not *I like very much reading.*

4.5 Food and drink (1) 4C 2 p36

a pizza

a burger and chips
(US: *French fries*)

a cheeseburger and chips

a tuna salad

a chicken salad

a mixed salad

a glass of white wine

a bottle of red wine

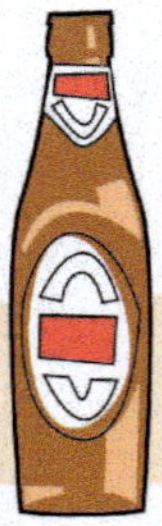

a bottle of beer

a bottle of still mineral water

a bottle of sparkling mineral water

an egg mayonnaise sandwich

a cheese and tomato sandwich

apple pie with cream

fruit salad

vanilla, strawberry, chocolate ice cream

tea and coffee

4.6 Food and drink (2) 4D 1 p38

Match the words to pictures a–y.

1. ☐ biscuits /ˈbɪskɪts/
2. ☐ milk
3. ☐ an apple
4. ☐ rice
5. ☐ yogurt /ˈjɒɡət/
6. ☐ sugar
7. ☐ toast
8. ☐ bread
9. ☐ fish
10. ☐ eggs
11. ☐ coffee
12. ☐ sausages /ˈsɒsɪdʒɪz/
13. ☐ soup
14. ☐ cheese
15. ☐ a banana
16. ☐ orange juice
17. ☐ a croissant /ˈkwæsɒ/
18. ☐ tea
19. ☐ jam
20. ☐ meat
21. ☐ fruit
22. ☐ cereal
23. ☐ olives
24. ☐ tomatoes
25. ☐ vegetables /ˈvedʒtəblz/

TIPS • biscuits (UK) = cookies (US)
• jam (UK) = jelly (US)

4.7 Countable and uncountable nouns 4D 5 p38

COUNTABLE NOUNS

- Countable nouns have a plural form: *biscuits, apples*.
- We use *a* or *an* with singular countable nouns: **a** *biscuit*, **an** *apple*.
- We don't use *a* or *an* with plural countable nouns: *biscuits* not **a** biscuits, *apples* not **an** apples.

UNCOUNTABLE NOUNS

- Uncountable nouns aren't usually plural: *milk* not milks, *rice* not rices.
- We don't use *a* or *an* with uncountable nouns: *milk* not a milk, *rice* not a rice.

TIP • Some nouns can be countable and uncountable: *I like coffee*. (uncountable = coffee in general) *Can I have a coffee, please?* (countable = a cup of coffee)

GRAMMAR

4.1 Present Simple (3): positive and negative (he/she/it) 4A 5 p32

POSITIVE (+)

- In Present Simple positive sentences with *he*, *she* and *it* we add **-s** or **-es** to the infinitive.

He **plays** video games.   She **emails** him every day.
He **watches** lots of DVDs.   It **starts** at ten o'clock..

TIP • The verb *have* is irregular. We say *he/she/it* **has**, not *he/she/it* **haves**: *He has tennis lessons every week.*

NEGATIVE (−)

- In Present Simple negative sentences with *he*, *she* and *it* we use:

subject + doesn't (= does not) + infinitive

subject	auxiliary	infinitive	
He	doesn't	like	the weather.
She	doesn't	talk	to him very often.
It	doesn't	start	at ten thirty.

4.2 Present Simple (3) positive: spelling rules (he/she/it) 4A 6 p33

spelling rule	examples
most verbs: add -s	play**s** write**s** phone**s** get**s** start**s** live**s**
verbs ending in -ch, -sh, -s, -ss, -x or -z: add -es	watch**es** /ˈwɒtʃɪz/ finish**es** /ˈfɪnɪʃɪz/
verbs ending in consonant + y: -y → -ies	stud**ies**
the verbs *go* and *do*: add -es	go**es** does /dʌz/
the verb *have* is irregular	ha**s**

4.3 Present Simple (4): questions and short answers (he/she/it) 4B 7 p35

QUESTIONS (?)

question word	auxiliary	subject	infinitive	
What	does	she	do	in her free time?
	Does	she	watch	TV a lot?
	Does	she	like	films?
What (music)	does	she	like?	

- Present Simple questions are the same for *he*, *she* and *it*:
Where does he live? What time does it start?
Does she like football? Does it start at nine o'clock?

TIP • We sometimes use a noun with some question words (*What*, *How many*, etc.): *What music do you like? How many children have you got?*

SHORT ANSWERS

Yes, he does.	No, he doesn't.
Yes, she does.	No, she doesn't.
Yes, it does.	No, it doesn't.

TIPS • We use *do* in questions with *I*, *you*, *we* and *they*. We use *does* in questions with *he*, *she* and *it*.

- We don't repeat the verb in short answers:
Yes, she does. not *Yes, she likes.*
No, she doesn't. not *No, she doesn't like.*

4.4 have or have got? 4B 7 p35

- We can use **have** or **have got** to talk about possessions and family:
She's got two dogs. = *She has two dogs.*
I haven't got any children. = *I don't have any children.*
Have you got a car? = *Do you have a car?*

- We can only use **have** to talk about meals and other activities:
I don't have breakfast. not *I haven't got breakfast.*
We often have coffee with friends. not *We often have got coffee with friends.*
Do you want to have a game of tennis? not *Do you want to have got a game of tennis?*

REAL WORLD

4.1 Requests and offers 4C 7 p37

REQUESTS

- We use **I'd/We'd like …** and **Can I/we have … ?** for requests (we want something).

> I'd/We'd like a bottle of mineral water, please.

> Can I/we have the bill, please?

OFFERS

- We use **Would you like … ?** for offers (we want to give something or help someone).

> Would you like to order now?

> What would you like to drink?

TIPS • *I'd like = I would like; We'd like = We would like.*

- We use a noun after *Can I/we have … ?*: *Can I have **the bill**, please?*

- We use a noun or the infinitive with *to* after *Would you like … ?* and *I'd/We'd like …* : *Would you like **a dessert**? I'd like **to order** now, please.*

- *the bill* (UK) = *the check* (US)

Language Summary 5

VOCABULARY

5.1 Adjectives (2) 5A 1 p40

Match these pairs of words to pictures a–j.

1. hot / cold
2. noisy / quiet
3. well / ill
4. short / tall
5. lucky / unlucky
6. different / the same
7. happy / unhappy
8. boring / interesting
9. friendly / unfriendly
10. terrible/awful / fantastic/amazing/wonderful

5.2 Years 5A 9 p41

1835 = eighteen thirty-five
1900 = nineteen hundred
1990 = nineteen ninety
2000 = two thousand
2005 = two thousand and five
2018 = twenty eighteen

TIPS • We use *in* with years: *I was born in 1990.*

• 2000–2009 = *two thousand, two thousand and one, two thousand and two,* etc.

• 2010–2099 = *twenty ten, twenty eleven,* etc.

5.3 Life events 5B 1 p42

leave school/university
meet my husband/my wife
get married/divorced
make a film/a lot of money
become a film director/famous
have children/a dream
move house/to a different country
study English/physics
write a book/a letter
win an Oscar/the lottery

TIP • *a film* (UK) = *a movie* (US)

5.4 Weekend activities 5C 1 p44

go for a walk
go for a run
clean the car
clean the house
do the washing
do your homework
write an email
write a report
go away for the weekend
go away for a couple of days
have a great time
have a bad cold
go to a party
go to your parents' house for lunch
stay with friends
stay at home all weekend

TIP • *do the washing* (UK) = *do the laundry* (US)

5.5 Adjectives (3)
5D 1 p46

Match these adjectives to pictures a–l.

1. bored /bɔːd/
2. crowded
3. *h* busy /ˈbɪzi/
4. comfortable
5. dirty
6. rich
7. dangerous
8. clean
9. poor
10. excited
11. *l* safe
12. empty

5.6 Adjectives with *very, really, quite, too* 5D 4 p47

It's **quite** big.   It's **very/really** big.   It's **too** big.

- *Too* has a negative meaning. It means *more than you want.*
- *Very, really, quite* and *too* come **after** the verb *be* and **before** adjectives: *I was **really** excited. The restaurant was **quite** dirty.*

TIP • We don't use *too* to mean *very very*: *She's really happy.* not *She's too happy.*

GRAMMAR

5.1 Past Simple (1): *be* (positive and negative)   5A 3 p40

POSITIVE (+)	NEGATIVE (–)
I was	I wasn't (= was not)
you/we/they were	you/we/they weren't (= were not)
he/she/it was	he/she/it wasn't

It was a fantastic party!
About thirty people were here.
Robert wasn't here because he was ill.
My two brothers weren't here.

5.2 Past Simple (1): *be* (questions and short answers)   5A 7 p41

QUESTIONS (?)

question word	was/were	subject	
When	was	Albert's 13th birthday?	
Where	was	the party?	
	Were	his friends	there?
	Was	the food	good?
Where	were	his grandparents?	

SHORT ANSWERS

Yes, I/he/she/it was.	No, I/he/she/it wasn't.
Yes, you/we/they were.	No, you/we/they weren't.

WAS BORN/WERE BORN

When were you born?   I was born in 1940.

Where was Matt born?   He was born in Liverpool.

TIP • We say *I was born in 1940.* not *I born in 1940.*

5.3 Past Simple (2): regular and irregular verbs (positive)   5B 4 p42

- We use the Past Simple to talk about the past. We know when these things happened.
- The Past Simple positive is the same for all subjects (*I*, *you*, *he*, *she*, *it*, *we*, *they*).

regular verbs: spelling rule	examples	
most regular verbs: add *-ed*	wanted started	worked visited
regular verbs ending in *-e*: add *-d*	moved	loved
regular verbs ending in consonant + *y*: *-y* → *-i* and add *-ed*	studied	married
regular verbs ending in consonant + vowel + consonant: double the last consonant	stopped	

TIP • There are no rules for **irregular verbs**. There is an Irregular Verb List on p167.

5.4 Past Simple (2): *Wh*- questions   5B 9 p43

- Past Simple questions are the same for all subjects (*I, you, he, she, it, we, they*).

question word	auxiliary	subject	infinitive	
What	did	James	study	at university?
When	did	he	make	*Terminator 2*?
Which (film)	did	he	make	in 3D in 2009?
Who	did	he	marry	in 1997?

TIP • Notice the difference between these questions:
Where *do* you live? (Present Simple)
Where *did* you live? (Past Simple).

REAL WORLD

5.1 Showing interest   5C 4 p45

I'm happy for you.	I'm sorry for you.	I'm surprised.	I'm not surprised.
Oh, nice. Oh, great!	Oh, dear. What a shame.	Wow! Really? You're joking!	Oh, right.

5.2 Asking follow-up questions   5C 6 p45

QUESTIONS YOU CAN ASK SOMEONE WHO …

… WAS ILL AT THE WEEKEND	… STAYED AT HOME	… WENT TO THE CINEMA	… WENT AWAY FOR THE WEEKEND
What was wrong? Are you OK now?	What did you do?	What did you see? What was it like? Who did you go with?	What was it like? Where did you go? Who did you go with? Where did you stay?

Language Summary 6

VOCABULARY

6.1 The internet — 6A 1 p48

- use the internet
- send emails
- get emails
- read a blog
- download videos or music
- go online
- have a favourite website
- chat to your friends online
- have WiFi
- use a search engine

TIPS • We can say *get emails* or *receive emails*.

• We *download music* or *videos* **onto** a *computer/laptop*. The opposite of *download* is *upload*.

• We can say *chat* **to** *someone* or *chat* **with** *someone*.

• Google is a popular *search engine*. We can also use *google* as a verb: *Why don't you google it?*

• *Email, download, video, chat* and *blog* can be nouns or verbs: *I email my brother a lot. She blogs every day.*

6.2 Mobile phones and TVs — 6B 1 p50

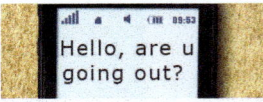

- send/get a text
- charge your phone 
- GPS 
- a channel 
- a TV programme 
- a battery  
- an app  
- turn on 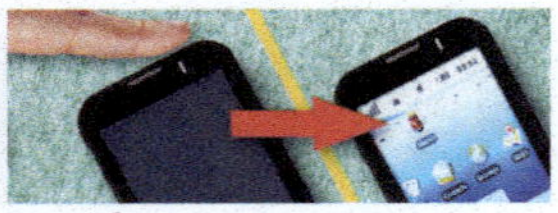
- turn off 
- record 

TIPS • You can *get* or *receive a text*. *Text* is also a regular verb: *He texted me yesterday.*

• You use *a charger* to charge your mobile phone.

• *TV programme* (UK) = *TV show* (US)

6.3 Past time phrases — 6B 2 p50

AGO
- We use *ago* to talk about a time in the past. We use it with the Past Simple: *I met him two years ago.* (= two years before now).

LAST
- We use *last* to say the day, week, etc. in the past nearest to now: *I met him last Friday.* (= the Friday before now).

- We use *last* with **days** (*last Monday*), **months** (*last March*) and in these phrases: *last night, last week, last weekend, last month, last year, last century.*

TIPS • We say *last night*, but *yesterday morning/afternoon/evening* not *last morning*, etc.

• We don't use a preposition with *last*: *last year* not *in last year*.

IN
- We use *in* with **years** (*in 1986*) and **months** (*in May*).
- We use *in the* with **decades** (*in the nineties*) and **centuries** (*in the eighteenth century*).

TIPS • We can use *on* with **days** (*on Monday*) to mean *last*: *I met him on Monday.* = *I met him last Monday.*

• *the day before yesterday* = two days ago

6.4 Verbs from news stories — 6C 2 p52

REGULAR VERBS
- damage /'dæmidʒ/ 
- sail
- die 
- receive 
- crash 
- save 

IRREGULAR VERBS
- buy (bought /bɔːt/) 
- lose /luːz/ (lost) 
- find (found) 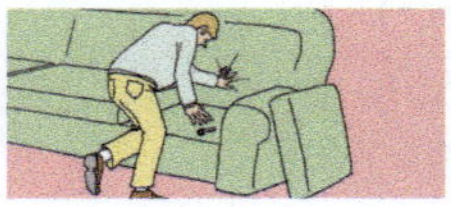
- put (put)  
- say (said /sed/) 
- tell (told)

6.5 Articles: *a*, *an* and *the* — 6D 4 p55

- We use *the* when we know which thing, person, place, etc. because there is only one: *People call him* **the father** *of video games.*

- We use *a* or *an* to talk about things or people for the first time: *The story always has* **a hero**, **a princess** *and* **a villain**.

- We use *the* to talk about a person or a thing for the second, third, etc. time: **The villain** *wants to marry* **the princess**.

TIPS • We use *the* in some fixed phrases: *at* **the** *weekend, in* **the** *evening, go to* **the** *cinema*, etc.

• We also use *the* with *first, second, third*, etc.: *Shigeru designed* **the** *first Mario Brothers game in 1983.*

GRAMMAR

6.1 Past Simple (3): negative 6A 3 p48

- To make the Past Simple negative of *be*, we use *wasn't* or *weren't* (see **GRAMMAR 5.1**):
*In the early days of the internet, search engines **weren't** very good and it **wasn't** easy for people to find the information they wanted.*

To make the Past Simple negative of all other verbs, we use:
subject + **didn't** (= did not) + **infinitive**

subject	auxiliary	infinitive	
They	didn't	like	each other at first.
They	didn't	finish	their course.
They	didn't	have	any money.

TIP • We use *didn't* for all subjects (*I, you, he, she, it, we, they*):
I didn't go out last night.
He didn't call me yesterday.

6.2 Past Simple (3): yes/no questions and short answers 6A 8 p49

YES/NO QUESTIONS (?)

auxiliary	subject	infinitive	
Did	you	go	to the cinema last week?
Did	Sergey	leave	Russia in 1978?
Did	he	go	to Maryland University?
Did	his parents	teach	computer science?

SHORT ANSWERS

Yes, I did.	No, I didn't.
Yes, you did.	No, you didn't.
Yes, he/she/it did.	No, he/she/it didn't.
Yes, we did.	No, we didn't.
Yes, they did.	No, they didn't.

TIP • Past Simple yes/no questions and short answers are the same for all subjects (*I, you, he, she, it, we, they*):
A *Did you go shopping last weekend?*
B *Yes, I did./No, I didn't.*

6.3 can/can't; could/couldn't 6B 4 p51

POSITIVE (+)

- We use **can** + **infinitive** to say that something is possible in the present.
You can choose from hundreds of TV channels.
You can watch TV programmes online.

- We use **could** + **infinitive** to say that something was possible in the past.
In the seventies you could only get three channels.
I could watch all my favourite programmes in colour!

NEGATIVE (–)

- The negative of *can* is **can't** (= cannot).
My son and daughter can't understand how people lived without them.
I can't explain this to my kids.

- The negative of *could* is **couldn't** (= could not).
You couldn't record TV programmes.
You couldn't watch TV all night.

TIPS • *Can/can't* and *could/couldn't* are the same for all subjects (*I, you, he, she, it, we, they*).

• We sometimes use *you* to mean 'people in general': *You could only get three channels.* = *People could only get three channels.*

YES/NO QUESTIONS (?)	SHORT ANSWERS
Can you watch TV online?	Yes, you can. No, you can't.
Could you record programmes in 1974?	Yes, you could. No, you couldn't.

- Yes/No questions and short answers with *can/could* are the same for all subjects (*I, you, he, she, it, we, they*):
A *Can he/she download videos?* **B** *Yes, he/she can.*
A *Could they record programmes?* **B** *No, they couldn't.*

- We can also use question words (*What, How many*, etc.) with *can/could*: *How many channels can/could you get?*

TIPS • We don't use *do, does* or *did* in questions with *can/could*: *Can you watch TV online?* not ~~*Do you can watch TV online?*~~

• We can also use *can/could* for ability in the present and the past: *My sister can speak Russian. How many languages could your grandfather speak?*

• We also use *can* for requests (*Can you help me?*) and offers (*Can I help you?*).

REAL WORLD

6.1 Talking about the news 6C 9 p53

- To start a conversation about the news, we can say:

Did you hear about that train crash?   No, where was it?

Did you read about the eighty-year-old couple and their boat?   No, what happened?

- To respond to good, bad and surprising news, we can say:

good news	bad news	surprising news
Oh, that's good.	Oh no, that's terrible. Yes, isn't it awful? Oh, dear. Are they OK?	Really? You're joking!

TIP • *News* is a singular noun. We say: *The news is terrible.* not ~~*The news are terrible.*~~

Language Summary 7

VOCABULARY

7.1 Places in a town 7A 1 p56

Match the words to pictures a–t.

1. c a building
2. ☐ a house
3. ☐ a flat
4. ☐ a square /skweə/
5. ☐ a market
6. ☐ a station
7. ☐ a bus station
8. ☐ a park
9. ☐ a museum
10. ☐ a theatre
11. ☐ a cinema
12. ☐ a hotel
13. ☐ a café
14. ☐ a shop
15. ☐ a restaurant
16. ☐ a bar
17. ☐ a pub
18. ☐ an airport
19. ☐ a beach
20. ☐ a road

TIPS • We can say *a station* or *a train station*.
• *a flat* (UK) = *an apartment* (US); *a cinema* (UK) = *a movie theater* (US)

7.2 Rooms and things in a house 7B 2 p58

Do you remember the things in the flat in Park Road? Check on p58.

rooms	furniture /ˈfɜːnɪtʃə/ and other things in a house
in the kitchen	a fridge /frɪdʒ/, a cooker, a sink, a washing machine, a table, four chairs, cupboards /ˈkʌbədz/
in the living room	a coffee table, two plants, a sofa, two armchairs
in the bathroom	a bath, a shower, a toilet, a washbasin
in the bedrooms	a double bed, a single bed, a desk, a plant, a chair, a shelf
on the balcony	three plants, a table, two chairs

TIP • The plural of *shelf* is *shelves*.

7.3 Shops 7C 1 p60

a bookshop   a clothes shop   a shoe shop   a supermarket

a kiosk   a newsagent's   a department store   a post office

a bank   a chemist's   a butcher's   a baker's

TIPS • We use **in** or **at** with shops: *You can buy magazines in/at a newsagent's.* But we say: *at a kiosk* not *in a kiosk*.
• *a shop* (UK) = *a store* (US); *a chemist's* (UK) = *a pharmacy* (US)

7.4 Things to buy 7C 3 p60

Match the words to pictures a–l.

1. ☐ stamps
2. [d] a map
3. ☐ a suitcase
4. ☐ tissues
5. ☐ aspirin
6. ☐ a lamp
7. ☐ postcards
8. ☐ a cake
9. ☐ a guide book
10. ☐ a newspaper
11. ☐ cigarettes
12. ☐ chocolate /ˈtʃɒklət/

7.5 Clothes 7D 1 p62

Match the words to pictures a–s.

1. ☐ trousers
2. ☐ shorts
3. ☐ jeans
4. ☐ a dress
5. ☐ shoes
6. ☐ a suit /suːt/
7. ☐ a skirt /skɜːt/
8. ☐ a jumper
9. ☐ trainers
10. ☐ a jacket
11. ☐ a hat
12. ☐ a tie
13. ☐ boots
14. ☐ socks
15. ☐ a T-shirt
16. ☐ a top
17. ☐ a coat
18. ☐ a cap
19. ☐ a shirt /ʃɜːt/

TIPS • We can say *a jumper* or *a sweater*.
• *trousers* (UK) = *pants* (US)
• *trainers* (UK) = *sneakers* (US)

7.6 Colours 7D 2 p62

white, black, red, blue
yellow, grey, pink, brown
orange, purple, dark green, light green

7.7 Plural nouns 7D 4 p62

nouns that look plural but can mean 'one thing'	nouns that can be singular or plural
jeans	a shoe/shoes
shorts	a sock/socks
trousers	a boot/boots
	a trainer/trainers

• We use **are** with plural nouns that mean 'one thing': *Those jeans are nice. These trousers are very big.*

• We use **some** or **any** with nouns that mean 'one thing': *I want some new shorts. Have you got any black jeans?*

TIPS • We can use **a pair of** … with both types of plural noun: *I've got a pair of red jeans/shoes.*

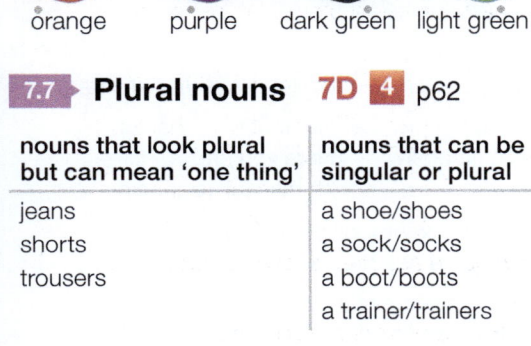

• The word *clothes* /kləʊðz/ is always plural: *These clothes are quite expensive.* If we want to use the singular, we can say *an item of clothing*.

GRAMMAR

7.1 there is/there are   7A 6 p57

	singular	plural
POSITIVE (+)	**There's** a nice beach.	**There are** lots of things to do.
NEGATIVE (–)	**There isn't** a station.	**There aren't** any restaurants.
QUESTIONS (?)	**Is there** a hotel?	**Are there** any good pubs?
SHORT ANSWERS	Yes, **there is**./No, **there isn't**.	Yes, **there are**./No, **there aren't**.

TIPS • We use *any* in negatives and questions with *there are*: *There aren't any restaurants*.
• We can say *lots of* or *a lot of*: *There are lots of/a lot of beautiful old buildings*.
• We can also make negative sentences with *no*: *There are no shops.* = *There aren't any shops.*
• The Past Simple of *there is* and *there are* is **there was** and **there were**: *There was a party last weekend. There were a lot of people at the party*.

7.2 How much … ? and How many … ?   7B 4 p58

• We use **How many … ?** with **plural countable** nouns (*tables, bedrooms, people, chairs, plants,* etc.):
How many bedrooms are there? How many people are in this room?
• We use **How much … ?** with **uncountable** nouns (*furniture, money, space, time,* etc.):
How much space is there in the flat? How much furniture have you got?

TIP • When we ask about prices we say: *How much is that?* not ~~*How much money is that?*~~: **A** *How much is that?* **B** *It's £25.*

7.3 some, any, a   7B 7 p59

• We use *a* (or *an*) in **positive** sentences, **negatives** and **questions** with singular countable nouns.
• We usually use *some* in **positive** sentences with plural countable nouns and uncountable nouns.
• We usually use *any* in **negatives** and **questions** with plural countable nouns and uncountable nouns.

	singular countable nouns	plural countable nouns	uncountable nouns
POSITIVE (+)	There's **a** cooker.	There are **some** chairs.	We'd like **some** information.
NEGATIVE (–)	There isn't **a** TV.	We haven't got **any** children.	I haven't got **any** money.
QUESTIONS (?)	Has it got **a** shower?	Are there **any** shops?	Is there **any** furniture?

REAL WORLD

7.1 What sales assistants say   7C 5 p60

Can I help you?
Do you need any help?
Yes, they're over there.
They're on the (second) floor.
Anything else?
Would you like anything else?
That's (£17.50), please.
Your pin number, please.
Would you like a bag?
Here's your change and your receipt. /rɪˈsiːt/

TIPS • *the ground floor* (UK) = *the first floor* (US)
• We say *the ground floor, the first floor, the second floor,* etc.

7.2 What customers say   7C 6 p61

SAYING WHAT YOU WANT

Have you got any (guide books for London)?
Can I have (four stamps for Europe), please?
Do you sell (suitcases)?
I'll have this one, please.

ASKING ABOUT PRICES

How much is this (map)?
How much are these (lamps)?

OTHER USEFUL PHRASES

No, that's all, thanks.
Here you are.
Thanks for your help.

TIPS • We use *one* in place of a singular noun:
A *Would you like a bag?* **B** *No, thanks. I've got one.*

• We use *ones* in place of a plural noun:
A *How much are these lamps?* **B** *The big ones are £25.*

Language Summary 8

VOCABULARY

8.1 Work 8A 1 p64

Match the words to pictures a–i.

1. a customer
2. a report
3. *g* notes
4. a letter
5. a message
6. a contract
7. a company
8. a meeting
9. a conference

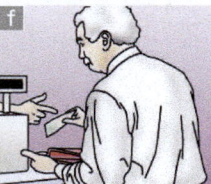

TIPS • We can **take** notes and **take** a message.
• We can **sign** a letter and **sign** a contract.
• We **work for** a company and **work in** an office.
• We **write to** a customer and **write to** a company.

8.2 Types of transport 8B 1 p66

- a car
- a plane 
- a train 
- a taxi 
- a bus 
- a tram 
- a bike 
- a scooter 
- a boat 
- a motorbike 
- a ferry 
- a coach 

TIPS • We can say *a taxi* or *a cab*.
• *a motorbike* (UK) = *a motorcycle* (US)

8.3 Travelling verbs and phrases 8B 2 p66

go by car = drive   go by bus/coach = take the bus/coach
go by bike = cycle go by ferry/boat = take the ferry/boat
go by plane = fly   go by train/tube/tram = take the train/tube/tram
go on foot = walk

TIPS • We say *go **by** bike, train*, etc., but *go **on** foot* not ~~go **by** foot~~.
• *the tube* (UK) = *the subway* (US)
• *public transport* = trains, buses, trams, etc.: *I usually travel by public transport.*

8.4 Indoor and outdoor activities 8D 1 p70

Match the verbs/phrases to pictures a–l.

1. swim
2. ski
3. surf
4. windsurf
5. sail
6. sing
7. cook
8. drive
9. speak another language
10. ride a horse
11. ride a motorbike
12. play a musical instrument

TIP • We use *can/can't* to talk about ability:
I can speak Japanese. I can't ride a horse.

8.5 Adjectives and adverbs 8D 4 p70

- We use **adjectives** to describe nouns. They usually come **before** the noun. *He's an **excellent** driver.*
- We use **adverbs** like *well, carefully*, etc. to describe verbs. They usually come **after** the verb. *He speaks Spanish **fluently**.*

spelling rule	adjective	adverb
most adverbs: add *-ly* to the adjective	careful fluent bad	careful**ly** fluent**ly** bad**ly**
adjectives ending in *-y*: *-y* → *-i* and add *-ly*	easy happy	eas**ily** happ**ily**
irregular adverbs	good fast hard	well fast hard

GRAMMAR

8.1 Present Continuous: positive and negative   8A 4 p64

- We use the Present Continuous to talk about things happening **now**:
  I'm waiting for a taxi. *They're sitting* in your office.
- We make the Present Continuous with:
  subject + **be** + **verb**+*ing*

POSITIVE (+)		NEGATIVE (–)	
I'm	verb+*ing*	I'm not	verb+*ing*
you/we/they're		you/we/they aren't	
he/she/it's		he/she/it isn't	

verb+*ing*: spelling rules	examples	
most verbs: add **-ing**	play → play**ing**	study → study**ing**
	look → look**ing**	go → go**ing**
verbs ending in -e: take off **-e** and add **-ing**	make → mak**ing**	write → writ**ing**
	live → liv**ing**	
verbs ending in consonant + vowel + consonant: double the last consonant and add **-ing**	sit → sit**ting**	run → run**ning**
	stop → stop**ping**	

TIP • We can also make negatives with **'re** or **'s** + **not**: *Danny's not doing anything. They're not looking very happy.* etc.

8.2 Present Continuous: questions and short answers
8A 9 p65

QUESTIONS (?)

question word	auxiliary	subject	verb+*ing*	
Where	is	Frank	calling	from?
	Is	the taxi	moving?	
	Are	they	having	the meeting now?
What	is	Danny	doing?	

YES/NO QUESTIONS (?)	SHORT ANSWERS	
Am I working here today?	Yes, you are.	No, you aren't.
Are you watching TV at the moment?	Yes, I am.	No, I'm not.
Is he/she/Janet answering his/her phone?	Yes, he/she is.	No, he/she isn't.
Are we going now?	Yes, you/we are.	No, you/we aren't.
Are they having the meeting now?	Yes, they are.	No, they aren't.

TIP • We can also make negative short answers with **'re** or **'s** + **not**: *No, you're not. No, she's not*, etc.

8.3 Present Simple or Present Continuous   8B 6 p67

- We use the **Present Simple** to talk about things that happen every day/week/month, etc.
- We use the **Present Continuous** to talk about things that are happening now.
- We usually use these words/phrases with the **Present Simple**:

> usually   sometimes   always   often   normally   never   hardly ever   every day/week/month

I normally go to work by train. I usually take the tube. It snows a lot in Canada every winter.

- We usually use these words/phrases with the **Present Continuous**:

> now   today   at the moment

He's watching TV now. I'm driving to work today. What are you doing at the moment?

REAL WORLD

8.1 Talking on the phone   8C 7 p69

asking to speak to people
Hello, can I speak to (Emily), please?
Hello, is that (Chris Morris)?

saying who you are
This is (Emily Wise) from (3DUK).
Speaking.
It's (Clare).

calling people back
Can I call you back (in an hour)?
I'll call you later. (I'll = I will)
Can you call me back?

other useful phrases
I got your message.
Call me on my mobile.
Hold on a moment.

TIP • When we answer the phone we say *It's (Clare).* not *I'm (Clare).*

Language Summary 9

VOCABULARY

9.1 Holiday activities   9A 1 p72

have a picnic
have a good/great/fantastic time

stay in a hotel
stay with friends or family

rent a car
rent a bike
rent a boat

go sightseeing /ˈsaɪtsiːɪŋ/
go diving
go skiing /ˈskiːɪŋ/
go camping

go to museums
go to the beach

go on holiday
go on a boat trip
go on a guided tour

travel by public transport
travel around

TIPS • We can **rent** or **hire** a car, bike, etc.
• go on holiday (UK) = go on vacation (US)

have a picnic   stay in a hotel   rent a car   go sightseeing
go diving   go skiing   go camping   go to the beach
go on holiday   go on a boat trip   go on a guided tour   travel around

9.2 Natural places   9B 1 p74

Match these words to pictures a–j.

1. [h] the countryside
2. [ ] a mountain /ˈmaʊntɪn/
3. [ ] a hill
4. [ ] a forest
5. [ ] a wood
6. [ ] a river
7. [ ] an island /ˈaɪlənd/
8. [ ] a lake
9. [ ] the sea
10. [ ] the desert

TIPS • A **mountain** is higher than a **hill**. A **forest** is bigger than a **wood**.
• **Countryside** is uncountable: *There's some beautiful countryside near the village.*
• We usually say **in** the countryside/a forest/a wood/the desert but **on** a mountain/a hill/an island.

9.3 Animals   9C 1 p76

Match these words to animals a–l.

1. [ ] a lion
2. [ ] a chicken
3. [ ] a tiger
4. [ ] a cow
5. [ ] a monkey
6. [ ] a sheep
7. [ ] a wolf
8. [ ] a rabbit
9. [ ] a mouse
10. [ ] a snake
11. [ ] a bird /bɜːd/
12. [ ] a gorilla

TIP • The plural of *sheep* is *sheep*. The plural of *wolf* is *wolves*. The plural of *mouse* is *mice*.

9.4 Verb patterns (*like doing*, *would like to do*, etc.)
9D 5 p79

- After some verbs we often use a second verb. The second verb is often in the **verb+*ing*** form (*going*, *doing*, etc.) or the **infinitive with *to*** (*to go*, *to do*, etc.): *Teenagers **like** going out on their own. I'**d like** **to go** back to the country one day.*

+ verb+*ing*	+ infinitive with *to*
like (doing)	would/'d like (to do)
enjoy (doing)	decide (to do)
love (doing)	want (to do)
stop (doing)	need (to do)
hate (doing)	would/'d love (to do)

TIPS • These verbs can also be followed by nouns or pronouns:
*You don't need **a car**.* (noun) *He hates **it**.* (pronoun)

• We can also use the infinitive with *to* after *like*, *love* and *hate*. In British English, verb+*ing* is more common: *I like **watching** TV.* In American English, the infinitive with *to* is more common: *I like **to watch** TV.*

GRAMMAR

9.1 Infinitive of purpose   9A 5 p73

- To say why we do something, we often use the infinitive with *to*: *We drove to a wildlife park **to see** some elephants. We went to Robben Island **to visit** the prison.*

TIPS • We often answer *Why … ?* questions with the infinitive with *to*: **A** *Why did you go there?* **B** ***To see** some elephants.*

• Sometimes we can also use *for* + noun: *We went to Table Mountain **for a picnic**.*

• We don't use *for to see* to say why we do something: *We drove to a wildlife park for to see some elephants.*

9.2 Comparatives   9B 4 p74

- We use comparatives to compare two places, people or things:
*Cairo is **hotter** than Sharm El Sheikh. Cairo is probably **noisier**.*

- When we compare two things in the same sentence, we use *than* after the comparative: *The Sels Hotel is smaller **than** the Shokran Hotel.*

type of adjective	spelling rule	comparative
most **1**-syllable adjectives	add *-er*	small**er** old**er**
1-syllable adjectives ending in *-e*	add *-r*	safe**r** nice**r**
1-syllable adjectives ending in consonant + vowel + consonant	double the last consonant and add *-er*	hot**ter** big**ger** but! new → new**er**
2-syllable adjectives ending in *-y*	*-y* → *-i* and add *-er*	nois**ier** happ**ier**
2-syllable adjectives not ending in *-y*	put *more* before the adjective	**more** crowded **more** common
adjectives with **3** syllables or more	put *more* before the adjective	**more** expensive **more** interesting
irregular adjectives	good bad	better worse

TIPS • The opposite of *more* is *less*: *The holiday in Sharm El Sheikh is **more** expensive. The holiday in Cairo is **less** expensive.*

• We can also use *more* with nouns: *There are **more** rooms in the Shokran Hotel.*

REAL WORLD

9.1 Deciding what to do
9C 4 p77

asking people what they want to do
What **would** you **like** to do?
Where **do** you **want** to go?
Would you **like** (to go to London)?
Do you **want** (to go to Regent's Park)?

saying what you want to do
I'**d like** (to go to the beach).
I **want** (to go to Longleat).
Yes, that's a good idea.
Not really. I'**d rather** (stay at home).

TIPS • *I'd like* = *I would like*; *I'd rather* = *I would rather*.

• *Would like* is more polite than *want*.

• We use *I'd rather* to say *I want to do this more than something else*.

• After *would rather* we use the infinitive (*go*, *do*, etc.): *I'd rather **rent** a bike.*

• After *would like* and *want* we use the infinitive with *to* (*to go*, *to do*, etc.): *I'd like **to go** swimming. I want **to rent** a car.*

Language Summary 10

VOCABULARY

10.1 Verb phrases 10A 1 p80

get fit
get stressed
spend time
spend money
carry the shopping
carry the bags
wash the windows
wash the car
take the lift
take the escalator
have a bath
have a shower
do the housework
do some exercise
get on/off a bus
get on/off a train

get fit    get stressed    carry the shopping
wash the car    take the lift    take the escalator 
do the housework    get on a bus    get off a train 

TIPS • carry the shopping (UK) = carry the groceries (US)
• take the lift (UK) = take the elevator (US)

10.2 Frequency expressions
10A 6 p81

once /wʌns/	a day		minute
twice	a week		day
three times	a month	every	week
four times	a year		month
ten times	an hour		year
etc.	etc.		etc.

TIP • We use **How often … ?** to ask about frequency:
A How often do you go to the gym? **B** Twice a week.

10.3 Appearance 10B 2 p82

age	height	body	appearance	race
He's/She's …	He's/She's …	He's/She's …	He's/She's …	He's/She's …
young	tall	thin	beautiful	white
middle-aged	short	slim	good-looking	black
old		fat	attractive	Asian
		overweight		/'eɪʒən/

eyes	hair /heə/	
He's/She's got …	He's/She's got …	He's got …
blue eyes	long/short hair	a beard /bɪəd/
brown eyes	dark/fair/blonde/grey hair	a moustache /mʊs'tɑːʃ/
green eyes		He's …
		bald /bɔːld/

overweight    slim    blonde hair    a beard    a moustache 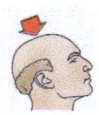   bald

TIPS • *Middle-aged* = the time in your life between young and old.

• *Slim* is more attractive than *thin*. *Overweight* is more polite than *fat*.

• *Beautiful, attractive* and *good-looking* all mean the same. *Beautiful* is usually for women. *Good-looking* is usually for men. *Attractive* can be for both men and women.

• *Asian* = from a country in Asia (India, Thailand, Japan, etc.)

• We say *long hair* not ~~long hairs~~ and *long dark hair* not ~~dark long hair~~.

10.4 Character 10B 6 p83

A **hard-working** person works very hard.
A **lazy** person doesn't like working.
A **kind** person likes doing things to help other people.
A **funny** person makes people laugh a lot.
Selfish people usually think about themselves, not other people.
An **outgoing** person is friendly and likes meeting new people.
When **reliable** people promise to do something, they always do it.
It's difficult for a **shy** person to talk to new people.
A **generous** person likes giving people money and presents.

10.5 Health problems 10C 2 p84

I've got …	a stomach ache /'stʌmək eɪk/ a headache /'hedeɪk/ toothache /'tuːθeɪk/ a sore throat /sɔː 'θrəʊt/ a cold a cough /kɒf/ a temperature /'temprətʃə/
I feel …	ill terrible sick better
my … hurts	back arm foot leg

TIPS • We can say *I've got **a** stomach ache/toothache* or *I've got stomach ache/toothache*, but not ~~I've got headache~~.

• We can also say: *I'm ill/sick/better* but not ~~I'm terrible~~.

• *I'm sick* can also mean the same as *I'm ill*. In American English, *sick* is more common: *I can't come to work today. I'm sick.* In British English *I feel sick.* usually means *I want to be sick.*

10.6 Treatment 10C 3 p84

go to bed
go home
go to the doctor
go to the dentist
stay at home
stay in bed
take the day off
take some painkillers
take some cough medicine
take some antibiotics

10.7 Seasons 10D 1 p86

spring   summer   autumn /ˈɔːtəm/   winter

TIPS • We use *in* with seasons: *in (the) winter*.
• *autumn* (UK) = *fall* (US)

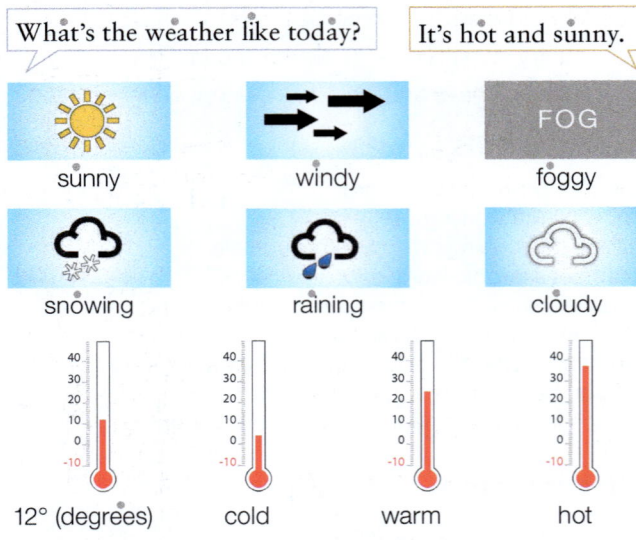

10.8 Weather 10D 4 p87

What's the weather like today?   It's hot and sunny.

sunny   windy   foggy
snowing   raining   cloudy

12° (degrees)   cold   warm   hot

10.9 Word building 10D 6 p87

noun	adjective	adjective	noun
sun	sunny	ill	illness
wind	windy	happy	happiness
cloud	cloudy	sad	sadness
fog	foggy	fit	fitness

Noun: *There isn't much **sun** today. His **illness** lasted a year.*
Adjective: *I love **sunny** days. He was **ill** on holiday.*

TIP • For *snow* and *rain* we usually use the verb, not the adjective: *It's snowing/raining.* not *It's snowy/rainy.*

GRAMMAR

10.1 Imperatives 10A 4 p81

- We often use imperatives to give strong advice.
- The positive imperative is the same as the infinitive (*go*, *do*, etc.):
Walk up and down stairs. *Get off* the bus one stop earlier.
- The negative imperative is *Don't* + infinitive (*Don't go*, *Don't do*, etc.):
Don't take lifts. *Don't drive* to the supermarket once a week.

TIP • We also use imperatives to give orders and instructions:
Go home! Don't write anything.

10.2 should/shouldn't 10A 9 p81

- We use *should* and *shouldn't* to give advice.
- We use *should* to say something is a **good** thing to do:
You should do some exercise three times a week.
- We use *shouldn't* to say something is a **bad** thing to do:
You shouldn't eat so many pizzas and biscuits.
- After *should* and *shouldn't* we use the **infinitive**: *You should eat more fruit.* not *You should to eat more fruit.*

TIPS • To ask for advice, we can say: *What should I do?*
• In spoken English, *should/shouldn't* is more common than the imperative for advice.

10.3 Questions with *like* 10B 8 p83

- We use *What's* (*'s = is*) *he/she like?* to ask for a general description. We often ask this when we don't know the person. The answer can include character and physical appearance:
She's friendly and outgoing. And she's very beautiful.
- We use *What does he/she look like?* to ask about physical appearance only: *She's tall and slim, and she's got long dark hair.*
- We use *What does he/she like doing?* to ask what people enjoy doing in their free time: *She likes clubbing and going to restaurants.*

TIPS • *How is he/she?* asks about health, not personality:
A *How's your mum?* **B** *She's fine, thanks.*

• We don't use *like* in answers to questions with *What's he like?* and *What does she look like?*
A *What's he like?* **B** *He's kind.* not *He's like kind.*
A *What does she look like?* **B** *She's very tall.* not *She's like very tall.*

REAL WORLD

10.1 Talking about health 10C 5 p85

asking about someone's health	expressing sympathy	giving advice
Are you OK?	Oh, dear.	Why don't you (go home)?
Are you alright?	I hope you get better soon.	You shouldn't (go to work today).
What's wrong?		You should (go to the doctor).
What's the matter?	Get well soon.	Take the day off.

TIP • After *Why don't you … ?* we use the infinitive:
Why don't you go home?

Language Summary 11

VOCABULARY

11.1 New Year's resolutions
11A 2 p88

get a new job
get fit

work hard
work less

lose three kilos
lose weight /weɪt/

have a holiday
have fun

do a computer course
do more exercise

stop working at weekends
stop smoking

move to another country
move house

not eat sweet things
not eat chocolate cake

TIPS • We can *do a course* or *take a course*, but not ~~make a course~~.

• We can also *do/take a course in* something: *I'm going to do a course in engineering.*

• *Exercise* is also a verb: *I exercise every day.*

lose weight  | have a holiday  | do more exercise
stop smoking  | move house  | not eat sweet things 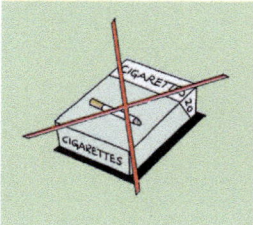

11.2 Studying   **11B** 1 p90

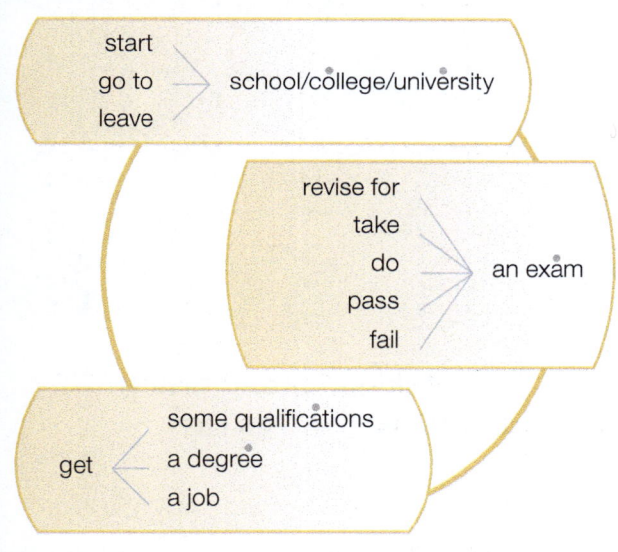

start
go to → school/college/university
leave

revise for
take
do → an exam
pass
fail

get → some qualifications
a degree
a job

TIPS • We *get a degree* when we finish university. We *get some qualifications* when we pass any official exams, for example when you leave school, do a course, etc.

• We can say *revise for an exam* or *study for an exam*.

revise for an exam  | take an exam
pass an exam  | fail an exam  | get a degree 

11.3 Collocations   **11D** 5 p95

• **Collocations** are words/phrases that are often used together. They can be:
verb + **noun** (book **a flight**, take **photos**, etc.)
verb + **preposition** (stay **in** a hotel, go **for** a run, etc.)
verb + **adjective** (get **married**, become **famous**, etc.)
verb + **adverb** (work **hard**, speak **fluently**, etc.)

book	stay	rent	get
a flight /flaɪt/	with (you)	a motorbike	to your place
a hotel room	in (the USA)	a car	a taxi
a train ticket	in a hotel	a flat	married
a seat on a train	at home	a house	home
a table in a restaurant			divorced

TIP • *A flight* is a journey by plane: *My flight to Los Angeles leaves at 10.30.*

GRAMMAR

11.1 be going to (1): positive and negative 11A 5 p88

I'm going to do a computer course.

I'm not going to eat sweet things any more.

- These sentences talk about the **future**.
- The people decided to do these things **before** they said them.
- We use *be going to* + infinitive for **future plans**.

subject	be (+ not)	going to	infinitive	
We	're (= are)	going to	get	fit.
Val	's (= is)	going to	stop	smoking.
David	's	going to	lose	weight.
I	'm (= am)	going to	do	more exercise.
I	'm not	going to	eat	sweet things any more.

TIP • With the verb *go*, we usually say *I'm going to Spain*. not *I'm going to go to Spain*. But both forms are correct.

11.2 be going to (1): Wh- questions 11A 8 p89

question word	be	subject	going to	infinitive	
What	are	you	going to	do	next year?
Where	's	she	going to	live?	
Where	's	he	going to	study?	
When	are	they	going to	start	getting fit?

11.3 be going to or might 11B 4 p91

- We use *be going to* to say a future plan is **decided**:
  I'm going to meet some friends in town at seven.
- We use *might* to say something in the future is **possible**, but **not decided**:
  I might go to the party or I might go out for a meal with Sam.
- After *might* we use the **infinitive**: *I might stay at home and watch a film.*

TIPS • *Might* is the same for all subjects (*I*, *you*, *he*, *she*, *it*, *we*, *they*).
• To make questions with *might*, we usually use *Do you think … ?*:
Do you think he might come to the party?

11.4 be going to (2): yes/no questions and short answers
11B 10 p91

YES/NO QUESTIONS (?)	SHORT ANSWERS	
Am I going to be late?	Yes, you are.	No, you aren't.
Are you going to look for a job?	Yes, I am.	No, I'm not.
Is he/she going to sell his/her car?	Yes, he/she is.	No, he/she isn't.
Are we going to stop working?	Yes, we/you are.	No, we/you aren't.
Are you going to move house?	Yes, we are.	No, we aren't.
Are his parents going to help him?	Yes, they are.	No, they aren't.

TIP • We can also answer *yes/no* questions with *(Yes,) I might*:
A *Are you going to buy it?* **B** *I might.*

REAL WORLD

11.1 Directions 11C 3 p92

Match the phrases to pictures a–i.

1. ☐ turn right
2. ☐ turn left
3. ☐ go over the bridge
4. ☐ go past the pub
5. ☒ c go along this road/street
6. ☐ it's on the/your left
7. ☐ it's on the/your right
8. ☐ it's opposite
9. ☐ it's next to

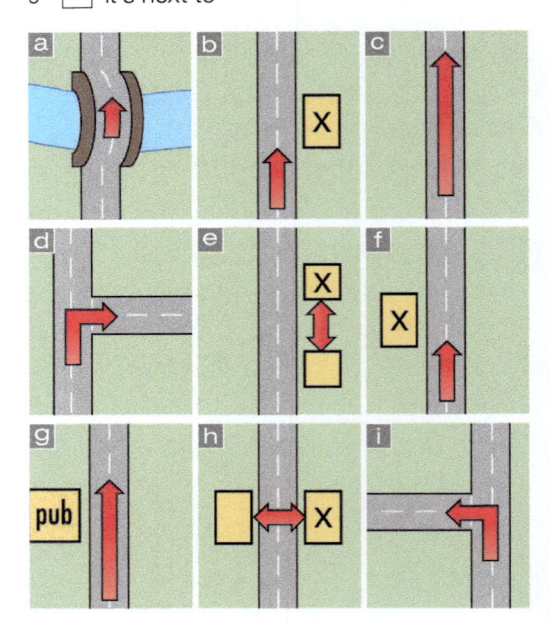

11.2 Asking for and giving directions 11C 7 p93

ASKING FOR DIRECTIONS

Excuse me. Is there (a newsagent's) near here?
Excuse me. Where's (the post office)?
Excuse me. How do I/we get to (the market)?

GIVING DIRECTIONS

There's one in (Berry Street).
Go along this road/street and turn right/left.
Go past the pub.
Go over the bridge.
(The newsagent's) is on the/your right/left.
It's opposite (the supermarket).
It's next to (the café).
It's over there.
You can't miss it.

IF YOU CAN'T GIVE DIRECTIONS

Sorry, I don't know.
Sorry, I don't live around here.

Language Summary 12

VOCABULARY

12.1 Big and small numbers   12A 1 p96

- For numbers with a decimal point (.) we say *point*:
  0.2 = *nought point two* or *zero point two*
  2.45 = *two point four five*

TIPS • 0 = *nought* /nɔːt/ or *zero* (or *oh* when we say phone numbers).

- In English we write *7.5* not *7,5*. We use a decimal point (.) not a comma (,).

- We can use **one** or **a** with *hundred*, *thousand* and *million*:
  100 = *a hundred* or *one hundred*
  1,000 = *a thousand* or *one thousand*
  1,000,000 = *a million* or *one million*

- For long numbers we use **and** after *hundred* (but not after *thousand* or *million*):
  127 = *a hundred and twenty-seven*
  850,000 = *eight hundred and fifty thousand*
  But 2,300 = *two thousand, three hundred* not ~~*two thousand and three hundred*~~

- We don't add a plural *-s* to *hundred*, *thousand* and *million*:
  32,470 = *thirty-two thousand, four hundred and seventy*
  50,000,000 = *fifty million* not ~~*fifty millions*~~
  But we can say: *hundreds/thousands/millions of* … :
  There were hundreds of people at the concert.
  We saw thousands of birds.

12.2 Things and places at an airport   12C 2 p100

Match the words/phrases to pictures a–m.

1. ☐ a passport
2. ☐ a boarding pass
3. ☐ hand luggage /ˈlʌɡɪdʒ/
4. ☑ d a ticket
5. ☐ pack your bags
6. ☐ passengers
7. ☐ a flight number
8. ☐ a gate
9. ☐ a check-in desk
10. ☐ a bag drop
11. ☐ a window seat
12. ☐ a middle seat
13. ☐ an aisle /aɪl/ seat

TIPS • We can say *a boarding pass* or *a boarding card*.
• When a flight is **on time**, it leaves or arrives at the correct time. When a flight is **delayed**, it leaves or arrives later than the correct time.

GRAMMAR

12.1 Superlatives   12A 5 p97

- We use **comparatives** (*bigger*, *more expensive*, etc.) to compare two things (see GRAMMAR 9.2).
- We use **superlatives** to compare three or more things.

type of adjective	spelling rule	superlative
most 1-syllable adjectives	add *-est*	long**est** short**est**
1-syllable adjectives ending in *-e*	add *-st*	safe**st** nice**st**
1-syllable adjectives ending in consonant + vowel + consonant	double the last consonant and add *-est*	big**gest** hot**test** but! new → newest
2-syllable adjectives ending in *-y*	*-y* → *-i* and add *-est*	heav**iest** happ**iest**
2-syllable adjectives not ending in *-y*	put *most* before the adjective	**most** boring **most** crowded
adjectives with 3 syllables or more	put *most* before the adjective	**most** expensive **most** beautiful
irregular adjectives	good bad	best worst

TIPS • We say: *The best place* **in** *the world.* not ~~*of the world*~~ or ~~*for the world*~~.

• Before superlatives in sentences we use:
the
Sanjay Kumar Sinha taught **the** *longest lesson in the world.*
The *shortest film in the world is 'Colin'.*

possessive 's
It was probably the **world's** *hottest soup.*
He's my **sister's** *oldest relative.*

possessive adjectives
Matt's **my** *best friend.*
It was **his** *most important book.*

• *the* + superlative is the most common form.

12.2 Present Perfect: positive and negative 12B 3 p98

- We use the **Present Perfect** to talk about experiences in life until now. We don't say when they happened:
I've been to about forty countries.
- We use the **Past Simple** if we say when something happened:
Two weeks ago I went to Mexico.

TIP • We can't use the Present Perfect if we say a time: *I went to England in 2011.* not *I've been to England in 2011.*

POSITIVE (+)

I/you/we/they + 've (= have) + past participle
he/she/it + 's (= has) + past participle

I've stayed in some of the world's best hotels.
We've had lots of other jobs.
He's written travel articles about lots of amazing places.

NEGATIVE (−)

I/you/we/they + haven't (= have not) + past participle
he/she/it + hasn't (= has not) + past participle

I haven't been to Australia.
They haven't had a holiday together.
He hasn't been to South America before.

TIP • We can say *I haven't …* or *I've never …* :
I've never been to Australia. They've never had a holiday together.

PAST PARTICIPLES

- For **regular verbs**, add -ed or -d to the infinitive: *work → worked, live → lived*, etc. The Past Simple and past participles of regular verbs are the same (see **GRAMMAR 5.3**).
- For **irregular verbs**, there are no rules. Look at the past participles in the Irregular Verb List, p167.

TIP • *go* has two past participles, *been* and *gone*. When we use the Present Perfect to talk about our experiences we usually use *been*:
I've been to Italy. (I went to Italy in the past and I'm not in Italy now).

12.3 Have you ever … ? questions and short answers 12B 7 p99

- We use the **Present Perfect** to ask about people's experiences. If the answer is *yes*, we use the **Past Simple** to ask for (or give) more information:
A *Have you ever been to Peru?*   B *Yes, I have./No, I haven't.*
A *Did you have a good time?*   B *Yes, I did./No, I didn't.*

YES/NO QUESTIONS (?)	SHORT ANSWERS	
Have I ever worked in a restaurant?	Yes, you have.	No, you haven't.
Have you ever been to Canada?	Yes, I/we have.	No, I/we haven't.
Has he ever lived in the USA?	Yes, he has.	No, he hasn't.
Has she ever written a book?	Yes, she has.	No, she hasn't.
Have we ever been there before?	Yes, we have.	No, we haven't.
Have they ever worked in an office?	Yes, they have.	No, they haven't.

TIP • *ever* + Present Perfect = any time in your life until now. We often use *ever* in questions.

REAL WORLD

12.1 At the airport 12C 3 p100

THINGS YOU HEAR AT THE CHECK-IN DESK OR BAG DROP

Can I have your passport, please?
How many bags are you checking in?
Did you pack your bags yourself?
And have you got any hand luggage?
Here's your boarding pass. You're in seat (16F).
No, (it's) an aisle seat.
Gate (twelve).
Boarding is at (fifteen thirty).
Enjoy your flight.

THINGS YOU CAN SAY AT THE CHECK-IN DESK OR BAG DROP

Is that a window seat?
Which gate is it?
Is the flight on time?

12.2 Saying goodbye 12C 6 p101

Have you got	everything? your passport? your boarding pass?	Yes, I have, thanks.
Have a	nice holiday. good time. good trip.	Thanks, I will.
Don't forget to send me/us	a text. an email. a postcard.	Yes, of course.
See you	in a month. soon. on the next course.	Yes, see you.

TIP • When we aren't going to see someone between Friday and Monday, we often say: *Have a nice/good weekend.* We often reply: *You too.*

Audio and Video Scripts

CD1 ▶ 4

Do exercise 6 on your own. | Listen and practise. | Look at the board. | Listen and check. | Work in pairs. | Match the words to the pictures. | Fill in the gaps. | Ask and answer the questions. | Work in groups. | Look at the photo on page 11. | Compare answers. | Open your book.

CD1 ▶ 6

class | photo | please | listen | nineteen

CD1 ▶ 7

MARCOS Hello. Sorry I'm late.
TEACHER No problem. What's your first name?
M It's Marcos.
T What's your surname?
M Fuentes.
T How do you spell that?
M F-U-E-N-T-E-S.
T Welcome to the class, Marcos.
M Thank you.

CD1 ▶ 8

A CAMILLE Hello, is this the English class?
   TEACHER Yes, it is.
C Oh, good. Sorry I'm late!
T No problem. What's your first name?
C Camille.
T How do you spell that?
C C-A-M-I-double L-E.
T And what's your surname?
C It's Laurent.
T And how do you spell that?
C L-A-U-R-E-N-T.
T Thanks, Camille. Welcome to the class.

B BARTEK Hello, sorry I'm late.
   TEACHER No problem. What's your name?
B My name's Bartek.
T How do you spell that, please?
B B-A-R-T-E-K.
T And what's your surname?
B Kowalski.
T OK. And how do you spell that?
B K-O-W-A-L-S-K-I.
T Thanks. Welcome to the class, Bartek.
B Thank you.

CD1 ▶ 11

ANSWER Tuesday

CD1 ▶ 15

ANSWERS 3 Spain 4 Australia 5 Italy, Brazil, the UK

CD1 ▶ 18

A A What's your phone number?
   B Er … wait a minute … it's 01221 960744.
   A 01221 960744?
   B Yes, that's right.
B A What's Tina's mobile number?
   B It's 07906 394896.
   A 07906 … er …
   B 394896.
C A What's the phone number of your hotel?
   B It's 0119 498 0691. I'm in room 302.
   A OK, thanks.
D A What's your number in Australia?
   B It's 0061 02 9967 2315.
   A So that's 0061 … 02 …
   B … 9967 2315.
   A OK. Thanks.

CD1 ▶ 20

ANSWERS 1 engineer 2 doctor 3 musician 4 police officer 5 accountant

CD1 ▶ 21

I'm not a teacher. | We aren't from the USA. | She isn't famous. | Are you from Spain? | Yes, I am. | No, I'm not. | Is she a musician? | Yes, she is. | No, she isn't. | Are you from New York? | Yes, we are. | No, we aren't.

CD1 ▶ 23

forty | seventeen | eighty | sixty | eighteen fourteen | sixteen | seventy

VIDEO ▶ 1   CD1 ▶ 26

WOMAN Right, first I need some personal details. What's your surname, please?
P It's Whatling.
W And how do you spell that?
P W-H-A-T-L-I-N-G.
W OK, thanks. What's your first name?
P Paul.
W And what's your nationality?
P I'm British.
W OK. What's your address?
P It's 29 Elmore Road, Bristol.
W How do you spell Elmore?
P E-L-M-O-R-E.
W And what's your postcode?
P BS13 6QT.
W I'm sorry?
P BS13 6QT.
W Great, thanks a lot. What's your mobile number?
P 07969 831016.
W 07969 …
P … 831016.
W OK. And what's your home number?
P It's 0117 480 6544.
W Could you say that again, please?
P 0117 480 6544.
W Right. And the last question … what's your email address?
P It's paul ninety-nine at webmail dot com.
W Could you repeat that, please?
P Yes, paul ninety-nine at webmail dot com.
W OK, thanks a lot. Now, what type of car would you like?

CD1 ▶ 30

this → What's this? → What's this in English? | that → What's that? → What's that in English? | these → What are these? → What are these in English? | those → What are those?

CD1 ▶ 32

British | teacher | thirty | mobile Japan | address | thirteen | Brazil bicycle | manager | Germany | Mexican computer | musician | umbrella | mechanic seventeen | engineer | Japanese | unemployed

CD1 ▶ 34

I've got an old car. | You've got a new mobile. | He's got a big TV. | She's got a new bicycle. | We've got a beautiful cat. | They've got an old DVD player. | I haven't got a laptop. | We haven't got a car. | He hasn't got a diary.

CD1 ▶ 35

INTERVIEWER Hello. Have you got time to answer some questions? It's a product survey about computers, cameras, TVs, that sort of thing.
MARY Yes, OK.
ALAN Sure.
I Oh, good. Thanks. Right, first question. Have you got a laptop?
A No, I haven't, but I've got an old computer.
I And you, madam? Have you got a laptop?
M Yes, I have, but it's not very good.
I Thanks. Right, next question. Have you got a camera?
M Yes, I have.
I And what about you, sir? Have you got a camera?
A No, I haven't. I take photos with my mobile.
I Right. And have you got an MP3 player?
M What's an MP3 player?
A They're for music. They're very small.
M Oh, those things. No, I haven't got one of those.
I And you, sir? Have you got an MP3 player?
A Yes, I have.
I Have you got a radio?
A No, I haven't. I listen to the radio on my mobile.
I And you, madam?
M Yes, I have.
I Thanks. Right, the last question. Have you got a DVD player?
A Yes, I have. I watch a lot of DVDs.
I And you, madam? Have you got a DVD player?

M Yes, I have, but it's very old.
I Right. Well, madam, we've got some very good DVD players at the moment …

CD1 ▶ 37

ANSWERS 2 children 4 daughter
5 father 6 mother 7 brother 9 sisters
11 grandchildren 12 grandsons
13 granddaughter 15 uncle 16 cousins
18 grandfather 19 grandmother

CD1 ▶ 38

Alan's → Pam is Alan's aunt. | Martina's → Greg is Martina's husband. | Florence's → Robbie is Florence's brother. | Ben's → Mary is Ben's wife. | Ben and Mary's → Florence is Ben and Mary's granddaughter.

CD1 ▶ 39

JILL Luke, come and look at these photos of my family.
LUKE OK.
J Right … This is my sister, Pam, and her husband, Nick.
L Pam's an English teacher, isn't she?
J Yes, that's right.
L What about Nick?
J He's a doctor.
L Oh, right. How many children have they got?
J Two. A boy and a girl. Look, here's a photo of them.
L Hmm. How old are they?
J Er, Robbie is six and Florence is about ten months old.
L They're beautiful.
J Yes, they are. And this is my brother, Greg. He's an engineer.
L And who's that?
J That's Greg's wife, Martina. She's from Italy. Oh, and that's their son, Alan.
L How old is he?
J Alan – he's nineteen. He's a student at Cambridge University.
L Really?
J Yes, he loves it there. And these are my parents. They're retired now.
L How old are they?
J Mum's seventy and Dad's seventy-three. And that's Lily, my favourite member of the family.
L Sorry, where?
J There.
L Oh, the cat!
J Yes, she's beautiful!

CD1 ▶ 40

1 A What time is it?
   B It's one o'clock.
2 A What's the time, please?
   B It's about half past seven.
3 A Excuse me, have you got the time, please?
   B Yes, it's four fifteen.
   A Thanks a lot.

CD1 ▶ 42 **CD1 ▶ 44**

A Thank you for calling Brent Gallery. We're open Mondays to Fridays from 10 a.m. to 6.30 p.m. and on Saturday and Sunday from 10 a.m. to 4.30 p.m. The exhibition now showing is Mexican Art. **[end of CD1 ▶ 42]** Ticket prices are £9.50 for adults and £6.50 for children. For more information about the exhibition go to our website at www.brentgallery.org.uk.

B Welcome to the FilmWorld information and booking line. Here are the films showing at this cinema from Friday June the 10th to Thursday June the 16th. *A New Day*, certificate 12, showing at 4.40, 7.00 and 9.20. *The Brothers*, certificate 15, showing at 5.00, 7.15 and 9.30. **[end of CD1 ▶ 42]** Ticket prices are £11.50 for adults and £8.25 for children under 16. To book tickets please press 1 or go to our website at www.filmworld.co.uk.

VIDEO ▶ 2 CD1 ▶ 45

JOSH Mum?
ALISON Yes, Josh?
J Can I have some popcorn?
A Yes, OK. Here's some money.
J And can I have a Coke?
A Yes, OK. But hurry up.
LOUISE Have you got any money, Chris? If not, I've got my credit card.
CHRIS No, it's OK. I've got some money. … Hi. Can I have two tickets for *The Brothers*, please?
TICKET SELLER Yes, of course.
C How much is that?
TS That's £23, please.
C Here you are.
TS Thanks.
L What time is the film?
TS It starts at seven fifteen. Here are your tickets. You're in screen 2.
C Thanks a lot.
TS You're welcome. Enjoy the film.
L We've got 20 minutes before the film starts.
C OK, let's have a drink first.
L Good idea.
A Hello. Can I have two tickets for *A New Day*, please? One adult and one child.
TS Yes, of course.
A How much are the tickets?
TS £11.50 for adults and £8.25 for children. So that's £19.75, please.
A Here you are. What time's the film?
TS It starts in two minutes. Here are your tickets. You're in screen 1.
A Thank you very much.
TS You're welcome. Enjoy the film.
A Thanks. Bye. … Hurry up, Josh. The film starts in two minutes.
J OK.

CD1 ▶ 47

NICK Pam, where's my suitcase?
PAM Here it is, behind the sofa.
N And have you got my keys?
P No, Nick, of course I haven't. They're on the desk. By the computer.
N OK, thanks. And where's my mobile?
P Oh, I don't know. Look, there it is, under my coat. There, on the sofa!
N Thanks.
ROBBIE Mum, where are my new shoes?
P They're under the chair by the window.
R And where's my bag?
P Oh, Robbie. It's by the door. Where it always is.
R Thanks, Mum.
N Right. Are you ready, Robbie?
R Yes.
P Have you got your school books?
R Yes, they're in my bag. Look.
N Oh no! Where's my passport?
P It's on the table by the window. In front of the plant.
N Oh yes, thanks.
P Bye, love. See you on Sunday.
N Bye.
P Right … hmm … where's the baby?

CD1 ▶ 53

FREDDIE Hello, Jeanette!
JEANETTE Oh, hello … er …
F Freddie. Freddie Roberts.
J You don't work in this office, do you?
F No, I work in the King Street office.
J Oh … er … yes, of course.
F Good party, isn't it?
J Yes, very nice.
F Er, Jeanette. Do you go out after work? On Fridays, maybe?
J No, I don't, sorry. I'm always very tired so I just go home.
F Right. What do you do in the evenings?
J I have dinner and watch TV.
F Do you go to the cinema?
J No, I don't. But I watch a lot of DVDs.
F Yes, me too. What do you do at the weekends?
J Well, on Saturday morning I go shopping. And I don't go out on Saturday evening. I stay in and watch TV.
F Right.
J And on Sunday afternoon I visit my parents.
F Oh, OK. Do you go to concerts?
J Yes, I do. You know, when I have time.
F Well, um … I've got two tickets for a concert on Sunday evening. Do you want to come with me?
J Er … thanks, Freddie, but there's a problem – well, 3 problems, actually.
F Oh?
J I'm married! And I've got two children!
F Oh … well, no problem. Oh look, there's Catherine. Er, I've got something I want to ask her. Excuse me.
J Really!

CD1 55
1. What do you do in the evenings? (x2)
2. Do you go to the cinema? (x2)
3. What do you do at the weekends? (x2)
4. Do you go to concerts? (x2)

CD1 56
1. A Do you go out a lot in the week?
   B Yes, we do.
2. A Do you visit your parents at the weekend?
   B Yes, I do.
3. A Do you go to concerts at the weekend?
   B No, we don't.
4. A Do you go shopping on Saturdays?
   B Yes, I do.
5. A Do your parents go out on Saturday evenings?
   B No, they don't. They stay in and watch TV.

CD1 58
1. I'm 30 today.
2. We've got a new baby daughter.
3. Today is our 40th wedding anniversary.
4. Guess what! We're getting married!
5. … 5, 4, 3, 2, 1 …

CD1 61
1. A What day is it today?
   B It's Wednesday.
2. A What's the date today?
   B It's the fifth of March.
3. A What's the date tomorrow?
   B It's March the sixth.
4. A When's your birthday?
   B It's on June the third.

CD1 62
1. A When do you start your English course?
   B On September the fifth.
2. A When's your birthday, Sam?
   B It's on the thirteenth of December.
   A Oh, that's on Tuesday!
3. A When's Mother's Day?
   B It's on the fourteenth of March.
   A Oh, that's next week.
4. A When do you start your new job?
   B On the second of July.
5. A Excuse me. What's the date today?
   B It's October the thirtieth.
   A Thanks a lot.
6. A When's Matt and Sarah's wedding anniversary?
   B I think it's the first of February.
   A Oh, no! That's today!

VIDEO 3   CD1 63
LOUISE Here's your tea.
CHRIS Thanks a lot.
L Chris?
C Yes?
L What's the date today?
C It's the twenty-ninth. Why do you ask?
L It's Sophie's birthday on Thursday.
C Is it?
L Yes, and I haven't got a present for her.
C Oh. Have you got a card?
L Yes, I have.
C Oh, well. That's OK, then.
L But I want to get her a present too. She's one of our best friends.
C OK then. Let's get her a present.
L Right. What shall we get her?
C Oh, I don't know. What about an MP3 player?
L No, I don't think so. I think she's got one.
C OK then. Why don't we get her a book?
L Maybe. But she's got lots of books.
C Hmm. This is difficult, isn't it?
L Yes, it is.
C I know! Let's get her a DVD.
L Yes, that's a good idea. Sophie and Marcus watch a lot of DVDs.
C And I think they've got a new TV.
L OK. Which DVD shall we get?
C Let's get her a film. Then we can watch it first!
L Chris!

CD1 65
JEANETTE Dominic, do you think I'm a happy person in the morning?
DOMINIC Yes, sometimes. Why do you ask?
J It's this questionnaire. 'Are you an early bird or a night owl?'. I'm sometimes happy in the morning, but I don't have a lot of energy … so that's b.
D What are the other questions?
J Here, come and have a look. Question two, well, that's easy. I hardly ever get up before nine at the weekend.
D Yes, that's true.
J The next question is about parties.
D Oh, that's easy. When we go to a party, you never stay to the end.
J Yes, that's true, I always leave early, don't I? OK, question four. Yes, I often watch films late at night.
D But you never see the end!
J Yes, you're right. So that's c.
D What about question five? When do you see friends at the weekend?
J Well, I usually see friends in the afternoon. Right, the last question.
D Ah, this is a good one.
J Yes, I'm always happy to talk to friends when they phone before eight in the morning.
D What? That's not true! *I* always answer the phone.
J Yes, *you* answer the phone, then *I* talk to my friends. So, it's a. Right, what's my score?
D OK, your score is … um …

CD1 68
POLLY Hi, Lorna. How are you?
LORNA I'm fine. But how are *you*? You're here and your husband's in Chile!
P Oh, I'm fine. And Trevor's back next month. He's got four weeks' holiday.
L So how is he?
P Well, he's very happy there. The job's great and the hotel's very good. And all of the people are nice. But he doesn't like the weather. It's hot and it hardly ever rains.

CD1 69
POLLY Well, he's very happy there. The job's great and the hotel's very good. And all of the people are nice. But he doesn't like the weather. It's hot and it hardly ever rains.
LORNA What does he do in his free time?
P Well, you know Trevor. He doesn't read a lot, but he plays video games, of course!
L Oh right.
P And he loves sport, so he watches a lot of sport on TV. They've also got a cinema there, so he sees a lot of new films.
L Oh, that's good.
P Yes, and he's got a very good camera, so he takes a lot of photos.
L But he's usually very active – does he do any sport?
P Oh, yes. He plays a lot of tennis. In fact, he has tennis lessons every week. And he goes to the gym every day. He says the gym at the hotel's great. And he goes swimming a lot. But he doesn't go running because it's hot in the day!
L What about running in the evening? It isn't hot then.
P No, he can't. He starts work in the evening! He studies the stars, remember?
L Of course! Do you talk to him very often?
P No, the time difference is a problem. But we email every day and he sends me lots of photos. Here's one I got this morning …

CD1 74
1. What does she do?
2. Does she like rock music?
3. What food does she like?
4. Does she like sport?
5. Does she have any animals?
6. What does she do on Saturday evenings?

VIDEO 4   CD1 77
CLARE This is a nice place.
PAUL Yes, it is, isn't it? I hear the burgers are very good here.
C Hmm. The salads look good too. Oh, it's difficult to decide … Yes, the chicken salad, I think.

[See exercise 6a p37]
1 What would you like to drink?
2 Would you like anything else?
3 Would you like a dessert?
4 Would you like tea or coffee?

P No, don't worry, Clare. Let me pay for this.
C Are you sure?
P Yes, of course.
C OK. Here's a tip.

CD1 79

Would you like to order now? | Yes, I'd like the chicken salad, please. | Can I have the cheeseburger and chips, please? | What would you like to drink? | We'd like a bottle of mineral water, please. | Would you like anything else? | Would you like a dessert? | Yes, I'd like the fruit salad, please. | And can I have the apple pie with cream? | Would you like tea or coffee?

CD1 80

CHEF Morning, Dylan. Good weekend?
DYLAN Yes, thank you. And you?
C Yes, thanks. So, what new nationalities have we got in school this week?
D New nationalities? Er, we've got Japanese, er French and Turkish.
C OK. Let's write the new breakfast menus.
D Yes, chef. So what do the Japanese have?
C Well, they usually have rice and fish and soup, and they drink green tea.
D Rice … fish … soup and … green tea. OK. And the French?
C They have a croissant or toast and jam. Oh and they usually have coffee with milk.
D Croissant … toast … jam … coffee. Well, that's easy. And what about the Turkish students? What do they have for breakfast?
C Well, they usually have big breakfasts. They have bread, cheese, eggs, olives and tomatoes.
D Wow! That's a lot! And to drink?
C They usually drink tea.
D OK. So that's bread, cheese, eggs, olives, tomatoes and tea.
C That's right. OK, Dylan, it's time to start cooking.
D Actually, it's time for my coffee break!

CD1 82

1 English | musician | Russia | nationality
2 cheese | chicken | sandwich | teacher
3 jam | vegetables | engineer | jazz

CD2 2

JASON Granddad, when were you born?
ALBERT I was born in 1953.
J So you were thirteen in … 1966.
A Yes, that's right.
J And where were you on your thirteenth birthday?
A I was in Liverpool with my parents.

Oh, I remember that birthday party very well. It was 30th July 1966, the day England won the World Cup.
J Really? Wow!
A Yes, the match was in the afternoon and my party was in the evening.
J That's amazing! Where was the party?
A It was at my parents' house – and in the street!
J Was it a big party?
A Yes, it was. All my friends were there and lots of my parents' friends were there too. There was music and food and dancing in the street – it was a very happy evening!
J It sounds like a great party. Was the food good?
A Yes, there were lots of sandwiches and chicken and ice cream, and a birthday cake with a big football on it.
J Were your grandparents there?
A No, they weren't. They were in London at the World Cup Final!

CD2 4

I was /wəz/ in Liverpool with my parents. | All my friends were /wə/ at the party. | Our house wasn't very big. | My brothers weren't there. | Where was /wəz/ the party? | Where were /wə/ his grandparents? | Were /wə/ his friends there? | Yes, they were. | No, they weren't. | Was /wəz/ the food good? | Yes, it was. | No, it wasn't. | When were /wə/ you born? | I was /wəz/ born in nineteen fifty-three. | Where was /wəz/ Matt born? He was /wəz/ born in Liverpool.

CD2 6

a August 16th b 1971 c two d 1986
e twelve f $2 billion g 1999

CD2 10

1 My parents study Italian. My parents studied Italian.
2 They finished work at six. They finish work at six.
3 They stayed in on Saturday. They stay in on Saturday.
4 I live in London. I lived in London.
5 My parents work in Germany. My parents worked in Germany.
6 I visit him every week. I visited him every week.

VIDEO 5 CD2 12

1 EMILY How was your weekend?
   TIM Terrible. I was ill all weekend.
E Oh, dear. What was wrong?
T I had a really bad cold.
E What a shame. Are you OK now?
T Yes, much better, thanks. And how was your weekend?
E It was OK. I stayed at home on Saturday.
T Oh, right. What did you do?
E I did the washing, checked my emails, watched TV – you know, the usual.

And then on Sunday I went to the cinema.
T Oh, nice. What did you see?
E It was called A Day in the Life.
T Oh, yes. What was it like?
E It was great. I really enjoyed it.
T Yeah, I'd like to see that. Oh, we're late for the meeting. Let's go!

2 SIMON Hi. How are you?
   RACHEL I'm very well, thanks. I went away for the weekend – to Spain!
S Wow! Where did you go?
R We went to Madrid. It was wonderful!
S Oh, great! Who did you go with?
R My friend, Ingrid.
S And where did you stay?
R We stayed with some friends from university.
S Oh, nice.
R What about you? How was your weekend?
S Oh, not very interesting. I worked all Sunday.
R Really? What did you do?
S I wrote that report you wanted. It took me 10 hours.
R You're joking! When did you finish it?
S At 11 o'clock last night. Here it is.
R That's great! Thanks, Simon.
S No problem.
R OK, let's start this meeting. Where are Emily and Tim?
S Here they are.
T Hi there. Sorry we're late. Emily wanted to get a coffee.
E Tim!

CD2 13

1 TIM I was ill all weekend.
   EMILY Oh, dear.
2 TIM I had a really bad cold.
   EMILY What a shame.
3 EMILY I stayed at home on Saturday.
   TIM Oh, right.
4 EMILY I went to the cinema.
   TIM Oh, nice.
5 RACHEL I went away for the weekend – to Spain!
   SIMON Wow!
6 RACHEL We went to Madrid. It was wonderful!
   SIMON Oh, great!
7 SIMON I worked all Sunday.
   RACHEL Really?
8 SIMON It took me 10 hours.
   RACHEL You're joking!

CD2 16

/ɒ/ hot | coffee | shopping | bottle
/əʊ/ old | sofa | mobile | open
/ʌ/ son | wonderful | sometimes | comfortable
/ə/ actor | tomato | computer | director

CD2 17
They didn't like each other at first.
They didn't finish their course.
They didn't have any money.
They didn't get the money for a month.
They didn't have a bank account.

CD2 18
PRESENTER Welcome to Book of the Day. Today we have the writer Wes Clark, talking about his new book, *Planet Google*. First of all, Wes, is it true? Did you really write this book in twelve weeks?
WES Yes, I did. And I enjoyed writing it because Larry Page and Sergey Brin are really interesting people.
P OK – so, let's start at the beginning. Where are they from?
W Well, Larry Page is American but Sergey Brin was born in Russia. His family went to live in the USA in 1979, when Sergey was six. But his mother wasn't very happy about going to the USA.
P Did she want to stay in Russia?
W Yes, she did.
P So did Sergey's parents find work in the USA?
W Yes, they did. Sergey's father got a job at Maryland University. He was a mathematics teacher there.
P And what about Sergey? Did he study mathematics?
W Yes, he did. He studied mathematics and computer science at the same university.
P At the same university as his father?
W Yes, that's right.
P Did Larry go to Maryland University?
W No, he didn't. He went to Michigan State University. His mother and father were computer science teachers there.
P Really? So Larry was at the same university as his parents!
W Yes, that's correct. And Larry's family always had computers in their home. He was the first student in his school to do his homework on a computer.
P Right. And then Page and Brin went to Stanford University, and now, of course, they're both very rich …

CD2 19
Did Sergey and Larry meet in nineteen ninety-four? | Did they like each other at first? | Did Sergey go to Maryland University? | Did Larry's parents teach mathematics? | Did Sergey study computer science? | Yes, he did. | No, he didn't. | Did Sergey and Larry launch Google in nineteen ninety-nine? | Yes, they did. | No, they didn't.

CD2 21
1 I can't find my mobile.
2 You can use my phone if you want.
3 A lot of people can't understand it.
4 You can buy 3D TVs online.
5 I can't turn off the TV!
6 Can you download TV programmes?

CD2 22
You can watch TV programmes online. | You can use my phone if you want. | I can't find my mobile. | A lot of people can't understand it. | You could only get three channels. | You couldn't record TV programmes. | Can you watch TV online? | Yes, you can. | No, you can't. | Could you record programmes in nineteen seventy-four? | Yes, you could. | No, you couldn't.

CD2 23
ANSWERS 2 could 3 could 4 could
5 couldn't 6 could 7 couldn't 8 can't
9 can 10 can 11 can't

CD2 24
damage, damaged | sail, sailed | die, died | receive, received | crash, crashed | save, saved | buy, bought | lose, lost | find, found | put, put | say, said | tell, told

CD2 25
ANNOUNCER It's one o'clock and here's George Lucan with the news.
NEWSREADER Over sixty people are in hospital after a train crash in Scotland this morning. The train was on its way to London but crashed only ten minutes after it left Edinburgh.
Fifty-three people died in storms in Florida last night. The storms damaged hundreds of homes and many people are without water and electricity.
Bill and Nancy Potter, who want to be the first eighty-year-old couple to sail round the world, are missing off the coast of Australia. Their family and friends became worried when the couple didn't arrive in Sydney last weekend as planned. Helicopters are now looking for the couple and their boat.
And finally, supermarket manager Joe Hall won over thirteen million pounds in last night's lottery – thanks to his dog! Joe told reporters today that his dog, Max, chose the numbers!
A That's the news this Thursday lunchtime. And now over to Jan Adams for the travel news.

VIDEO 6 CD2 26
1 PAUL I really enjoyed that burger.
   CLARE Yeah, the salad was good too.
P By the way, did you read about the winner of this week's lottery?
C No. How much did he win?
P Over 13 million pounds.
C Really?
P Yeah, and guess what? His dog chose the numbers for him!
C You're joking! How?
P He wrote 50 numbers on envelopes, put biscuits in them and put them around the house.
C Right.
P And then he used the numbers of the first six envelopes that the dog found. And now he's a millionaire!
C That's amazing!

2 WAYNE Did you hear about that train crash?
   ALISON No, where was it?
W Somewhere near Edinburgh.
A Oh, dear.
W Yes. Over sixty people are in hospital.
A Oh no, that's terrible.
W Yes, I know.
JOSH Mum, Dad, can we talk about the holiday now?
W Yes, OK. Let's have a look …

3 TIM Here's your coffee.
   EMILY Thanks a lot.
T You have family in the USA, don't you?
E Yes, why?
T Did you hear about the storms in Florida?
E Yes, isn't it awful? I saw it on the news this morning.
T Is your family OK?
E Yes, they're fine. They don't live in Florida. They live near Washington.
T Oh, right. Oh, we're late for a meeting *again*!
E Come on, let's go.

4 CHRIS Did you read about the eighty-year-old couple and their boat?
   LOUISE No, what happened?
C Their boat was damaged in a storm and they were missing for two days.
L Oh, dear. Are they OK?
C Yes. A helicopter found them yesterday off the coast of Australia.
L Oh, that's good.
C Maybe we can sail around the world when we're eighty.
L You're joking, I hope.
C Yes, of course.

CD2 27
Did you hear about that train crash? | No, where was it? | Did you read about the eighty-year-old couple and their boat? | No, what happened? | Oh, that's good. | Oh no, that's terrible. | Yes, isn't it awful? | Oh, dear. Are they OK? | Really? | You're joking!

CD2 28
Tonight's programme looks at the work of Shigeru Miyamoto, the world-famous video game designer. Shigeru was born in Kyoto, Japan, on November 16th 1952. He studied art at Kanazawa College of Art from 1970 to 1975. Between 1998 and 2010 he won awards for his work in the USA, the UK, France and Spain. But Shigeru lives a very

ordinary life. He's married with two children and he usually goes to work by bike. In his free time he plays the guitar and he writes music. He once said, "They say video games are bad for you. But that's what they said about rock 'n' roll." Shigeru designed the first Mario Brothers game in 1983 and he says Mario is his favourite video game character. Shigeru was the first video game designer to tell a story in his video games. All Mario Brothers video games have a hero, a princess and a villain …

CD2 ▶ 31

Listening Test (See Teacher's Book)

CD2 ▶ 32

TIP • Words in pink are weak forms.

A JOSIE Where were you born, Clive?
   CLIVE I was born in a small town called Burford, near Oxford.
J   How long did you live there?
C   We lived there for 12 years and then we moved to London. But my grandparents still live in Burford.
J   What's it like?
C   Oh, it's really nice. There are lots of beautiful old buildings and interesting shops. There isn't a station, but there's one at Charlbury, about five miles away.
J   Are there any good pubs in Burford?
C   Yes, there are. In the town centre there are four or five really nice pubs and all of them have fantastic food.
J   So when did you last go there?
C   About six months ago. I was at my grandparents' house for New Year.
J   Oh, nice.

B VANESSA Hi, James. Did you have a good weekend?
   JAMES Yes, it was OK, thanks. I stayed at home all weekend. What about you?
V   I went to visit my brother in Ireland.
J   Really? Where does he live?
V   In a small village called Eyeries. It's about two hours from Cork airport.
J   Oh, right. What's it like?
V   Well, there's only one road, and all of the houses are different colours!
J   Really? It sounds lovely.
V   Yes, it is. There are lots of beautiful beaches nearby and it's a good place to go for walks.
J   Is there a hotel?
V   No, there isn't. And there aren't any restaurants. But there are two bars and a couple of shops.
J   Oh, OK.
V   If you want to go there one day, I'm sure you can stay with my brother.
J   Oh, thanks a lot.

C BRIAN Hi, Aunt Alice. Happy birthday!
   ALICE Hello, Brian. You remembered!
B   Of course. I couldn't forget my favourite aunt's birthday!
A   Oh, thank you. And how are things with you? Do you like living in Brisbane?
B   Yes, I love it here. There are lots of things to do and the people are very friendly.
A   And how's your new flat?
B   It's great. There's a nice beach about five minutes away and there are lots of bars and restaurants. It's a great place to go out at night.
A   Oh, that's nice, dear. I'm pleased that you're happy there.
B   Yes, I am. And how's Uncle Thomas?
A   Oh, he's very well, thanks …

CD2 ▶ 37

ESTATE AGENT Hello. Can I help you?
JOHN Hi, I'm John, and this is my wife, Becky.
BECKY Hello.
EA Nice to meet you.
J   You too. We'd like some information about the flat in Park Road, please. We saw it on your website.
EA Of course. What would you like to know?
J   Er, firstly, is there any furniture?
EA Yes, there are some chairs, a sofa, beds – it's fully furnished. But, er, there isn't a TV.
J   Oh, that's OK. And the bedrooms – are they big?
EA Er, well, one bedroom's very big, but the other is, er, quite small. It's fine for a child.
B   That's OK. But we haven't got any children.
EA Right. Well, there's a lot of space for two people.
J   Hmm. And the bathroom. Has it got a shower?
EA Yes, there's a shower and a bath. It's very nice.
J   OK. Is there anything else, Becky?
B   Yes, what's in the kitchen?
EA There's a cooker, a fridge and a washing machine. And I think there are some chairs and a table.
B   Right. And are there any shops near the flat?
EA Yes, there are some shops only 5 minutes away. And it's near the station.
J   That's not bad for £800 a month.
B   Yes, maybe.
EA It is a beautiful flat. Would you like to see it?
J   Er, yes I think so, don't you?
B   Yes, definitely.
EA Great! What about, er, today at 3 o'clock?
J   Yes, 3 o'clock is fine. Can we meet at the flat?

CD2 ▶ 39

ANSWERS 2 some 3 any 4 some 5 any 6 some 7 some 8 any 9 a 10 any 11 some 12 some 13 a

VIDEO ▶ 7 CD2 ▶ 40

1 SALES ASSISTANT 1 Hi. Can I help you?
   PAUL Yes, please. Have you got any guide books for London?
SA1 Yes, they're over there.
P   Oh yes, I see. Thanks. … I'll have this one, please. How much is this map?
SA1 This one is … £5.95.
P   OK, I'll have the map too.
SA1 Sure. …
P   And can I have four stamps for Europe, please?
SA1 I'm sorry, we don't sell stamps for Europe.
P   No problem.
SA1 Anything else?
P   No, that's all, thanks.
SA1 Right, that's £19.45, please.
P   Here you are.
SA1 Would you like a bag?
P   No, thanks. I've got one.
SA1 OK. Here's your change and your receipt.
P   Thank you.
SA1 Have a nice day.
P   You too. Bye.
SA1 Bye.

2 SALES ASSISTANT 2 Do you need any help?
   CLARE Oh, yes, please. How much are these lamps?
SA2 The big ones are £25 and the small ones are £17.50.
C   Um, OK. I'll have this one, please.
SA2 Of course. Would you like anything else?
C   Yes, do you sell suitcases?
SA2 Yes, we do. They're on the second floor.
C   OK. I'll buy this first.
SA2 Right. … Right, that's £17.50, please.
C   Thanks.
SA2 … Your pin number, please. … OK. Here you are. Your receipt's in the bag.
C   Great. Thanks for your help. Bye.
SA2 Goodbye.

CD2 ▶ 43

/ɔː/ shorts | strawberry | tall | August | bought | divorced
/ɜː/ shirt | Thursday | word | birthday | person | skirt

CD2 ▶ 45

FRANK Janet? It's Frank.
JANET Frank! Where are you?
F   I'm at the station. The train was late. I'm waiting for a taxi.
J   But we've got that meeting with the Tamada brothers at 10 o'clock!
F   Yes, I know. Are they there yet?
J   Yes, they're sitting in your office.
F   Oh no!
J   And they aren't looking very happy.
F   Hold on … here's a taxi. Start the meeting without me, but take notes.

J   Oh, and Janet?
J   Yes?
F   Remember – this isn't your contract. It's *my* contract!
J   Of *course* it is, Frank … bye! Liz?
L   Yes?
J   Where's Adriana?
L   Oh, she's working at home today.
J   Oh, dear. I need someone to take notes at the Tamada meeting.
L   I'm not doing anything important at the moment. Do you want me to do it?
J   Actually, I want you to finish those reports.
L   Well, Danny isn't doing anything. I can ask him.
J   OK, thanks.

CD2 46

I'm waiting for a taxi. | They're sitting in your office. | They aren't looking very happy. | She's working at home today. | I'm not doing anything important at the moment. | Danny isn't doing anything.

CD2 47

ANSWERS 2 's reading 3 isn't reading ('s not reading) 4 's studying 5 'm waiting 6 aren't working ('re not working) 7 'm going

CD2 48

FRANK   Hello, Liz, it's Frank.
LIZ   Hi, Frank. Where are you calling from?
F   I'm in a taxi. There was an accident or something. We're not moving.
L   Oh, dear.
F   Look, Janet isn't answering her phone. What's she doing?
L   She's talking to the Tamada brothers. And Danny's taking notes.
F   Oh, right. Where are they having the meeting?
L   Er … in Janet's office.
F   In *Janet's* office? Oh no! Liz, please go and tell Janet *not* to sign that contract.
L   OK, Frank. See you soon. And hurry up!

CD2 49

FRANK   Hi, Liz. Are they still in Janet's office?
LIZ   Yes, they are. Good luck!
F   Right … Hello, everybody. Sorry I'm late.
J   Er, hello, Frank. Mr Tamada and I are just signing the contract.
F   No, you're not, Janet. *I'm* signing the contract.
J   OK, Frank. It's all yours.
F   I'm so sorry I wasn't here when you arrived. There was an accident and I …

CD2 50

ANSWERS 2 Are you having a nice time?
3 What are you doing? 4 Are the kids doing their homework? 5 What are they doing?

CD2 51

Are you working late this evening? | Are you having a nice time? | What are you doing? | Are the kids doing their homework? | What are they doing?

CD2 52

PRESENTER   And with all this snow, let's go over to Jan Adams in the centre of London for this morning's traffic news.
JAN   Well, people aren't very happy here in the city – there aren't any trains, traffic isn't moving and there are problems on the tube and the buses. Excuse me, sir, are you on your way to work?
FIRST MAN   Yes, I am. I usually go by train, but I'm taking the bus today and I'm very late.
J   What time do you usually start work?
FM   I start at eight. And it's eight thirty now. And I'm still waiting for a bus! Why can't they do something about the roads?
J   Thank you, sir. Excuse me, madam, are you going to work?
WOMAN   Yes, I am.
J   And do you always walk to work?
W   No, I usually cycle, but I'm walking today because the roads are so bad.
J   So how long is your journey to work on a normal day?
W   About twenty minutes.
J   OK. And how long is it taking today?
W   Well, I left home at half past seven, that's about an hour ago.
J   Well, good luck. Excuse me, sir, are you on your way to work?
SECOND MAN   Yes, I am.
J   And how do you usually travel to work?
SM   When I'm working in London, I usually take the tube.
J   Right. And how are you getting to work today?
SM   Well, today I'm walking because of the snow.
J   And where are you from?
SM   I'm from Canada.
J   Oh, so you know all about snow.
SM   Yes, it snows a lot in Canada every winter. And we never have these problems! Why isn't anyone doing anything about the roads?
J   Thank you. Well, as you can hear, everyone's asking the same question today – why can't they do something about the roads?
P   Thanks, Jan. That was Jan Adams reporting from the centre of London.

CD2 54

ANSWERS 2 work 3 'm working
4 'm sitting 5 'm writing 6 don't work
7 's snowing 8 drive 9 visit 10 're staying
11 is answering 12 'm watching
13 don't watch

CD2 55

ANSWERS 2 Is (she) working … 3 … is (she) doing … 4 Does (she) work … 5 … do (Lenny and Eve usually) do … 6 … are (they) doing … 7 Does (Eve normally) watch …
8 … is (she) watching …

CD2 56 CD2 57

1   MESSAGE   Hello, this is Alan Wick's voicemail. I'm sorry I can't take your call at the moment. If you leave a message, I'll get back to you. Thanks for calling. [end of **CD2 56**]
EMILY   Hello, it's Emily Wise here, from the contracts office at 3DUK. Can we meet tomorrow morning at about 10? I need to talk to you about the new contract with Morris Computers. Can you call me back? Thanks. Bye.
2   MESSAGE   Welcome to the NRL voicemail service. I'm sorry, but the person you called is not available. Please leave your message after the tone. [end of **CD2 56**]
EMILY   Hi, Clare, it's Emily. Would you like to meet for coffee after work? Call me later – I'm at work. Bye!
3   MESSAGE   Thank you for calling the Queen's Theatre. Please choose one of the following 3 options. For ticket information, press 1. To book tickets by credit card, press 2. For all other enquiries, press zero. [end of **CD2 56**] You are in a queue. Please hold. Your call will be answered as soon as possible.
TICKET SELLER   Hello, Queen's Theatre. Can I help you?
EMILY   Oh, hi. Are there any tickets available for *Not Now* on Saturday?
TS   Yes, there are.
E   How much are they?
TS   They're £24.50 and £38.
E   £24.50 and £38. OK, thanks a lot. I'll think about it. Bye.
TS   Goodbye.
4   [**CD2 56 only**] I'm sorry. There's no one available to take your call. Please try later.

VIDEO 8 CD2 58

1   TIM   Did you check that contract for Morris Computers?
EMILY   Yes, I did. It's fine, I think.
T   Good. We need to check this with Alan Wick too. … Hello, 3DUK. Can I help you?
CLARE   Hello, can I speak to Emily, please?
T   Hold on a moment. She's here.
E   Hello. Emily Wise.
C   Hi. It's Clare. I got your message.
E   Good. Do you want to go for a coffee after work?
C   Sure. Is six o'clock OK?

161

E Yes, that's fine. Let's meet at Café Uno.
C OK. See you there at six. Bye.
E Bye. … Sorry about that, Tim. Right, where were we?
T The Morris Computers contract. We need to talk to Alan Wick.
E Yes, I'm waiting for him to call me back.
T Great. And we need to talk to Chris Morris.
E Yes, I know. I'll call him now.

2 LOUISE Hi, love.
   CHRIS Hi.
L I'm going to Sophie's for a coffee. Do you want to come?
C No, I can't, I'm sorry. I've got a conference call in a minute and it's quite important.
L OK, see you later.
C Bye.
L Bye.
C … Hello?
EMILY Hello, is that Chris Morris?
C Speaking.
E This is Emily Wise from 3DUK.
C Hello, Emily. Look, I've got a conference call in an hour. Can I call you back in an hour?
E Of course. Call me on my mobile.
C Right. I'll call you later.
E Thanks a lot. Bye.
C Bye. … Hello? … Hello? … Jason, good to hear from you. … Hello, Andrea. How are things?

CD2 ▶ 61

1 milk | his | ill | excited | window | interesting | chicken
2 teeth | he's | ski | beach | meeting | thirteen | machine

CD3 ▶ 1

JESSICA When did you last go on holiday, Andy?
ANDY In September last year.
J Where did you go?
A I went to Cape Town for two weeks.
J Oh, great! I really want to go to South Africa. Did you have a good time?
A Yes, I did. It's a fantastic city and the people were really friendly.
J Who did you go with?
A Nigel, a friend from university.
J Oh, right. What did you do there?
A Well, on the first day we went on a guided tour of the city, which was very interesting.
J Right.
A And the next day we went to Table Mountain for a picnic. Lots of tourists do that.
J Did you walk up the mountain?
A No, we went by cable car. The view from the top was amazing!
J And where did you stay?
A We stayed with Nigel's brother. He lives in the centre of Cape Town.

J Oh, that was lucky. And how did you travel around?
A For the first week we travelled by public transport, and then we rented a car for the second week. We drove to a wildlife park to see some elephants. It was a beautiful place – and there were elephants outside our room every morning!
J Ah, that sounds fantastic! What else did you do?
A Well, we went to Robben Island to visit the prison. That was really interesting. We saw the cell where Nelson Mandela lived for 27 years.
J Wow!
A And on our last day we went on a boat trip to see the whales. That was the best day of the holiday, I think – I took lots of photos.
J It sounds like you had a great time.
A Yes, it was amazing. I didn't want to come home.

CD3 ▶ 3

to see some elephants → We drove to a wildlife park to see some elephants. | to visit the prison → We went to Robben Island to visit the prison. | to see the whales → We went on a boat trip to see the whales.

CD3 ▶ 4

PATRICK OK, so it's a week in Cairo or a week in Sharm El Sheikh.
JULIET Most people just call it Sharm, I think.
P OK. Where do you want to go, Juliet? Sharm or Cairo?
J Well, I think Sharm's more beautiful than Cairo.
P Yes, it is. But Cairo's more interesting.
J Yes, maybe. But Sharm looks nicer than Cairo. It's a beautiful place and the diving looks amazing!
P Yes, but Cairo's a fantastic city. There are lots of things to do there. We can go on boat trips along the Nile, visit the Pyramids, go to the Egyptian Museum, and, er, go shopping?
J Maybe. But Cairo's busier than Sharm.
P Well, all capital cities are busy. And the hotel in Cairo is cheaper.
J We don't need to spend a lot of money when we're there. I'm happy to go to the beach every day and go snorkelling.
P OK, but you know I'm not really a beach person.
J Well, you can rent a motorbike and go into the desert, or, er, go on a camel ride.
P Yes, I know. But I still think Cairo's better than Sharm.
J Sharm's probably safer too, especially at night. And it's more popular with young people. I just want go to the beach and relax, Patrick. It's a holiday!
P Well, maybe we can go to the beach near Cairo, you know, just for a day or two.

And there are islands on the Nile, I think – maybe you can go snorkelling there. And then next year we can go anywhere you want.

CD3 ▶ 6

VIC Hi, Patrick, how are you?
PATRICK Hi, Vic. I'm fine, thanks. Just back from holiday, actually.
V Really? Where did you go?
P Er, we went to Egypt, a place on the Red Sea called Sharm El Sheikh.
V Yes, I know it. Very nice. But I thought you didn't like beach holidays.
P Me? Oh yes, I love the beach. I chose the holiday, actually – Juliet wanted to go to Cairo!
V Really?

VIDEO ▶ 9 **CD3** ▶ 7

WAYNE Well, it's Saturday tomorrow. What would you like to do?
ALISON I'd like to go to the beach.
JOSH Oh, no. Not the beach again. We went to the beach last weekend.
W He's right. I'd rather go somewhere different.
A Well, would you like to go to London?
W Yes, that's a good idea.
A We can spend the day at Regent's Park. It's really beautiful and there's lots to do there.
W That sounds good. Do you want to do that, Josh?
J Do what, Dad?
W Do you want to go to Regent's Park?
J Not really. I'd rather stay at home.
A But Regent's Park is a great place to visit. You can go on boat rides and there's a really good open air theatre.
J Mmm. Theatre. That's really interesting. Anyway, what about Daisy? Why aren't you asking her?
W You know your sister works at the restaurant every Saturday.
J Lucky her.
W OK, so where do you want to go?
J I want to go to Longleat.
W Oh, I don't think so. It's a long way.
J But some friends from school went there last week. And there's a safari park where you drive around and look at all the lions and tigers and monkeys from your car.
A That sounds quite dangerous.
J It isn't if you don't open the windows!
W And you can see animals in Regent's Park – that's where London Zoo is!
J But I went to London Zoo last year with the school. I want to go somewhere different.
A OK, let's go to Longleat. Would you like to ask a friend to come?
J Yeah, OK. Can I ask Elliott?
A Fine. Tell him to be here tomorrow morning at eight.
J Great. Thanks, Mum.

W OK, that's decided, then. Now, what's on TV?

CD3 11

2 mountain 3 Wednesday 4 answer
5 wrong 6 postcard 7 friendly 8 breakfast

CD3 12

DOCTOR Hello, Mrs Lee.
MRS LEE Hello, doctor.
D So – you're here for a check-up.
L Yes.
D Right. First let's see what you weigh. Over here, please. Mmm. 70 kilos. Four kilos more than six months ago.
L Really?
D Yes. Do you do much exercise?
L Well, with three children, I don't really have time.
D Do you walk to school with them?
L No, not very often. Maybe once or twice a month. That's because we're usually late, so I take them in the car. Then I drive to work.
D And you work in an office, is that right?
L Well, yes.
D A lot of sitting … Ah, but you started going to a gym last March. How often do you go?
L Er, not very often. Perhaps three times a month.
D You should do some exercise three times a *week*, really.
L Yes, I know, but my husband works away from home, so it's difficult to get to the gym.
D Maybe … you should get a dog. Then you and the children can take it for walks twice a day.
L Maybe. The children would love a dog.
D And what about food? What do you usually eat?
L I don't have much time to cook in the week so we have things like pizzas and sausages. And I eat quite a lot of biscuits. I know I shouldn't, but they're so nice with coffee.
D Well, you shouldn't eat so many pizzas and biscuits. And you should eat more fruit and vegetables and do more exercise. But you probably know that.
L Er, yes, I'll try.
D Right. Let's listen to your heart.

CD3 13

ANSWERS 1 should 2 shouldn't 3 should
4 shouldn't 5 should 6 shouldn't

CD3 14

TINA OK, Leo. I've got four people for the *Break* poster. See what you think.
LEO Right. Where's the first one? Hmm, he's not bad.
T Yes, I quite like him. He looks friendly, the type of person who buys a lot of chocolate.
L I can see that!
T Yes, he's a bit overweight, isn't he? Is that a problem?
L Er, I'm not sure. Who else have you got?
T Well, there's him.
L He's better, maybe. He's tall and good-looking.
T Yes, he's very good-looking. But I don't know about the long hair.
L Yes, you've got a point there. Who's next?
T What about her?
L Yes, she's nice. Slim, long dark hair, and she's very attractive.
T Yes, she's beautiful – but, do we want a beautiful person on this poster?
L I'm not sure. Is that all of them?
T No, there's one more.
L Hmm, she's older than the other models, isn't she?
T Yes, but maybe that's good. Older people buy a lot of chocolate. And she's attractive – she looks very friendly and happy, I think.
L Yes, she does.
T And eating chocolate makes people feel happy.
L Yes, you're right. Well, let's choose.
T OK. Do we want a man or a woman?

CD3 15

TINA OK. Do we want a man or a woman?
LEO I think that we want a woman.
T Why's that?
L Well, women buy more chocolate than men. So they want to see a woman on the poster.
T Yes, good point.
L And people know that chocolate can make you overweight – but everyone wants to be thin.
T So we want someone slim.
L And people always think they're young – so they want to see young people on posters. Which means …
T Zoë. OK. Let's have Zoë. Fine. Shall I ask her to come for a meeting?
L Yes, good idea. Right, what else do we need to talk about?

CD3 16

TINA Hi, Leo. I hear everyone really likes the *Break* posters. Well done.
LEO Thanks a lot.
T And I hear you've got a new girlfriend.
L Er, yes, I have.
T **What's she like?**
L Well, she's friendly and outgoing. And she's very beautiful.
T Oh, right. **When did you meet her?**
L Er, about three weeks ago.
T **And what does she like doing?**
L Well, she likes clubbing and going to restaurants. The same as me, really.
T OK. **What does she look like?**
L Well, she's tall and slim, and she's got long dark hair.
T **How did you meet her?**
L Oh, er, we met here, you know, in the office.
T Really? **What does she do?**
L Er, she's a model.
T Leo, **what's your new girlfriend's name?**
L It's, er, Zoë. You know, from the *Break* advert.
T Oh, really.

CD3 18

1 What's she like? 2 What does she look like? 3 What's he like? 4 What does she like doing? 5 What does he look like? 6 What are they like?

CD3 19

I've got a stomach ache. | I've got a headache. | I've got toothache. | I've got a sore throat. | I've got a cold. | I've got a cough. | I've got a temperature. | I feel ill. | I feel terrible. | I feel sick. | I feel better. | My back hurts. | My arm hurts. | My foot hurts. | My leg hurts.

VIDEO 10 CD3 20

1 SIMON Hi, Rachel.
   RACHEL Hello, Simon. You don't look very well. Are you OK?
S No, I feel terrible.
R Oh, dear. What's wrong?
S I've got a terrible stomach ache.
R Well, maybe you shouldn't go to work today.
S I know, but Emily and I have got an important meeting this morning. It's with some people from Morris Computers.
R Well, why don't you call them and cancel it?
S Yes, maybe you're right. We can have the meeting next week instead.
R Good. And then go home.
S OK. That's a good idea.
R And maybe you should go to the doctor.
S Yes, perhaps.
R OK. Bye, Simon. I hope you get better soon.
S Bye, Rachel. Thanks a lot. … Hello, is that Chris Morris? … Look, I'm sorry, but we can't have our meeting today. I'm not very well. … Yes, next Tuesday morning's fine with me too …

2 EMILY Hi, Tim.
   TIM Hi, Emily. Are you alright?
E No, I don't feel very well.
T Oh, dear. What's the matter?
E I've got a headache and a sore throat.
T Why don't you go home?
E I can't. I've got a meeting this morning. It's really important.
T Who's your meeting with?
E Simon, and some people from Morris Computers.

163

T Well, Simon called about ten minutes ago and left a message. He's ill and he's not coming in today.
E Oh, no!
T And the meeting with Morris Computers is next Tuesday morning now.
E Oh, so there isn't a meeting today. That's great. So I *can* go home.
T Yes. Take the day off. You should be in bed. And don't come to work tomorrow.
E OK. Thanks a lot.
T No problem. Get well soon.
E Thanks, Tim. Bye.

CD3 22

ANSWERS 2b 3a 4b 5a 6b

CD3 25

/æ/ hat | rabbit | contract | family
/ɑː/ bath | answers | arm | dance
/eɪ/ lazy | radio | games | famous
/ə/ ago | another | elephant | island

CD3 27

1 MEG Happy New Year, Jack!
   JACK Thanks, Meg. And happy New Year to you.
M Any New Year's resolutions?
J Yes, I have, actually. I'm not going to work until ten every night. I'm going to work less and have more fun. And I'm going to have a holiday this year.
M Good! Where are you going?
J I don't know. Somewhere I can relax.
M Good idea.
J And what about you? What are you going to do this year?
M I'm going to move to Australia.
J Wow! When did you decide that?
M Oh, a couple of months ago.
J That's fantastic news! Where are you going to live?
M In Melbourne. I've got family there.
J Well, that's great. Good luck.
M Thanks a lot.

2 ED Hello, David. Hi, Val.
   DAVID Hi, Ed. Happy New Year!
E Happy New Year to you too!
VAL Have you got any New Year's resolutions?
E Yes, I'm going to do a computer course.
D Oh, right. Why computers?
E I want to get a new job. The one I've got now is really boring.
V Where are you going to do the course?
E I don't know. I'm going to start looking for courses next week.
D Right. Well, good luck with that.
E Thanks. And what about you? Any New Year's resolutions?
D Yes, we're going to get fit.
E Oh, right.
D And Val's going to stop smoking.
V Yes, I am. And David's going to lose weight. Well, he says he is.

D Er, yes, I want to lose eight kilos. I'm going to do more exercise and I'm not going to eat sweet things any more.
WOMAN Chocolate cake, anyone?
D No, not for me, thank you.
W Oh, go on. It's really good!
D Well, er … just a little, thank you.
V David!
D Oh, didn't I say? I'm going to start my New Year's resolution *after* the party.

CD3 30

ERIC Wow, Jenny, that was a difficult exam. And I revised really hard for this one.
JENNY Yes, me too. Do you think you passed?
E I don't know. The first part was OK, but I couldn't answer the last two questions.
J Yes, they were really difficult. Hi, Melanie. How did it go?
MELANIE It wasn't easy, was it? But it's over, that's the important thing!
J Absolutely! So how are you going to celebrate tonight, Melanie?
M Well, there's a big end-of-exams party at Caroline's house, so I might go to that. Or I might stay at home and watch a film. What about you, Eric?
E Well, first I'm going to go home and sleep.
M Yes, good idea.
E Then I'm going to meet some friends in town at seven. After that, I don't know. We might go to Caroline's, or we might go to that new club on Market Street.
M And what about you, Jenny?
J Well, first I'm going to phone my mum. But I'm not sure what I'm going to do this evening. I might go to the party or I might go out for a meal with Sam.
M Anyway, I'm sure of one thing.
E What's that?
M That's the last exam I'm ever going to take in my life!
J Yeah, me too.
E And what about the summer? Have you got any plans? …

CD3 31

I might go to the party. | I might stay at home and watch a film. | I might go out for a meal with Sam. | We might go to Caroline's. | We might go to that new club on Market Street.

CD3 33

ANSWERS 2a 3b 4a 5b 6a

CD3 34

ERIC And what about after the holidays? Are you going to look for a job?
JENNY Yes, Sam and I are going to Spain in September. We're going to look for a job there.
MELANIE What kind of job?

J I don't know. We might work for a holiday company or something. Sam wants to teach English.
M My cousin's going to teach English in Argentina next year.
J Yes, that's a good idea. I might do that.
M And what about you, Eric?
E I'm going to do a business course in London.
M Really? How are you going to pay for it?
E Good question. My parents are going to help me.
M Oh, that's lucky. Business courses are really expensive.
E Yes, I know. I need to get £10,000 before September.
J So are you going to sell your car?
E Yes, I am, actually. Why, do you want to buy it?
J I might. How much do you want for it?
E Oh, about thirty thousand pounds.
J Yeah, right. You mean the cost of a business course!
E Well, and the rent for a nice flat in London.
M You don't need to do a course, Eric. You're already a businessman!

CD3 35

PAULINE Hello, Seaton Holiday Homes, can I help you?
ALISON Oh, hello, I'm phoning about your advert for Benton House.
P Of course. When would you like to stay there?
A From July 14th for 2 weeks. Is it available then?
P Let me have a look. Er, yes, it is.
A Great. How much is it?
P Two weeks in July, er, that's £620 per week.
A Oh, that's more expensive than the advert.
P Well, it's the school holidays, you see. Everything's more expensive then.
A OK. Is Hill Place cheaper?
P Yes, it is. In July it's, er … £595 per week.
A And is it available for those two weeks?
P Let me check … Oh, it's available the first week, but not the second. Sorry.
A Right … OK, can I book Benton House, please?
P Certainly. Can I have your name, please?
A Yes, my name's Alison Wilson.
P And do you have an email address, Mrs Wilson? …

CD3 36

1 Go along Abbott Street and it's on the right, next to the bus station.
2 Go along the High Street, past the station, and it's on the left, opposite the department store.
3 Go along the High Street, past the department store, and turn right. Go along North Road and it's on the left.

164

4   Go along Abbott Street and turn right by the river. That's West Street. Go along that street for about 100 metres and it's on the right, next to the car park.

VIDEO 11 CD3 37

1   ALISON   Excuse me. Is there a newsagent's near here?
    MAN 1   Yes, there's one in Berry Street.
A   Where's that?
M1 Go along this road and turn right. That's Berry Street. Go past the pub and the newsagent's is on the right, opposite the supermarket.
A   So I go along this road and turn right. Then I go past the pub and …
M1 And the newsagent's is on the right.
A   Opposite the supermarket. Oh, great, thanks a lot.
M1 No problem.

2   WAYNE   Excuse me.
    MAN 2   Can I help you?
W   Yes, where's the post office?
M2 The post office? It's over there, next to the café.
W   Ah yes, I can see it. Thanks. Sorry, I'm on holiday here and I don't know my way around.
M2 No problem. Bye.
W   Goodbye.
M2 And have a nice holiday!
W   Thanks a lot.

3   DAISY   Excuse me. How do we get to the market?
    WOMAN   You go along this street and over the bridge. That's New Road, and the market's on your left.
D   So that's, er, along this street, er …
JOSH   Over the bridge and the market's on the left.
W   Yes, in New Road. You can't miss it.
D   How far is it?
W   Oh, it's not far. Only about five minutes' walk.
D   Great. Thanks a lot. Right, let's go. Do you remember the way? I never listen when people give me directions …

CD3 39

ELLIE   Hello?
MIKE   **Hello, Aunt Ellie. This is Mike. I'm calling from England about Ian and Amy's wedding. Is this a good time to call?**
E   **Mike! Yes, of course it is.** Oh, dear. I never replied to your email, did I? Sorry, I'm very bad at emails. But we're all very happy that you're coming over for Ian's wedding.
M   Yes, that's what I'm calling about. Can I stay with you when I get there? Or should I book a hotel?
E   Oh, I'm afraid there isn't any room in our house because Amy's parents are staying with us for a week.

But if you want, I can book a hotel room for you nearby.
M   Yes, that would be great, thanks a lot.
E   And your uncle says you can use his motorbike if you want to travel around after the wedding. He doesn't use it much any more and he'd love you to ride it.
M   Wow, that's fantastic! And what about getting to your place from Los Angeles airport? Should I get a taxi?
E   No, of course not! Just tell us what time your flight arrives and we can come and get you.
M   That's very kind of you, thanks a lot.
E   And I'm going to book a table at our favourite restaurant that evening so you can meet Amy's family.
M   Great! I'll email you my flight details this evening.
E   OK. See you in a couple of months. Would you like to speak to your uncle?
M   Yes, of course. … Hello, Uncle Sid, how are you?

CD3 41

/ʊ/ look | book | woman | should | wood | sugar | good-looking
/uː/ room | blue | June | suit | food | boots | choose

CD3 43

sixteen million | four point two three | five hundred thousand | seven thousand, six hundred and fifty | three hundred and ninety | nought point one five | a hundred and seventy-two | ninety-eight thousand, five hundred

CD3 44

ANSWERS   a 73 hours   b 5,350 litres
c 182 kg   d 35.6 kg   e $399   f one second
g 152 hours   h £8,000

CD3 46

ABBY   Do you like doing quizzes, Len?
LEN   Yes, I love them. Ask me the first question.
A   OK. What's the world's most expensive city? Moscow, Tokyo or Milan?
L   Mmm, that's a difficult question. Er … this is a guess – Milan.
A   Just a minute. Er, no, it's Tokyo. Wow, it says here that a typical two-bedroom flat is about six thousand dollars a month.
L   Really?
A   Yes. OK, next question. Which of these countries is the hottest – Libya, the USA or Australia?
L   The hottest? I think it's Libya, isn't it?
A   Yes, that's right. It can have temperatures of fifty-seven point eight degrees. That's really hot!
L   OK, what's the next question?

A   Question three. Which of these cities is the oldest – Athens, Rome or Damascus?
L   Oh, I know this one. It's Damascus.
A   Yes, you're right!
L   It's eight thousand years old.
A   How do you know that?
L   I just read it in the newspaper.
A   Er, question four. Which of these countries is the most popular with tourists – Spain, China or France?
L   Oh, I don't know – France?
A   Yes, it's France, with seventy-four point two million visitors. That's three you've got right. Ah, this one is easier. Which is the longest river in the world? The Nile, the Amazon or the Yangtze?
L   Well, it's not the Yangtze. Er, I think it's the Amazon.
A   No, it's the Nile and it's six thousand, six hundred and fifty kilometres long.
L   Oh, right. So, is that the last question?
A   No, there's one more. Which is the world's most crowded country – Bangladesh, Singapore or Monaco?
L   Well, Monaco is the smallest country – so perhaps it's the most crowded too.
A   Yes, that's right! Monaco has seventeen thousand people per square kilometre. You got four out of six right. Not bad!

CD3 49

LUCY   Are you enjoying the food?
STEVE   Yes, it's wonderful. Guy's a great cook. How's business?
L   Oh, it's fine. Busy, you know. I really need a holiday.
S   Yes, me too.
L   But you're always on holiday!
S   No, I'm not. People always say that. I work very hard when I'm travelling.
L   Yeah, right. Have you ever been to Peru?
S   Yes, I have.
L   Did you have a good time?
S   Yes, I did. It's a fantastic country. The mountains are beautiful and the people are really friendly.
L   When did you go there?
S   About three years ago. Why do you ask?
L   Guy and I would like to go there for a holiday next year.
S   Yes, it's a great place to visit. I'd like to go to Australia. Have you ever been there?
L   Yes, I have, actually. I went there about eight years ago, with my brother.
S   And did you enjoy it?
L   Oh, yes, we had a wonderful time. We travelled around in an old car for three months and camped every night.
S   Mmm, it sounds great.
GUY   Is the food OK, Steve?
S   Yes, very good, as usual. Guy, have you ever been to Australia?
G   No, I haven't. I never leave this restaurant!

CD3 50

Have you ever been to Peru? | Yes, I have. | Have you ever been to Australia? | No, I haven't. | Have you ever worked in a restaurant? | Yes, I have. | Have you ever met someone from Ireland? | No, I haven't. | Have you ever seen a Japanese film? | Yes, I have. | Have you ever worked in an office? | No, I haven't.

VIDEO 12.1   CD3 51

MAN Hello. Can I have your passport, please?
DAISY Yes. Here you are. …
M How many bags are you checking in?
D One. …
M Did you pack your bag yourself?
D Yes, I did. …
M And have you got any hand luggage?
D Yes, this bag.
M OK. … Here's your boarding pass. You're in seat 16F.
D Is that a window seat?
M No, an aisle seat.
D Oh, OK. Which gate is it?
M Gate 12.
D Is the flight on time?
M Yes, it is. Boarding is at 15.30. Enjoy your flight.
D Thanks. Bye.
M Bye.

VIDEO 12.2   CD3 53

ALISON Now, have you got everything?
DAISY Yes, I have, thanks.
A Have you got your boarding pass?
D Yes, I have, thanks.
WAYNE So, is the flight on time?
D Yes, it is.
W OK. Well, have a good trip.
D Thanks, I will.
W And don't forget to send us a text when you get to Thailand.
D Yes, of course.
A And don't forget to send your grandmother a postcard.
D I will. Don't worry.
A OK, have a good time, Daisy.
D Thanks, Mum, I will.
W See you in a month.
D Yes, see you. Bye, Mum. Bye, Dad.
A Bye.
W Bye.

CD3 54

/iː/ cheese, leave, week
/əʊ/ boat, note, snow
/ɒ/ cough, often, wash
/ʌ/ sunny, money, young
/ə/ sofa, second, woman
/ɔː/ shorts, call, four
/ɜː/ shirt, heard, word
/ɪ/ build, live, thin
/æ/ hat, bank, hand
/eɪ/ hate, great, train
/ʊ/ look, would, foot
/uː/ room, fruit, lose

CD3 55

Listening Test (See Teacher's Book)

Phonemic Symbols

Vowel sounds

/ə/	/æ/	/ʊ/	/ɒ/	/ɪ/	/i/	/e/	/ʌ/
father ago	apple cat	book could	on got	in swim	happy easy	bed any	cup under

/ɜː/	/ɑː/	/uː/	/ɔː/	/iː/			
her shirt	arm car	blue too	born walk	eat meet			

/eə/	/ɪə/	/ʊə/	/ɔɪ/	/aɪ/	/eɪ/	/əʊ/	/aʊ/
chair where	near here	tour mature	boy noisy	nine eye	eight day	go over	out brown

Consonant sounds

/p/	/b/	/f/	/v/	/t/	/d/	/k/	/g/
park soup	be rob	face laugh	very live	time white	dog red	cold look	girl bag

/θ/	/ð/	/tʃ/	/dʒ/	/s/	/z/	/ʃ/	/ʒ/
think both	mother the	chips teach	job page	see rice	zoo days	shoe action	television

/m/	/n/	/ŋ/	/h/	/l/	/r/	/w/	/j/
me name	now rain	sing think	hot hand	late hello	marry write	we white	you yes

Irregular Verb List

infinitive	Past Simple	past participle
be	was/were	been
become	became	become
begin	began	begun
break	broke	broken
bring	brought /brɔːt/	brought /brɔːt/
buy	bought /bɔːt/	bought /bɔːt/
can	could	been able
catch	caught /kɔːt/	caught /kɔːt/
choose	chose	chosen
come	came	come
cost	cost	cost
cut	cut	cut
do	did	done /dʌn/
drink	drank	drunk
drive	drove	driven
eat	ate	eaten
fall	fell	fallen
feel	felt	felt
find	found	found
fly	flew /fluː/	flown /fləʊn/
forget	forgot	forgotten
get	got	got (US: gotten)
give	gave	given
go	went	been/gone
have	had	had
hear	heard /hɜːd/	heard /hɜːd/
hold	held	held
know	knew /njuː/	known /nəʊn/
learn	learned/learnt	learned/learnt

infinitive	Past Simple	past participle
leave	left	left
lose	lost	lost
make	made	made
meet	met	met
pay	paid	paid
put	put	put
read	read /red/	read /red/
ride	rode	ridden
run	ran	run
say	said /sed/	said /sed/
see	saw /sɔː/	seen
sell	sold	sold
send	sent	sent
sing	sang	sung
sit	sat	sat
sleep	slept	slept
speak	spoke	spoken
spell	spelled/spelt	spelled/spelt
spend	spent	spent
stand	stood	stood
swim	swam	swum
take	took	taken
teach	taught /tɔːt/	taught /tɔːt/
tell	told	told
think	thought /θɔːt/	thought /θɔːt/
understand	understood	understood
wear	worn	worn
win	won	won
write	wrote	written

Cambridge Dictionary

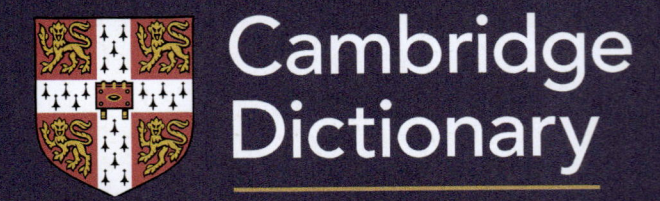

Make your words meaningful

Free, trustworthy, corpus-informed dictionaries, grammar reference and language learning resources.

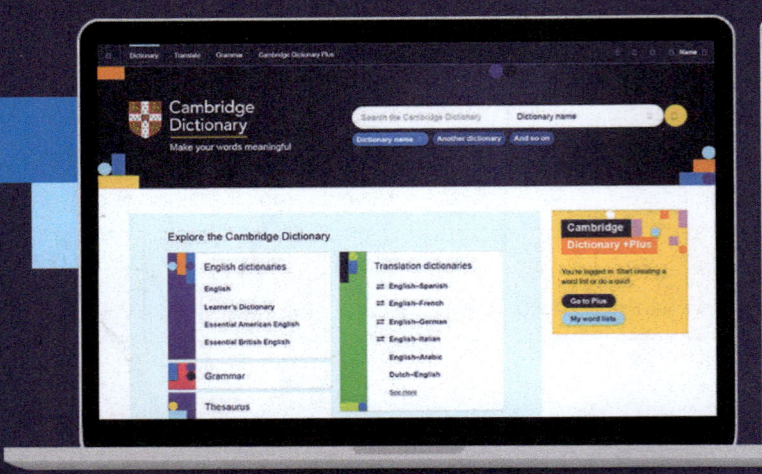

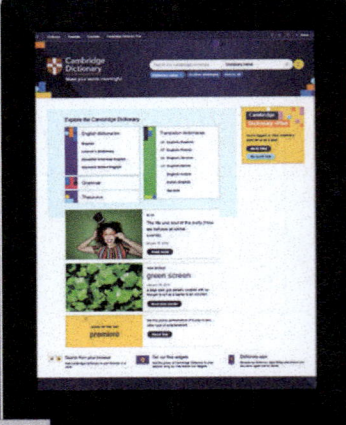

Definitions, audio, translations and grammar

Written especially for learners of English, our definitions are clear and easy to understand. You'll also find American and British English audio pronunciations for each word, grammar advice, lots of example sentences, and translation dictionaries in more than 20 languages.

Optimised for smartphones

Perfect for looking up definitions, checking grammar and listening to pronunciations on the move. Cambridge Dictionary is as easy to use on a mobile phone as it is on a tablet or laptop.

Always up to date

Follow our blog to find out about new words and to get advice on grammar, vocabulary, phrasal verbs and idioms. Join us on Facebook, Twitter and Instagram for our Word of the Day and to become part of our community.

Personalised for you

Create and share personalised wordlists, quiz yourself and be the first to receive information about new features by signing up for Dictionary +Plus.

- @cambridgewords
- @cambridgewords
- @cambridgedictionariesonline
- Cambridge Dictionary

dictionary.cambridge.org